D0214210

Loyalty in America

John H. Schaar

LOYALTY IN AMERICA

GREENWOOD PRESS, PUBLISHERS
WESTPORT, CONNECTICUT

Library of Congress Cataloging in Publication Data

Schaar, John H.
   Loyalty in America.

   Reprint. Originally published: Berkeley : University
of California Press, 1957.
   Includes index.
   1. Allegiance—United States. 2. Loyalty.
I. Title.
JK1726.S33 1982   323.6'5   82-972
ISBN 0-313-23416-7 (lib. bdg.)   AACR2

Copyright, © 1957, by The Regents of The University of
California.

Reprinted with the permission of University of California Press.

Reprinted in 1982 by Greenwood Press,
A division of Congressional Information Service, Inc.
88 Post Road West, Westport, Connecticut 06881

Printed in the United States of America

10 9 8 7 6 5 4 3 2 1

Preface

LOYALTY IS A GRAND AND PROTEAN WORD, A WORD TO CON-
jure with. Moralists praise it, politicians plead for it, philosophers analyze it. Loyalty is among the noblest of virtues, as any Boy Scout
knows, and disloyalty the basest of crimes. Definitions of loyalty range
from the doggerel sentiment of popular song and ballad to the metaphysical profundities of Josiah Royce's categorical imperative: "Be
loyal to loyalty." And yet we know little enough about it: its pro-
nouncement evokes images more dazzling than enlightening.

Nor has contemporary discussion contributed more to clarity than
to confusion. Loyalty has become a pawn in the political struggle.
When that fate overtakes any word, its later career is bound to be
devious. Moreover, during the last few years some men have arrogated
authority to assess the loyalty of their fellows, and many outrages
have been excused in the name of loyalty. What those events reflect
is public bewilderment on matters concerning the rights and obligations of citizens. The time is appropriate for an appraisal of the problem of loyalty.

But the discourse must be adapted to the subject. Although clarity
and precision of thought are needed, it would be false wisdom to pre-
tend that a subject so abundant in meanings, so lavish in implications,
could be reduced to severe forms and rigid categories. There is little
reward to be won from a search for some presumed "essence" of
loyalty. It would be equally debilitating to focus inquiry around some
fixed definition, for then appears the danger of confusing words with
actualities. Moreover, such enterprises too easily degenerate into dogmatic defenses of one's asserted definition against all comers. The
question with words is which is to be master—he who uses them, or
they themselves.

So it must be said at the outset that this is not an exercise in definition. Of loyalty there are definitions aplenty, and some will be exhibited in this study. But the very fact that definitions are so numerous, and so various, should warn against taking a narrow view of the subject at the start. The portion of human experience dealt with is of spacious dimensions and teeming content. It will not admit of over-abstraction. It must be known in its particularity and multiplicity.

That is a formidable task. But the scope of the inquiry is not so broad as the foregoing remarks might suggest. It is, first of all, confined to political loyalty, that is, to those loyalties directed toward political objects and of importance in the life of the political community. Secondly, the empirical field is limited to the United States. In the third place, greatest, though not exclusive, attention is devoted to recent events. Finally, only some of the most prominent and decisive features of the subject will be treated. This is a study of some of the most prominent features of the problem of political loyalty in contemporary America.

What are the "prominent and decisive features of the subject"? On that question there is ample area for differences of opinion, and no answer would be acceptable to all. Throughout the study two principles of choice were used: select those aspects of the subject that are basic to and generative of others, and select those features that are most neglected in current discussions. The two criteria admittedly are of different orders. Yet, the conclusions reached by applying both at once are often the same as though only one were employed. Most current writing on the federal loyalty program, for example, or on the congressional committees whose job it is to expose "un-American" activities, has dealt with their procedural and legal aspects. Other matters, such as the historical background and social determinants of present problems, and the concepts of loyalty employed by the committees and loyalty boards, have received much less attention. But the latter topics are precisely those of supreme objective importance. They stand to the former as causes to effects, as substances to procedures. This, however, is not the place for a tedious defense of my answer to the puzzle of selection. The study must serve as its own advocate and each reader must judge how well it speaks.

The project divides into a number of distinct though related parts. First there is a brief introduction to the psychology and sociology of loyalty. Following that comes a more extensive discussion of political loyalty, including an analysis of the relations between loyalty and a few other concepts, and a description of the diverse forms loyalty assumes under different political regimes. There follows an excursion into the historical development of political loyalty in the United States. After this background has been sketched in, the study moves forward to consider some of the chief factors determining the current stress on loyalty. Then the chief concepts of loyalty currently operative in the federal loyalty program are examined. Finally, these concepts are checked against the conditions that were supposed to have generated the current concern with loyalty, thereby making it possible to probe the relations between ideas and sociological determinants, to compare what is new with what is old, and to draw conclusions about the nature and significance of the role of loyalty in the recent period.

Such is the design of the project. Broadly conceived, the study is of a philosophic and synthetic character. If one could distinguish between the philosophy and the politics of loyalty, this study would belong in the first category. It is an effort to organize and understand a vast and inchoate complex of ideas and events in recent American politics. It is philosophic and synthetic in the additional sense that it tries to fuse some traditional concerns of political philosophy with more modern concepts and techniques of analysis. Discouragingly often it was impossible to adhere to that first precept of science and conscience: "Prove all things: Hold fast that which is good." So, manifestly, final answers are rarely asserted. Rather than being able to hold fast that which is good, it is often necessary to stand with that which seems better than the alternatives.

Finally, the project could be undertaken only with the aid of workers in fields of knowledge but little known to the writer. Doubtless, delicate professional toes have been trod upon. For that, sincere apologies. And this defense: I strived to draw my materials, as Burton put it in his curious treatise on the *Anatomy of Melancholy,* "not from circumferanean rogues and gipsies, but out of the writings of worthy philosophers and physicians, yet living some of them . . . who are able to patronize what they have said, and vindicate themselves from all cavillers and ignorant persons."

One may not presume to "dedicate" a work so slight, nor to distribute responsibility for its errors of fact and reason. It was composed originally as a doctoral dissertation in political science at the University of California, Los Angeles. Whatever strengths the study has are largely the fruits of the knowledge of those who so generously and patiently aided the efforts of a novice. Its weaknesses are my own.

J. H. S.

Contents

LOYALTY IN THE VOCABULARY OF
POLITICAL SCIENCE

Loyalty occupies the ground between patriotism and obligation. It is something less than the uncritical adulation and defense of one's own land which is the essence of patriotism. It is something more than the formal duty to obey law which is the meaning of obligation. Loyalty is more rational and less comprehensive in its objects than patriotism, less rational and more comprehensive than obligation.

Patriotism appears to be the inevitable companion of the development of solidarity sentiments in human groups. "Communities of all types," writes William Aylott Orton, "as they become organized and self-conscious, have a tendency also to become closed. The 'I belong' tends increasingly to imply 'you don't.' Consciousness of kind becomes increasingly consciousness of difference. And consciousness of difference tends . . . to be translated in terms of superior and inferior." [2] It is this sense of superiority in difference that most closely expresses the essence of patriotic feeling and action. Each community feels itself unique and inherently above the other communities in its environment —there are always "Greeks" and "Barbarians." These feelings may be expressed in the tolerant paternalism of Pericles' Funeral Oration which pictured Athens as the school of Greece, in the missionary ardor of the medieval Church for the conversion of the infidel, in Hitler's rabidly nationalistic tirades, in the historical mission and elite qualities conferred upon the proletariat by Marx, or in various other forms. They need rest on no objective basis to be vehement in expression— who can prove the Germans better than the Jews? Patriotic sentiment, the special political name for this sense of superiority in difference, rests more on emotion than on reason, and comprehends many facets of the life and culture of a group.

The question of obligation is the question of why political authority should be obeyed. T. H. Green, at the outset of his study of political obligation, defines the scope of his subject as including ". . . the obligation of the subject towards the sovereign, the obligation of the citizen towards the state, and the obligation of individuals to each other as enforced by a political superior." [3] Men have not been content to rest obedience merely on the given fact that the only life we know is life lived in society and thus under the restraints of authority and law. It is not enough to obey out of habit or custom; obedience must have moral grounds as well. Brute obedience must be transmuted into moral obligation. Inquiries into the grounds and limits of obligation are, in this respect, the political analogue of Milton's effort to "justify the ways of God to man." Such inquiries direct their appeal as much to the mind as to the heart and often rest on close argument and reasoning. Moreover, obligation is usually limited in its objects to political authority as expressed in validly enacted laws and does not enclose the broad and shifting objects of patriotism.

Loyalty, then, lies between the two, partakes partially of each, yet differs from both. But to insert loyalty at its proper place in the vocabulary of political science is not to go far toward understanding all that the word implies. Although it makes communication easier, strict adherence to traditional categories may also imprison the mind within a cell which excludes much of the realm of reality. Emancipation from accepted forms is often the first step toward knowledge. No discussion of loyalty can dwell long on the heights of political speculation without falling victim to the vertigo that comes from abandoning the concrete for the abstract. The empirical phenomena collected under the rubric "loyalty" are, in the first place, data of psychology and sociology, and must be examined as such before analysis can proceed to other aspects.

LOYALTY AS AN ATTITUDE

Josiah Royce, who perhaps had a sharper perception of the meaning of loyalty than most moral philosophers, defined it as "*. . . the willing and practical and thorough-going devotion of a person to a cause.*" [4] Each descriptive carries a special cargo of meaning: loyalty must be freely given; must manifest itself in action; and is intense in emotional tone. Each also raises a number of questions which this section will try to answer.

Another writer points out additional factors which cast Royce's conception into fuller and more precise form and bring to view other aspects of loyalty:

> Man in society finds himself the focal point of innumerable loyalties. . . . Each one of these represents some special aspect of his nature which seeks outlet in association with others of similar interest. A loyalty, then, would appear to be the identification of one's own interest with that of a group. It implies the associated necessity of furthering both the larger purpose which the group fosters and the integral unity of the individual himself with the group and the group purpose. [5]

These two definitions direct attention to a number of related problems important in the psychology of loyalty. Each insists that loyalty has at least two dimensions, internal or personal, and external or social. This means that loyalty is a relation between subject and object and is manifested both in internal mental states and in external behavior. It means also that loyalty has consequences for both individual and society. Both definitions view the relation of loyalty as similar to the process which the psychologist calls identification. Royce draws attention to the affective tone of loyalty whereas Bloch reminds that loyalty serves the interests of individual and group. Bloch pictures man-in-society as the focal point of innumerable loyalties and points out that each loyalty serves a particular aspect of one's nature. This suggests the possibility of conflicts among loyalties together with changes in the content of individual loyalties. It is these psychological problems of loyalty—its formation, growth, tone, functions, and conflicts—that will concern us here. Although it is true that loyalty also has moral dimensions, they are best left for later treatment. We can plead for clarity on the facts before plunging into the values.

But before plunging anywhere, one caution. The difficulties in presenting the psychology of loyalty are not so much substantive as procedural. They inhere in the tools of inquiry, not in the subject itself. We must deal here not with linear cause and effect but with relations of mutual dependence. Yet our language, and thereby our "natural" patterns of thought, is a language of cause and effect.* We must treat of multiple variables ever changing in quantity and relation one to the other, but the logic of our grammar treats of fixed states and distinct entities. There is here a practical difficulty which cannot be solved with entire satisfaction. For at the very outset of inquiry we must break into the circle of loyalty at some point and push onward from

---

* Compare with this the following: "The common inherited scheme of conception which is all around us, and comes to us as naturally and unobjectionally as our native air, is none the less imposed upon us, and limits our intellectual movements in countless ways—all the more surely and irresistibly because, being inherent in the very language we must use to express the simplest meaning, it is adopted and assimilated before we can so much as begin to think for ourselves at all." F. M. Cornford, *From Religion to Philosophy: A Study in the Origins of Western Speculation* (London: Edward Arnold, 1912), p. 45, as quoted in C. K. Ogden and I. A. Richards, *The Meaning of Meaning: A Study of the Influence of Language upon Thought and of the Science of Symbolism* (10th ed.; London: Routledge and Kegan Paul, 1952), pp. 25–26. Also, "A Cause indeed, in the sense of something which forces another something called an effect to occur, is so obvious a phantom that it has been rejected even by metaphysicians. The current scientific account, on the other hand, which reduces causation to correlation, is awkward for purposes of exposition, since in the absence of a 'conjugating' vocabulary constant periphrasis is unavoidable." (P. 55.)

there, knowing even as we do so that a circle is without beginning, end, or direction.

It can be said, as a first approximation, that the psychology of loyalty is a branch of the psychology of attitude and identification. This proposition affords the amateur in psychology a measure of security, since both attitudes and identification have been studied extensively by the psychologists and there is general agreement on their nature.[6]

Granted the assertion that loyalty is but a special type of attitude, it is possible to derive a typology of loyalty by reference to the psychology of attitude. After this typology is firmly in mind, the different task of studying the formation and growth of loyalty can be undertaken. The attempt here is to describe the general structure of loyalty rather than to analyze the detailed properties of loyal word or deed. To this end, it is suggested that loyalty has five major characteristics.[7]

1. Loyalty implies a subject-object relationship and the content of loyalty, which changes with that relationship, can be highly various. Loyalty is always the loyalty of some person for or toward something else. That "something else"—the object of loyalty—can be another person, a group, a cause, an ideal, an institution, and so forth. The content of a loyalty is established by the subject-object relationship and varies with it. Thus, for example, Protestant and Catholic may worship the same God in principle but display their worship in quite different ways inasmuch as the religious practices of each are prescribed by different religious institutions to which they are loyal. Or, by way of further illustration, the content of loyalty may be described as political or religious according as it runs to the institutions of government or of God.

2. Loyalties vary in intensity of emotional tone. This proposition asserts that loyalty may be manifested in diverse ways and degrees. Loyalty in its richest expression is the passionate devotion of an individual to a cause combined with zealous exertions to advance its projected aims. In its more meager manifestations it may be an almost habitual, barely conscious, and diffuse sense of sharing in a common purpose. Within this range, intensity of loyalty will vary.

This idea contains further implications. First, it suggests that loyalties might be measured along a scale ranging from fanaticism at the one pole to resigned acceptance at the other. The behavioral components useful in measuring the tone of a given loyalty might include, for example, the degree of participation and absorption of a person in his object of loyalty, and the sacrifice he will endure for it. It suggests, secondly, that the strength of loyalty has considerable impact on behavior. Loyalties are programs of action and the strengths of a man's loyalties must be known before permitting him to undertake certain tasks. As Sidney Hook warns, it would be unwise to staff an institution for the aged and infirm with doctors who believe wholly that the old should not continue the burdens of this life. Nor will a society that cares for its own well-being fill positions of trust with agents dedicated to its destruction.[8]

3. *Loyalties differ in specificity and particularity.* Loyalties develop as by-products of experience and thought. As a result, the extent and diversity of stimuli to which a loyalty is related will vary in accordance with the situation in which the loyalty originated and with the kind of cognitive connections established between the loyalty and the immediate stimulus situation. If the original matrix from which a loyalty emerged is capable of partial representation in other situations, then the loyalty may be evoked in these other contexts. The relation between the generative matrix and the specificity of a loyalty is direct: as the matrix tends toward formlessness, the loyalty becomes less specific; conversely, as the matrix increases in precision of structure, the loyalty increases in specificity. The less specific a loyalty, the more easily it is transferred to a greater number of situations.

Although some few loyalties may be evoked only in face of the situation in which they originated, it is more usual that an established loyalty will be related to objects not directly present and influential in its original crystallization. An original loyalty of a particular son for a particular father may be evoked in an altered form when that son enters other situations where authority is exercised over him by persons of greater age and higher status. Many loyalties are operative in a wide variety of situations because the stimulus field in which the loyalty originally grew was itself extensive and diffuse and therefore capable of representation or reproduction in many other contexts.

Particularity refers to the degree of relatedness one loyalty has with others. The more particular a loyalty is, the less connection it has with other loyalties. The relevant consideration is whether a loyalty stands sharply alone or as part of a larger constellation of attitudes. Thus, my loyalty to political authority may stand quite apart from my loyalty to family but closely connected with my loyalties to political party or religious society.

4. *Loyalties differ in precision and endurance.* Some loyalties are tightly structured, clearly formulated, and highly articulate; others

are amorphous and flowing, vague, nearly inarticulate. Some loyalties have but a short life while others endure through long time, ending only when he who holds them ends. There is no clear relation between these two qualities, for even the deepest and most enduring loyalties may not be highly articulate and organized. Conversely, it often happens that the explicit profession of a systematic and idealized loyalty is but the mask of one more deeply concealed and profoundly rooted in the most fundamental attitudes of one's character.

It is a material point that the clearest fact about a loyalty is its persistence through time. Our loyalties are not easily escaped, for they are rooted in our deepest sentiments and needs. Man in his pride may admire his intellect as an engine of limitless liberating power, but he must recognize still that his very thought modes and life habits can never shake the bonds of existing loyalties and the attitudes implicit in them. Even though he in his freedom revolt, the bounds of that revolt are circumscribed by past loyalties and attitudes. Still, loyalties do change. Even our dearest convictions are not spared the awful necessity of adapting to novel circumstances. From this it can be seen that the processes of loyalty formation and alteration are central to the process of social change itself. Although the point will be elaborated later, it should be noted here that the complexity and instability characteristic of modern political institutions are basic to an understanding of contemporary issues of loyalty.

5. *Loyalties vary in importance.* This proposition requires little embellishment. The point is simply that from the standpoint of their impact on political behavior all loyalties are not of equal importance. In addition, the same loyalty may acquire different weights in accordance with the person holding it as well as with the situation in which it receives expression.

FORMATION AND MODIFICATION OF LOYALTY

Freud remarks somewhere in his writings that from his earliest history man has been "forced into coöperation" with his fellows. This, although it savors of a paradox similar to Jean Jacques's famous attempt to force men into freedom, is perhaps as good a place as any to open a discussion of the formation and modification of loyalty. For the sentiment of loyalty, although it emerges from a social matrix and binds men together in adherence to prescribed ideals and patterns of action, also affords bountiful opportunities for free choice and responsible action. Loyalty is Janus-faced. In this duality some of the deepest problems of human conduct and social organization find their roots.

No matter where we look, nor how far back in time we go, man is never seen alone but always is found in association with others of his kind. It is unnecessary to posit any "gregarious instinct" to explain this phenomenon when other more easily verified hypotheses will do as well. Indeed, little would be lost by foregoing attempts to explain the origins of group living and holding with Dewey that "associated activity needs no explanation; things are made that way." [9] Men have always combined in social units because it was necessary and, if we can infer from our own lives, because it was pleasant. Necessary because "there must be," on the authority of Aristotle, "a union of those who cannot exist without each other; namely, of male and female, that the race may continue. . . ." Necessary, secondly, because the lone individual lacks adequate defenses against the hazards of nature and the aggressions of other men. Association is pleasant in that it seems good and satisfying to live in communion with others. It was Aristotle, again, who said that the solitary is either a god or a beast. Furthermore, in this calculus of pleasure one should not forget that the human sexual drive, being continuous rather than intermittent in its demand for expression, also urges toward permanent association. Association, then, can be accepted as a datum of fact without probing further into its causes.

Loyalty in its primordial forms grows from association. It is a felt sentiment of attachment to something outside the self, usually other persons or an ideal. Only at later and higher levels does it acquire more complex and rational layers of meaning. The sentiment grows naturally, that is, it flows effortlessly from the basic and repeated interactions one has with his fellows. At the earliest stage this growth is largely unconscious; there is little or no awareness that it is occurring and there are few or no agencies with the specific social function of instilling loyalty. The individual wears his loyalties comfortably and becomes intensely aware of them only when social changes push them to the forefront of consciousness.[*]

---

[*] Writing of primitive society, one anthropologist states: "Until the rise of civilization, mankind lived in communities so small that every adult could, and no doubt did, know everybody else." Under such conditions, men are held in community by strong bonds of status, kinship, and shared attitudes concerning the moral ends of life. Thus: "We may say that the members of the precivilized community had a strong sense of group solidarity." Robert Redfield, *The Primitive World and Its Transformations* (Ithaca: Cornell University Press, 1953), pp. 7, 8.

It is not enough to gloss over this subject with the declaration that loyalty emerges from a social matrix. The subject deserves more care than that. In the following pages an attempt will be made to delineate at least the outlines of these processes of growth and change. The discussion rests on the previously stated premise that, considered psychologically, loyalty is but a particular type of attitude. The analytic problem, therefore, becomes one of applying existing knowledge concerning the nature of attitudes to the immediate problem.*

It is clear, first of all, that one's beliefs and attitudes are in great measure shaped by the culture in which he lives. This proposition is supported by both empirical studies and basic psychological theory. Many correlational studies have been made between attitudes and such cultural components as family background, education, religion, socioeconomic status, and so forth. A few such studies might be cited. (1) P. F. Lazarsfeld, B. Berelson, and H. Gaudet have shown that if a person's economic status, place of residence, and religious affiliation are known, a reasonably reliable index of his "political predisposition" can be constructed.[10] (2) T. M. Newcomb and G. Svehla showed that there are high positive correlations between parents and children in their attitudes about internationalism.[11] (3) A 1936 study by E. L. Horowitz on the formation of attitudes toward the Negro concluded that ". . . attitudes toward Negroes are now chiefly determined not by contact with Negroes, but by contact with the prevalent attitude toward Negroes."[12] Horowitz applied a series of attitude tests to children and adolescents from various groups—e.g., rural and urban Southern white children, white children in New York City, and New York children of Communist parents. It is not the point of least interest in his study that he discovered that only the children of Communist parents were innocent of anti-Negro prejudice.

The point is upheld also by certain theoretical considerations. One's needs, perceptions, and tensions are affected by the stimulus patterns he confronts. The cultural environment is a main stimulus source for

---

* The analysis here would not placate the professional conscience of the psychologist. A fully satisfactory treatment would begin with a study of motivation, perception, and learning, move on to examine the structural properties of social-psychological fields, and only then consider the final problem of how norms and sentiments emerge from social interaction. Such a comprehensive presentation is beyond the scope of this study. The analysis here deals mainly with the final level and neglects the prior levels, even while confessing that to do so is without any justification other than convenience. One wishes he might remedy these omissions by performing the legislator's adroit trick of "incorporation by reference" and merely cite the rich psychological literature available.

the individual. Since no social environment is composed of factors selected in a purely random fashion (i.e., there is a *pattern* of culture), it follows that each society presents its members with stimulus *patterns* which encourage the emergence of only certain kinds of needs, emotions, goals, and attitudes. Therefore, variations among social patterns will be reflected in differences in the beliefs and attitudes held by individuals in those societies.

The idea hardly requires emphasis for it is a germinal doctrine of much modern social science. It does require modification. Sociologists and educators, particularly, have accented cultural influences in explaining individual beliefs and attitudes. Indeed, there is a school of thought in modern sociology, marching under the banner of "cultural determinism," which holds that individual character is entirely the creature of culture. Here, perhaps, the doctrine runs too far and is vulnerable to criticism:

> Modern sociology has an inherent disposition to regard the human individual as a mere by-product of social or cultural forces, a mere overlapping point of innumerable groups; and so to deny him any significance or efficacy in his own right. A large body of fact supports this view: the sort of fact that the methods of sociology are adapted to discover.[13]

That is the crucial point—"the sort of fact that the methods of sociology are adapted to discover." The result of such methods is to reduce the individual to the pallid existence of an epiphenomenon. When viewed in historical perspective, this phenomenon is recognized as an exact analogue of the "reductive fallacy" so widespread in nineteenth-century social thought. Someone has called the nineteenth the "nothing but" century, for social theory then was often an effort to reduce social problems to a single simple base. Marx explained that all social change was basically nothing but economic change. Likewise, Spencer demonstrated that society was nothing but the struggle for existence and the survival of the fittest. Now, in our own more enlightened day, we learn that human character is nothing but the product of cultural forces.* Yet, the individual resists

---

* In Tolstoy's monumental *War and Peace* there appears a passage keenly appreciative of the durability and strength of this urge to reduce complex situations to single causes. He writes: "The combination of causes of phenomena is beyond the grasp of the human intellect. But the impulse to seek causes is innate in the soul of man. And the human intellect, with no inkling of the immense variety and complexity of circumstances conditioning a phenomenon, any one of which may be separately conceived of as the cause of it, snatches at the first and most easily understood approximation, and says here is the cause." (Modern Library ed.; New York: Random House, n.d.), p. 918.

this aggression and pleads for salvation from the forces of culture. And surely he is right: exposure to a regular and patterned range of stimulations does not, in and of itself, issue in uniform beliefs and attitudes among those exposed. There are still individual differences.

Beliefs and attitudes develop selectively. The process of perception itself is selective. No person perceives and registers everything in the external environment. This selectivity is systematic. As Krech and Crutchfield state, ". . . the objects that are accentuated are usually those objects which serve some immediate purpose of the perceiving individual." [14] The success of "projective techniques" in diagnosing personality corroborates this notion. The technique itself depends upon the fact that responses to stimuli reflect personal needs and demands. Since one's beliefs and attitudes must be built on his perceptions, it is apparent that attitudes and beliefs too will vary with individual needs and demands. Therefore, attitudes will not reflect with perfect fidelity the "real" stimulus conditions presented by cultural patterns. Beliefs and attitudes are formed selectively, are intimately related to individual needs, and are not a simple "carry-over" from cultural patterns.

Furthermore, the very heterogeneity of cultural influences to which one is exposed will make for large individual variations in held attitudes. Culture is not an assembly line which turns out identical human products as Ford produces automobiles. No culture is a single, homogeneous pattern. The cultural influences to which one is exposed are diverse and not infrequently contradictory. Thus, even if beliefs and attitudes mirrored objective stimulations, there would still be great individual differences within the same culture. What is true of individuals here is equally true of subgroups within the same social system.

The tenable conclusion is that beliefs and attitudes are products of complex interactions between cultural and functional determinants. Functional determinants include such things as an individual's needs, emotions, and specific personality traits. Under cultural factors are bunched such items as family and educational background, socioeconomic status, and religious affiliation. One selects from the stimulations presented by culture those that have most relevance for himself. Both types of factors must be included in any analysis of attitude formation.

Over and above the functional meanings that particular attitudes and beliefs may have for particular individuals, there are general needs which beliefs and attitudes fulfill for human personality as such. First of all, they impart structure and continuity to existence. Human existence without enduring beliefs is inconceivable. Without lasting belief structures, each experience would be novel and the individual would be a "new" person in each situation. Second, there is a very important cluster of attitudes that define the individual to himself, telling him who he is and how he is related to others. These are the "ego-attitudes" which Sherif and Cantril explain as follows:

> In brief, the ego consists of many attitudes which from infancy on are related to the "I," "me," "mine" experiences. These attitudes, which may be designated as ego-attitudes, are constituent components of the ego. Apart from the constellation of these ego-attitudes, there is no such entity as the ego. . . . They are attitudes that define and qualify an individual's relative standing to other persons or to institutions in some more or less lasting way. They are attitudes that determine the more or less enduring character of one's personal identity with the values or norms incorporated in him.[15]

Third, beliefs and attitudes aid in the human search for meaning. The modern psychologist's concept of man as a striver for meaning echoes Aristotle's classic definition of man as the rational animal. There is in human nature an insistent urge to understand, to find meaning and significance in the events of life. Man does not accept events as just so many unrelated phenomena; he builds of them not a catalog, but a story, with a plot and a moral. Man is not only a thinking but a believing creature. This search for beliefs which can impart meaning to life may be explicit and systematic, as in the search of the philosopher for "fundamentals"; or it may be only the inchoate wonderings we all engage in when faced with the unfamiliar.

Before moving on to other subjects, it is necessary to treat, however briefly, the problem of change in attitudes. It has been mentioned previously that this problem is inseparably bound to the whole process of social change. Anything learned about the former problem, therefore, should indicate some of the workings of the latter.

It is a part of everyday knowledge that beliefs and attitudes tenaciously resist change. So important is this phenomenon that it should be examined in some detail. The subject can be approached by specifying the major factors that account for the resistance of attitudes to change.

1) One has a "vested interest" in his attitudes and beliefs. It was noted above that attitudes and beliefs provide a structure of meaning for the self in its journey through the world of experience. When the structure is shaken, personal insecurity often results; therefore, one relinquishes established attitudes with reluctance.

2) Beliefs and attitudes influence perception.[16] New facts hostile to one's beliefs may not even be perceived. If perception is impaired in this way, reorganization of beliefs will not automatically occur with changes in the real environment. Each of us views the world through a special pair of glasses and what we "see" is tinted by our beliefs and attitudes. If the attitudes are of great functional significance, they can even occlude factors in the external environment. Or, if contradictory data are perceived, they will be interpreted in such a way as to produce the slightest possible impact on existing belief and attitude configurations.

3) Finally, beliefs and attitudes tend to persist if they receive social support. It was pointed out earlier that beliefs and attitudes are affected by cultural patterns. This correlation operates so as to offer social support to one's attitudes if they are consonant with the group mores. Attitudes and beliefs thus often function to meet the needs of social acceptance and approval. When attitudes receive social approval, it is exceedingly difficult to force changes in them. Sometimes it can be done only by the substitution of a different approval group.[17]

Although the foregoing pages have been framed in the language of the general psychology of attitudes, their bearing on the topic of loyalty is easily determined. One's loyalties emerge from the dynamic interaction of cultural and functional determinants. We can therefore expect the members of a social unit to share a common cluster of loyalties. But this does not mean uniformity. Cultural diversity, plus special functional determinants, produces individual variations. A man's loyalties perform for him the supremely important tasks of providing self-definition and interpreting experience. Shared loyalties facilitate communication among members of a social group and provide the cement of unity. Once formed, loyalties are not easily changed, not only because they receive social support but also because individuals build up vested interests in them, and because established loyalties predispose those who hold them to perceive their environment selectively. These are the basic principles of the psychology of loyalty; with them in mind, we can advance to a broader frame of analysis.

GEMEINSCHAFT AND GESELLSCHAFT LOYALTIES

Ferdinand Tönnies contributed to modern sociology a pair of concepts which can further an understanding of loyalty in larger contexts than those considered thus far.[18] Tönnies began with the proposition that social relationships are products of human will. He moved on to divide social structures into two major categories dependent upon the type of will and the quality of the inner relationships that compose them. A group can be created (i.e., willed into being) for limited and definite ends and without regard for sentimental values in the relations among members. Then the structure created is a Gesellschaft and the type of willing operative is *Kurwille*—the rational will which distinguishes between ends and means and is based upon expedient calculations of interest. On the other hand, there may be willed into being a group felt to be valuable in and of itself and in which inner relationships are charged with sentimental values. In this instance, the structure created is a Gemeinschaft, and the type of willing operative is *Wesenwille*—the emotional will which springs from temperament and looks not solely toward expedient calculations of interest but toward relationships with moral and sentimental values.[19]

Although some have not been so cautious, Tönnies himself was careful to explain that the two categories are "pure concepts" or abstractions; they are not found *as such* in reality. They are useful abbreviations for phenomena which, in varying proportions, appear in social entities. For example, the observer should not label the family or the tribe a Gemeinschaft, and the trading company a Gesellschaft, but should ascertain to what extent the family under particular conditions (e.g., the middle-class urban family) partakes more of the Gemeinschaft type than it does under other (e.g., rural) conditions.

Corresponding to these type divisions of social structures, there are divisions of loyalty. Different social entities vary as to the types of loyalty dominant in them. To some groups, the individual's loyalty runs only so far as interest dictates. But to others his loyalty transcends personal interest and takes on complex overlays of sentiment. The social units to which strongest loyalty is given are of the Gemeinschaft type. The particular entities of Gemeinschaft character vary in time and place but are most frequently family, clan or tribe, religious body, and nation. These units usually include ". . . solidarity sentiments making it a magical, sacred, or moral obligation of the members to give such sentiments priority over all considerations of expediency."[20] Thus, many legends are woven around those who have sacrificed even the precious gift of life itself for family or religion. Organizations of the Gesellschaft type do not arouse this kind of loyalty; few indeed are the martyrs for the limited liability corporation. Individuals, then, may be attached to institutions or causes in two general ways which are dependent upon the nature of the object of loyalty itself.

It is obvious that in the modern nation-state loyalty is largely of the Gemeinschaft character. The nation-state can usually muster more of the loyalties and energies of its members than any other social structure. But, as is well known, this was not always so. In Western Europe, for example, religious institutions commanded more loyalty than their secular counterparts for a great many centuries. The Gemeinschaft loyalty of the national community is inherently aggressive and exclusive; it is the modern manifestation of that sense of in-group versus out-group that has always been part of the meaning of loyalty.

Another modern social structure which tends increasingly toward the creation of Gemeinschaft loyalty is the political party. This is most evident in certain of the totalitarian parties and movements, such as the Russian Communist party or the former German National Socialist movement, but is not restricted to them. Certain continental Social Democratic parties, as in Germany and Austria, have displayed the same tendencies. The modern party tries to attract loyalties of this sort by fostering *Weltanschauung* ideologies, by extensive propaganda campaigns, by programs of cadre training, and other like techniques. The party strives to become for its membership the object of supreme loyalty and the fountainhead of all other loyalties. In National Socialist Germany and Communist Russia the parties attained this tremendous goal. The whole society became, as it were, a magnified version of the patriarchal family, with all loyalties ultimately directed to, and all power and prestige flowing from, one leader at the apex of a monolithic and elitist party structure.

One further cognate point should be made before leaving this subject. Just as different types of social entities elicit different types of loyalty, so do different social circumstances condition the strength with which loyalties are expressed. It appears that the strength of the members' loyalty to an organization varies directly with the felt needs of the group.[21]

Within limits which cannot be fixed with precision, but which are undoubtedly broad, this holds true regardless of whether loyalty aids or injures a member's private interests. For many millions of men loyalty to nation offers no obvious and immediate benefits. Frequently, such loyalties are actually destructive of personal interest, as when the youth is asked to give his life in war. Yet our loyalties are often most strongly expressed when the entities to which they are given

are threatened. During times of peace, national loyalties may seem
to weaken and dissolve under the corrosive effects of individualism,
sectionalism, or class conflict. But—let the nation be threatened with
foreign attack; particularisms diminish and the populace rises to new
heights of effort and sacrifice in a massive display of common loyalty.
Observing this phenomenon, some moral philosophers have concluded
that war is the noblest endeavor of nations. Herein too lies the wisdom
of that notorious political maxim which holds that the final solution
for internal crisis is foreign adventure. This same phenomenon explains
the secret of the spectacular success of the demagogue's cry for
sacrifice in time of real or contrived danger. The point should be
made also that in a period like the present, when each nation conceives itself to be living in a world fraught with perils and threats,
we should not expect a reduction in the temperature of national
sentiment. It is during such times that the cry for loyalty swells,
and those who look hopefully toward the creation of the grand and
spacious world community must either alter these perilous conditions
or resign themselves to a lengthy residence in the cramped quarters
of the nation-state.

By now the outlines of the processes of loyalty formation, expression, and change should be fairly clear. The word itself has
many shades of meaning, and the phenomena it signifies are not
simple. But loyalty is not a supernatural manifestation; it is only
complex and entangled. What is called loyalty is really a kind of
norm containing the properties ascribed to it by Royce and Bloch,
and resting upon the familiar processes of attitude formation and
change. The roots of loyalty are to be found in social interaction.
Expressed briefly, shared activities evoke shared sentiments of sympathy. As the group lives together as a social unit, members experience mutual debts of gratitude, mutual likes and dislikes, and shared
interests which bind them together. This culminates in the simply
stated and profoundly felt emotion of owing much to each other
and to the group as a whole. Who can forget Socrates' sublime statement of his duty to remain and accept death rather than flee the
community which had given him life and being? "Well then," he
represents the Laws as asking, "since you were brought into the world
and nurtured and educated by us, can you deny in the first place that
you are our child and slave . . . ? Has a philosopher like you failed
to discover that our country is more to be valued and higher and
holier far than mother or father or any ancestor, and more to be

regarded in the eyes of gods and of men of understanding?" [22]

One's earliest and strongest loyalties are formed in his childhood primary groups. In these groups too are generated many of the broadest general attitude complexes carried throughout life. Our loyalties are first attached to objects within immediate experience, later radiating outward to enclose more distant objects as experience and knowledge expand. But there are always objects outside the circle of loyalty. *Our* language, *our* customs, *our* beliefs, *our* gods, *our* leaders evoke loyalty from the individual and distinguish him and his group from outsiders. Those outside the group are strangers to whom no loyalty or obligations are owing. Since there is always present a powerful current of feeling which binds the group together against an outside world which—because unknown—is nearly always suspected of hostile designs, it is an easy matter to channel the group into aggressive or defensive measures against the strangers. It is no mere etymological accident that *hospes* (stranger) and *hostis* (enemy) share the same root. As Ranyard West put it, "Human loyalty and human strife came to this world together. . . . And no economic or political organizations of history have checked man's passionate devotion to his 'ain folk'—his little group." [23] Loyalty has an inherent propensity toward exclusionism and aggressiveness.*

Even at the most primitive level loyalty can be a very strong emotion quite capable of overriding the so-called selfish motives. Loyalty is felt to impose obligations which must be fulfilled if one is to please others and be judged worthy in their eyes. There are few explicit and formal sanctions against breach of loyalty; the controls are, as it were, worked into the very fabric of the group life. A breach of loyalty is a disruption of the usual pattern of life, a dissonance in the collective harmony. When such a dissonance sounds in the life of the small group there is an automatic retuning to

---

* A fascinating sidelight on this point is provided by the etymology of the word "rival." Its Latin root, *rivalis,* meant an associate or companion, and *rivales* signified two neighboring communities. Shakespeare too used it to mean colleague or companion. Thus:

> Well, good-night.
> If you do meet Horatio and Marcellus,
> The rivals of my watch, bid them make haste.
> —*Hamlet,* Act I, Scene I

Today, of course, a rival is a competitor or opponent. We tend to think of two communities or groups in close proximity as not only neighbors in the sense of being friends, but also as competitors.

restore the original harmony.* These restorative forces can range
from simple disapproval and admonition to that most terrible of all
punishments—ostracism. He who suffers this affliction is cast beyond
the pale of society; he is Homer's "tribeless, lawless, heartless one,"
and his path thereafter must move in those dark and shaded regions
outside the friendly fires of clan and kin. Human societies have always saved their harshest punishments for betrayal and disloyalty,
for these crimes turn the knife in the vitals of the social organism.
Rebecca West, in richly metaphorical language, plumbs the depth of
this feeling when she describes betrayal as ". . . that sin which is
the dark travesty of legitimate hatred because it is felt for kindred,
just as incest is the dark travesty of legitimate love." In another place
she writes of treachery as ". . . the betrayal of familiars to strangers,
of those who are near to those who are far, of those to whom one
is bound by real interest to those who, being foreign, will treat one
as a foreigner and maybe, in the end, turn against one." [24] For the
sin of disloyalty, then, harsh penance is exacted.

---

* Redfield, *op. cit.*, p. 14, writes: "In the most primitive societies of living
men . . . the controls of action are informal; they rest on the traditional obligations of largely inherited status, and are expressed in talk and gesture and in
the patterns of reciprocal action. Political institutions are few and simple, or
even entirely absent. . . . People do the kind of things they do, not because
somebody just thought up that kind of thing, or because somebody ordered them
to do so, but because it seems to the people to flow from the very necessity
of existence that they do that kind of thing."

2
Political Loyalty

To see loyalty as a general phenomenon in human intercourse is a first step toward the fuller view of political loyalty which is the object of this essay. It affords a broader view of the terrain without which lesser features cannot be seen in their proper places and relations. With that first step, the perspective shifts from the general to the partial, from the larger to the smaller, narrowing down to focus on loyalty in its specifically political forms.

LOYALTY AND COMMUNITY

In the vocabulary of political science loyalty resides between patriotism and obligation. Political loyalty is a devoted attachment to the political ideals and institutions established in a community. In most of its manifestations political loyalty is a complex mixture of tradition and sentiment, choice and reason. Most of our loyalties are acquired in the course of social conditioning and are integrated into the character structure without conscious thought. We know, for example, that the largest portion of adherents to the Republican party derive their allegiance originally from tradition and justify their continued support by a process which the psychologist would coldly label "rationalization." On the other hand, some loyalties are products of choice, choice which may be based on rational calculations of interest or on emotional considerations. Such a chosen loyalty is illustrated by the conversion of the nonbeliever to religious faith, and by the choice, in contemporary America, of membership in the Communist party. But most loyalties are compound rather than simple and the broadest generalization possible, as will be elaborated later, is that different polities prefer one over another of the components.

Since political loyalty is a devoted attachment to the established political institutions of a community, it is itself a foremost component of community. Through political institutions, policies and ends binding on the whole social order are prescribed.[1] Therefore, popular attachment to these institutions, together with agreement upon the ideals they embody, forms one of the essential elements of group unity. It is loyalty that defines the community and preserves its integrity in the face of changing conditions. Shared loyalty to political ideas and institutions gives to members of a group that faith and confidence in their fellows which lubricates social relations and makes consensus in other projects possible. Shared loyalties are the basis of a man's faith in his fellows and, as Barth writes, "When men lose faith in one another, they lose the substance of what constitutes a community among them." [2]

These ideas, of course, are merely embroideries on the standard argument that "agreement upon the fundamentals" is a precondition of successful community. Lord Balfour has given the proposition its classic political rendering. Referring to the British system, Balfour wrote:

> Our alternating Cabinets, though belonging to different Parties, have never differed about the fundamentals of society. And it is evident that our whole political machinery presupposes a people so fundamentally at one that they can safely afford to bicker; and so sure of their own moderation that they are not dangerously disturbed by the never-ending din of political conflict.[3]

He who seeks empirical confirmation on a grand scale of the disastrous effects an absence of shared loyalties can produce in other areas of

---

[1] For numbered notes to chap. 2, see pp. 194–196.

social life need only consult the history of post-Revolutionary France.

Loyalty, then, is a great good from the standpoint of community. It is equally a good from the standpoint of the individual as it gives him an ease of communication with his fellows and a set of goals which help impart purpose to his life. Through loyalty one becomes related to something outside of and larger than himself. And, through this connection, life acquires meaning and direction. Royce announces this theme early and returns to it repeatedly in his treatise on loyalty.

> Loyalty, again, tends to unify life, to give it centre, fixity, stability.
>
> Now, a loyal man is one who has found, and who sees . . . some social cause . . . so rich, so well knit, and, to him, so fascinating, and withal so kindly in its appeal to his natural self-will, that he says to his cause: "Thy will is mine and mine is thine. In thee I do not lose but find myself, living intensely in proportion as I live for thee."
>
> Wherever loyalty is, there is selfhood, personality, individual purpose embodied in a life.
>
> Disloyalty is moral suicide.[4]

Loyalty is a good for the individual in the additional sense that through it he learns to orient his life toward the achievement of ideal projects. By a process similar to Stendahl's notion of crystallization, loyalty formation always includes the idealization of the object of loyal attachment. The object of loyalty is seen as beautiful and noble beyond all others and as offering great promise for the future good of its adherents. From the viewpoint of the loyal individual this holds true regardless of how the object of loyalty may appear to the external observer. Shaw's cynical definition of love as an exaggeration of the differences that distinguish one woman from another may seem cold truth to the cold man, but the lover knows otherwise. So too is it with the man of loyalty and his cause.

This point should not be passed over casually. The psychology of loyalty, it was explained in the previous chapter, is related to the psychology of identification. And the impulse to identify with a person, a cause, an ideal, possesses nearly everyone at one or another time, with greater or lesser intensity. Given the inherent tendency for loyalty to include idealization of its objects, it is clear that identification with objects of loyalty raises the spiritual tone of life. In serving the idealized objects of loyalty with which we identify ourselves, our lives are made richer, more radiant, more altruistic. We demand much from ourselves, and are satisfied only when we give greatly of what we have. Life and thought are elevated above the lowlands of an existence where we use but a small portion of our capacities to the pinnacle where potency is greater, the inner life more vital.

In summary, loyalty is a good-in-itself for both individual and society. It is the cement that binds men together in harmonious union. It is through shared loyalties that man can break through the shell isolating him from his fellows, enabling him to become a vital part of the ongoing collective process. Through this sharing he becomes part of the organic social being and works for its ends while striving for his own. Violence is done neither to individual nor to social ends; shared loyalties make them identical. It is not rhetoric to say that loyalty is the great design by which anarchy becomes order and isolation communion. Through loyalty, in the words of St. Paul, "We are members one of another."

LOYALTY AND LIBERTY

Perhaps the most hallowed word in the liberal democratic lexicon is liberty. Closely associated with it is consent. Philosophers and laymen alike agree that these two ideas, however defined, are of the essence of the liberal democratic way of life. Nonetheless, the level of understanding concerning their nature is not high; and when men come to compare meanings, the level of agreement on content is often disturbingly low. Given this, little in the way of a contribution to clarity or consensus should be expected from the efforts of a novice. Still, something of the nature of liberty and consent can be understood by connecting the two concepts with loyalty.

In preparation for writing his projected history of freedom, Lord Acton gathered hundreds of definitions of liberty. From this voluminous collection he adopted the following as his own:

> By liberty I mean the assurance that every man shall be protected in doing what he believes his duty against the influence of authority and majorities, custom and opinion. . . . The most certain test by which we judge whether a country is really free is in the amount of security enjoyed by minorities.[5]

Acton's formulation goes to the heart of the matter: one has liberty when he has assurance of protection against outside interference in the performance of his felt duty. Duty is a moral concept; it is something we *should* do, a service we *ought to* perform for ourselves or others. Acton's statement lifts liberty above the realm of mere whim and assertion, placing it on the higher plane of morality. The free man, Acton declares, is he who is free to do what he thinks he should do.*

The free man has a duty. But this alone is not enough; he must have protection in the execution of that duty. To be free one must know that others will not simply tolerate but will respect and defend him so long as he performs what he conceives to be his duty. Protection is a concept with an empirical referent. It directs attention to the physical conditions of freedom. The question is whether men are secure against arbitrary infringements on the actions they take in discharging the dictates of duty. It is here that the relation between liberty and loyalty becomes of concern. But first, a preliminary matter requires attention.

There is a line of political thought running from Aristotle, through Montesquieu, and on to the Pluralists of the twentieth century, which argues that the major *physical* condition of freedom is division of power in society and government. This is the premise behind Aristotle's defense of the mixed constitution, Montesquieu's regard for the separation of powers, and Gierke's analysis of the role of corporations in society. The doctrine is summed up in Madison's maxim: "The accumulation of all powers . . . in the same hands . . . may justly be pronounced the very definition of tyranny." [6] It is the protection provided by divided power which is the first condition of freedom. We shall see that it is one of the leading reasons for support of numerous loyalties in society.

The major *spiritual* condition of freedom is loyalty. The essence of loyalty, it may be repeated, is devotion to a cause, a devotion requiring action which furthers the cause. But the only meaningful loyalty is a loyalty freely granted, a loyalty to which one gives himself rather than into which he is forced. Loyalty, therefore, involves choice, and is the very antithesis of slavish subjection and unthinking conformity. It was the great insight of Royce to see that he who is truly free is freely loyal. A man who has genuinely found freedom is one who has freely bestowed loyalty upon a cause and who realizes himself through realizing his cause. Authentic freedom is not a free-

---

* It should be clear that this is not the same as saying the free man is the man who does what others think he should do. It is to say that meaningful freedom means not only absence of restraint, though that is part of it, but also an idea of what freedom is for. As André Gide, most clamorous of the French immoralists, wrote: "To know how to free oneself is nothing; the arduous thing is to know what to do with one's freedom." (*L'Immoraliste,* 1921.)

dom of undisciplined and unchanneled action, but a freedom defined within freely accepted limits. What we feel to be our duties are in essence deductions from our loyalties. When we are loyal to something it means we have accepted a duty to support it by our actions and thoughts. In carrying out this duty we realize our freedom. Our loyalties, in brief, give content to freedom. They answer the question "freedom for what?" Liberty and loyalty are thus inextricably bound together.

These ideas suggest other reflections on the relations between liberty and loyalty. As political theory is translated into popular ideology and embodied in institutions, it loses its shadings and subtleties and becomes gross and crude. The precise formulations of the theorist, his careful qualifications and subtle refinements, his nice distinctions, are brushed away by impatient hands. They are debased into formulas and given universal application. Soon the original body of ideas is all but consumed by the glittering generality, the cliché, and the slogan. Is there not a Gresham's law of ideas, whereby the cheaper drive the better out of circulation?

This Gresham's law has operated with conspicuous results in the theory and practice of liberal democracy. The careful thought of a Locke on the qualifications of majority rule, of a Jefferson or Mill on the meaning of representation and equality, of a Montesquieu on the limitations of freedom, is obscured. We inherit, rather, the magisterial assertions of a Declaration of the Rights of Man and Citizen, or of a Declaration of Independence. Here we are particularly concerned with this process as it has affected the concept of liberty. Liberty was taken first to mean intellectual freedom, then abolition of arbitrary despotic power, then liberty of action under the law. It became, under the contract theory and the exigencies of politics, something far different. It came to imply a sovereignty of the individual, an individual endowed with reason and possessed of both an inalienable right and a natural urge to freedom. Such individuals might, in their discretion, contract over to the political community some portion of their absolute freedom. In nineteenth-century America physical conditions joined with this contract theory to spawn an idea of liberty which was nearly identical with defiance of all efforts to inhibit the activities of individuals. The idea is defective and disruptive in two senses; as it applies to society, and as it applies to the human being. Let de Madariaga explain the first sense:

> Since it [this concept of liberty] is due to an over-development of individualism, i.e., of the centrifugal force of society, it is one of the most disruptive factors in contemporary life, and at bottom one of the most inimical to true liberty; for not only does it call forth, as a reaction, an over-development of authority, leading to tyranny, but, in practice, it always takes the form of an attack of one set or class of citizens against the liberty of another set or class.[7]

It is false as it applies to the individual because it assumes all men desire freedom and abhor its opposite. A host of modern psychologists and sociologists testifies that the human being lacks any such instinctive urge. Rather, their testimony reads, most men feel lonely and lost if they are unlimited by authority, by custom, and by institutions. We are even being accustomed to deal with the type of the "authoritarian personality," the man who loathes and fears freedom and yearns for slavery. But for assistance here, one can look elsewhere than to the academicians. The intuitive genius of Fyodor Dostoevsky, nourished and goaded by suffering, plumbed the human psyche to depths where others feared to follow. In *The Possessed* he laid bare the relentless and criminal frenzy of the men who repudiate all traditional restraints and sanctions. The fanatic, he insisted, is precisely the man who is blemished by the limited freedom permitted him in even the most rigid society and who in his wrath and terror would destroy all. In *The Brothers Karamazov* his insight into the meaning of freedom is even more profound. In one chapter of that unfinished book he outlined his enormous conception of Christ's return to earth and of His imprisonment by the austere and ancient Grand Inquisitor. The Inquisitor abuses Christ for the harm He did men in His first incarnation. Christ gave men liberty and, in so doing, bestowed a gift too heavy for their tired shoulders. But the Church is kinder and more generous. If men will but accept its authority, the Church will liberate them from the dreadful responsibility of freedom. Most men cannot bear freedom; sooner will they accept destruction or slavery.

> Oh, ages are yet to come of the confusion of free thought, of their science and cannibalism. For having begun to build their tower of Babel without us, they will end, of course, with canni-balism. But then the beast will crawl to us and lick our feet and spatter them with tears of blood. And we shall sit upon the beast and raise the cup, and on it will be written, "Mystery." But then, and only then, the reign of peace and happiness will come for men. . . . Oh, we shall persuade them that they will

only become free when they renounce their freedom to us and
submit to us. And shall we be right or shall we be lying? They
will be convinced that we are right, for they will remember
the horrors of slavery and confusion to which Thy freedom
brought them. Freedom, free thought and science, will lead
them into such straits and will bring them face to face with
such marvels and insoluble mysteries, that some of them, the
fierce and rebellious, will destroy themselves, others, rebellious
but weak, will destroy one another, while the rest, weak and
unhappy, will crawl fawning to our feet and whine to us: "Yes,
you were right, you alone possess His mystery, and we come
back to you, save us from ourselves. . . ." [8]

In this passage Dostoevsky foretold what many moderns have repeated, that unlimited liberty is insupportable. For present purposes,
it is enough to mark its relevance to the immediate point. If liberty
is not combined with loyalty—loyalty to institutions, to causes, to
ideals—it leads first to anarchy, then to total submission. Montesquieu,
in his insistence upon the necessity of "corporations" as a preventive
of tyranny, put the concept in political terms. Tocqueville saw the
same thing when he underlined the importance of voluntary associations in American life. Erich Fromm has employed the concept
in his analysis of the flight from empty freedom into total order.
Thus, in conclusion, the theory of loyalty is necessary to round out
the theory of liberty.

Although often hinted at in previous pages, the relation between
liberty and multiple loyalties now should be made explicit. It has
been argued that freedom for the individual is the right and ability
to take action in furtherance of his loyalties. The necessary—it may not
be sufficient—social condition making such freedom possible is the
presence of a variety of loyalties in the social order.

No firmer proof of this thesis could be found than that provided
by the theory and practice of totalitarianism. By totalitarianism is
meant, of course, the theory of the limitless state, the state that transcends and encompasses the whole of society. And, to make the state
supreme, it is first necessary to destroy all potential centers of resistance. The would-be totalitarian despot must "atomize" the social
order, must break down all strong free corporations and convert society
into a pile of individual particles. After this work of destruction is
completed, it is a relatively easy matter to re-form the particles into
new associations under the sway of the state. This procedure was
followed in totalitarian Japan, Germany, and Russia. Thus did the

Japanese destroy local centers of opposition by establishing the "neighborhood associations" as channels through which the state could manipulate the citizenry. Hitler put to rest the remnants of German federalism, debased the integrity of the free cities, and demolished all strong popular organizations. This done, the populace was easily herded into "estates" where they could be "coördinated," that is, dominated, by political authority. In Russia the same course has been followed. The integrity of traditional national and ethnic loyalties was destroyed by a false federalism; workers' organizations were made a mere adjunct of state administration; the ancient peasant *mir* saw its lands and properties expropriated and its members compelled into vast collectives. In all three states the corollary of social atomization was an ideology which clamored that all allegiance must be delivered over to the state, a state embodied in one superhuman figure, whether the Emperor, the Führer, or the Great Comrade. The state became an all-embracing unity; if individuals or groups thought they had interests which the state disturbed, that was because they did not understand their "true" interests. Private interests and loyalties were the results of error or of treason. "The state is all," cry the totalitarians. "It embodies the ideal, the objective, and the real. All else is mere subjectivity. Citizens must live for the state; and in so living they achieve true freedom."

Such are the practice and doctrine of totalitarianism. That practice and doctrine fall from two fatal defects: the failure to distinguish between society and state, and the failure to distinguish between individual and society. The individual is conceived as a cell in an organic social body, without separate being and function, and the social body is in turn identified with the state. Private loyalties are subordinated. This is the way of totalitarianism; and for all the totalitarians may prate of liberty, their freedom seems much like slavery.

Let the theorem that variety of loyalties is a necessary precondition of liberty be supported by positive argumentation. Everywhere humans are found they are found as members of groups. But the group is not all: no person is totally absorbed by his groups; each retains some individuality and separateness. Moreover, group membership is usually plural. Even in the most primitive of societies men are at the same time members of several groups: family, kin-group, totem, tribe. And in more complex societies multiplicity of memberships is so conspicuous as to require no illustration. Various groupings develop

to satisfy the various needs of man and it is false to see one group
as incorporating all others. To be sure, the various groups must function within a common social order, but each retains in itself some
separateness of value and function. It is as Robert MacIver writes:
". . . There is no one group, no single form of organization, that
incorporates all the rest and wholly circumscribes the social life of
man. . . . Man needs a matrix of society, say the range of community
within which he has significant relations, but this matrix is not a
form of organization, not a corporate or integral unity." [9]

In this multiplicity of groups grows freedom. Where many groups
are permitted to exist, no one of them can usurp the powers of the
others and draw unto itself all individual allegiances. Where the
individual holds membership in many groups, each erects a barrier
against the imperialisms of the others. Although one still devotes
himself to the particular cause, he does so in accordance with his
own will, and his devotion is qualified by the existence of other, often
competing, objects of loyalty. He attains freedom and self-development
in the service of numerous objects of loyalty. If there were but one
such object, it is likely that his freedom would be reduced to subjection. Moreover, as a very practical matter, a multiplicity of groups
offsets the tendency toward oligarchy within each group. When
groups must live in an environment characterized by competition
for men's loyalties, no group can afford the stigma of being labeled
undemocratic or authoritarian. In the climate of toleration and individualism fostered by multigroup society, any group so branded loses
its prestige in the public mind.

It is true of course that variety of loyalties militates not only
toward freedom but also toward conflict. Indeed, the basic problem
of such a system is that of adjusting competing loyalties within
some common frame of reference. As society grows more complex,
so does the problem. With this we come to the everyday work of
politics. The claims of these competing loyalties must be adjusted,
and this has become the chief task of government in the modern liberal democracies. It is useless to yearn for a return to some pristine
state of social simplicity; the single-group society is a myth that
cannot be breathed into life by the efforts of fanatics or sentimentalists.
"We have left behind the one-room social habitation of our ancestors.
We have built ourselves a house of many mansions. Somehow we
must learn to make it ours." [10]

The argument must move one step more before reaching its
denouement. Since loyalty is a good for both individual and society,

since loyalty involves freedom of choice and action, and since as an empirical matter there are always numerous and sometimes competing loyalties, it follows that if a given loyalty is considered undesirable, the only ethical way to alter that loyalty is to alter its object. Not the sentiment of loyalty itself, but the object of loyal attachment, should be the target of attack. One may criticize a cause, reduce it to its constituent elements, expose its inadequacies and dangers, but *never* attack the emotion of loyalty as such. To attack one's sentiment of loyalty per se is to reduce to a mockery the good of loyalty itself. To require one to betray his loyalty is to demand that he violate the moral code that enables men to live together in mutual trust and confidence. But all objects of loyalty are subject to criticism in the open society. This is to say, for example, that the way to separate the Communist from his cause is to point out the evils of the cause, not to attack his loyalty as such. There is something mean and contemptible in efforts to wrest a man from his cause by impugning his character and questioning the motivations behind his conferral of loyalty. Can it be assumed that the loyalty of the Communist to his cause is evil, insincere, and less worthy than the loyalty of other men to their causes? His loyalty may be as pure, as noble, as important to him as yours is to you. It is not his loyalty, not his sentiment of devotion, that must be called into question. What can and must be doubted is the cause to which loyalty has been granted. That cause may be despicable; it may even be dangerous. It is, in the open society, always subject to discussion and criticism. The categorical imperative of the morality of loyalty is, as Royce knew, "Be loyal to loyalty."

Much vain and sterile discussion of liberty might be avoided if these connections between liberty and loyalty were kept in mind. Too often freedom is held to apply to abstract entities called individuals and is regarded as freedom against others. This school of thought usually concludes by remarking that no freedom is unlimited, but that freedom is subject to the equal freedom of others. Freedom of speech, for example, is not absolute but conditioned by circumstances and the rights of others. Thus freedom is left at the mercy of those who judge the circumstances, or who comprise the "others" —especially if they are stronger, or are in a majority. This is the sharp trap into which John Stuart Mill stumbled in his essay *On Liberty*. Many before and since have followed him there.

The "contradiction" between individual liberty and the needs or rights of the community is resolved when loyalty is introduced into the equation. As has been said previously, loyalty is the cement that binds men together in harmonious union. It is shared loyalties that make a community. It is action in pursuit of such loyalties which brings self-realization and freedom. Liberty and loyalty, then, are equally essential in the life of the social individual—the only life and the only individual we know.*

LIBERAL DEMOCRATIC AND AUTHORITARIAN LOYALTY COMPARED

It is not enough to talk of political loyalty as if it were an abstract manifestation, a category existing independently of conditioning forces. For the fact is that the character of the behavior described as loyal differs from place to place. In order to make that point clear, and to provide groundwork for later discussion, some of these differences as they appear in liberal democratic and authoritarian polities will be pointed out.

The concept of loyalty operative in a society can be understood only within the full cultural context and seen as part of the "design for living," the "pattern of culture," of a human group. Hegel was aware of this unity of cultural expressions long before certain anthropologists canonized it as a dogma of modern social science. In the following passage he is writing, in that heirophantic and stupefying style at which he excelled, of the web of interrelations between philosophy and other aspects of culture.

> The definite form (*Gestalt*) of a philosophy is not only contemporaneous with the definite form (*Gestalt*) of the nation within which it appears, with its constitution and form of government, its ethics, its social life, aptitudes, customs and forms

---

* As a necessary and obvious qualification of this discussion, it should be stated that in the final reckoning, liberty must mean the right to choose and act for oneself. It means the absence of compulsion. It includes the right to misbehave, to make a fool or a menace of oneself. For, where compulsion begins, responsibility ends. And no theory of democracy can be built upon premises that do not admit personal responsibility. It is suggested here only that this is but the foundation of the theory of liberty. Its upper stories, because they must house the individual-in-society, compel recognition of the connections between liberty on the one side, and loyalty on the other. D. H. Lawrence has put the point well: "Men are free when they are in a living homeland, not when they are straying and breaking away. Men are free when they are obeying some deep, inward voice of religious belief. Obeying from within. Men are free when they belong to a living, organic, believing community, active in fulfilling some unfulfilled, perhaps unrealized purpose." Quoted in Van Wyck Brooks, *The Flowering of New England* (Everyman's ed.; New York: E. P. Dutton Co., 1952), p. 541.

of leisure, with its efforts and labors in art and science, with its religions, with its belligerent and other external relations, with the decline of states, in which this particular principle had asserted itself, and finally with the origin and emergence of new views in which a higher principle is created and developed. Rather the spirit works and spreads out the principle of this stage of its many-sidedness. It is a rich spirit, the spirit of a people, an organization—a cathedral which has many vaults, passages, columnades, halls, and other subdivisions; it all has been created as one whole, with one purpose or end.[11]

First, then, a concept of loyalty must be set within its entire cultural context. And, since we are dealing with political loyalty, it is necessary to relate the concept of loyalty to other values in a political society. At the center of every society reposes a complex of values and attitudes regarded by its members as superior to other possible alternatives. These core values supply the group with an image of itself which differentiates it from other groups and endows it with a unique character and destiny. This cluster of core values aids in determining esteemed goals and in marking paths of action toward achieving them. These core values are basic to and creative of norms of more modest ambit just as a constitution is fundamental to other laws in a constitutional polity; or, to use another analogue, as Professor Kelsen's *Grundnorm* is basic to derived norms in the legal order. In fine, these supreme values define group character and channel collective activities. Nor could any functions be more vital in the service of community life, for, as the learned Maritain writes, "No society can live without a basic common inspiration and a basic common faith." [12]

The structure of political loyalty varies with the manifold of values central to each political arrangement. There is no need here to elaborate the full catalog of such central norms in authoritarian and liberal democratic societies; it is enough to suggest a few. Such values as order, obedience, hierarchy, inequality, and leadership are awarded a premium in the authoritarian society. In the liberal democratic polity the panel would feature liberty, moral and political equality, individual dignity, respect for reason, and popular participation in the political process. Joined to these different constellations of values are opposed conceptions of loyalty.

The authoritarian sees loyalty as virtually identical with unquestioning acceptance of established authority and follows a path of thought that comes uncomfortably close to reducing loyalty to obedient service. In personal relations this type of allegiance is portrayed faithfully in the network of relationships between the "loyal" servant and his master. Obedience becomes in and of itself a prime virtue and a source of pride. In a larger context, obedience—nay, servility —remains the essence of authoritarian loyalty. Psychologist Henry V. Dicks, in his engrossing study of the functional relations between personality and ideology among German citizens, embellishes this idea. In National Socialist Germany, he reports, "Conformity and 'loyalty,' as of a servant to his master, are rated among the highest virtues, and demonstratively stressed in home and institutional life, almost as synonymous with 'honour' on the one hand and with un-questioning obedience on the other." He later refers to this virtue as "'loyalty-conformity' (*Treue*)." [13]

If the National Socialist state be regarded as pathological rather than normal authoritarianism, other illustrations can be marshaled to repel the objection. Monarchical authoritarianism, the dominant po-litical order known to European peoples for centuries, can be taken as typical of the authoritarian type. Has anyone ever felt and portrayed the pageantry and temper of kingly sway more acutely than Shake-speare? In his magnificent historical dramas appear all the life and all the color, all the greatness and the baseness of the ascendant English monarchy. Nowhere has the meaning of authoritarian loyalty for the plain-folk been more poignantly expressed than in a simple colloquy in *Henry V.* When told the king's war was just, William retorts: "That's more than we know." His comrade in arms counters: "Ay, or more than we should seek after." The doctrine is completed when a common soldier, also discussing the rightness of the struggle, absolves himself and those of his estate from all blame for its con-sequences by a convenient renunciation: "If his cause be wrong, our obedience to the king wipes the crime of it out of us." [14] This is the loyalty that exalts obedience, insists upon conformity, demands unreflective acceptance, and absolves the individual from personal responsibility for actions performed in the service of political superiors.

Such loyalty, as Graham Greene has pointed out in his novel, *The Power and the Glory,* is easily confused with instinct. Perhaps Professor Pavlov's famous dogs make a more accurate analogue: with this loyalty there is no pause for thought, only automatic response to command. The task of the loyal citizen-servants is to obey orders without question and to the letter: "Theirs not to reason why, / Theirs but to do and die."

Authoritarian loyalty frequently renders a saga of selected portions of the past—as in both Shakespeare's drama and Hitler's *Reich*—and frames present loyalties in terms of reverence for that saga. With this traditionalism there is sometimes combined a veneration of the *status quo*. In both cases, intrinsic to the authoritarian conception is a belief that the object of loyalty is full and entire in itself, a finished product that cannot be improved and that must not be bared to critical examination.

This doctrine is in a very real sense negative and restrictive. It seeks to define loyalty by reference to a fixed criterion and content rather than a dynamic principle, and aims to imprison the meaning of loyal thought and deed in a single pattern, repudiating experimentation and diversity. This model of loyalty often is accompanied by an insistence that specified symbols be accepted and that behavior pursue a prescribed course. If these imperatives are met, then the demands of loyalty are fulfilled. Externals are taken as a full and accurate representation of internals. Justice Jackson has warned of the fallacy inherent in this equation: "A person gets from a symbol the meaning he puts into it, and what is one man's comfort and inspiration is another's jest and scorn. . . ." [15]

Between authoritarian and democratic loyalty there are substantial differences. Perhaps Marcel's words will offer an introduction to them:

> Concerning loyalty, one fundamental error or illusion ought to be eliminated immediately: we are over-inclined to consider it as an internal disposition oriented exclusively toward the maintenance of an existing state of things, as a simple safeguard of the *status quo*. But, in reality, the most authentic loyalty is a creative loyalty. [16]

Whether or not one cares to admit Marcel's normative distinction between authentic and (by implication) counterfeit *fidélité*, his statement does suggest the meaning of loyalty in a democracy. Democratic loyalty begins—but only begins—in obedience to ordained authority. Obedience is admitted as an instrumental virtue, as the necessary foundation of service in the cause of the object of loyalty. Democratic loyalty, Marcel's *fidélité authentique*, is also a *fidélité créatrice;* it transcends its humble origins in obedience, ascending to a superior plane of affirmation where creativity becomes its identifying emblem.

Loyalty. in this sense is a dynamic principle—as opposed to a static content—of belief and action. It is the principle of voluntary and wholehearted devotion to the best interests of the object of loyal attachment. And therein lies a decisive distinction between the two styles of loyalty. To speak of devotion to the "best interests" of the object of loyalty is to say that the citizen has both the right and the duty to determine for himself what those best interests are. He may seek advice and heed counsel; in the end the decision is his. This creed tolerates critical examination of political authority. Professor Henry Steele Commager, in a much discussed essay, expertly develops this theme. Viewing the current situation, he asks:

> What is the new loyalty? It is, above all, conformity. It is the uncritical and unquestioning acceptance of America as it is— the political institutions, the social relationships, the economic practices. . . .

But, he argues, this new identification of loyalty with conformity is false. "It is narrow and restrictive, denies freedom of thought and of conscience, and is irremediably stained by private and selfish considerations." What then is the meaning of loyalty in the liberal democratic state? It is far easier, Commager acknowledges, to describe what it is not than what it is. However, this much can be said with assurance that it is in sympathy with basic democratic values:

> Loyalty is a principle, and eludes definition except in its own terms. It is devotion to the best interests of the commonwealth, and may require hostility to the particular policies which the government pursues, the particular practices which the economy undertakes, the particular institutions which society maintains.[17]

Loyalty in the liberal democratic regime, then, does not carry with it any implication that the objects to which it attaches are complete and perfect. Quite the contrary: he whose loyalty is of this quality recognizes—even searches for—imperfections in his objects of devotion and assumes responsibility for their eradication. Rather than stand in rapt contemplation of the perfection already there, he asks how perfection can be brought closer. This is not passive acquiescence in the *status quo*, not automatic participation in ceremony, not unreflective adulation of whatever happens to be just because it is. It is devotion to the general framework and principal values of whatever may be the object of loyalty, together with vigorous and creative action to press the given ever nearer to the ideal.

By easy stages the discussion has advanced to the point where the chief distinction between democratic and authoritarian loyalty rises into full view. That distinction is the relative rationality—for want of a better term—between the two types of loyalty.

The theory of democracy maintains a belief in the power of reason. Nor, unlike some other political ideologies, does it fear to see that reason turned against itself. This philosophy is confident that intelligent men, given the facts and arguments for valid comparison, will conclude that the claims of democracy outweigh those of alternative systems. Liberal democracy assumes that its own superiority may be established through open inquiry into its own principles and practices. It is as though the democratic state said to its members: "Go. Use the reason which nature has given you and which education has trained to measure my virtues against my competitors'. Determine for yourself whether it is not so that my achievements far outweigh theirs. I am confident that your faith in me will be all the greater for your initial doubt and inquiry."

In its origins democratic loyalty, like any other, emerges from environment and social interaction; it is the product of habit and social atmosphere. But for loyalty in a democracy that is only the beginning. What begins as mere habitual or traditional loyalty is elevated into a devotion founded upon reasoned inspection of the democratic system. Democracy gives its citizens the right and power to evaluate, firm in the belief that a loyalty based originally on habit and tradition will be transformed into one founded on reason and intelligence. The highest type of loyalty to democracy issues from a reasoned consideration of the triumphs and failures of democracy as compared with those offered by competitors. Loyalty based on habit, or on mere ignorance of alternatives, is not congenial to the genius of democracy nor so highly prized as loyalty rationally given after full and intelligent consideration of alternatives.

This, of course, is not to argue that all members of democratic communities attain this superior loyalty based on reason, but that rational loyalty is the ideal and the standard of measurement. The contrast here between democratic and authoritarian loyalty is patent. Authoritarian loyalty begins, as does its democratic counterpart, in habit and emotional conditioning. And there it also ends. The authoritarian system does not invite its subjects to expose its claims to the probe of reason. It attempts to forestall inquiry into its legitimacy, and asks not for criticism but conformity. Indeed, the contention of authoritarianism is that most men are incapable of forming reasonable judgments about political issues. Therefore, authoritarianism makes its appeal not to reason but to tradition, to emotion, and to force; when the methods of exhortation fail, there remains the sword. The democratic state wins loyalty by permitting its citizens to convince themselves that the democratic way is worthy of devotion because, in the light of intelligence, it is superior to its rivals. "This means," as Sidney Hook points out, "that ultimately a democracy is committed to facing the truth about itself. Preaching and edification have their holiday uses but they do not inspire initial loyalty—only practice does—nor do they sustain loyalty against critical doubts, for they present no rational grounds. . . . A democracy is the only society which in principle believes that men can accept the truth in every realm of thought, and live with it." [18]

There is a final striking difference between authoritarian and liberal democratic ideals of loyalty.[19] As a first formulation, it might be put this way: just as democracy permits the individual wide discretion in action and thought, so does it exact from him much in the way of responsibility. We noted the facile way Shakespeare cleansed his soldiers of moral stain for deeds committed while faithfully executing the will of their political superiors. If loyalty is synonymous with obedience and conformity, then personal responsibility ends where loyalty begins. But the democrat cannot travel that easy road; for him, where loyalty begins, there also begins personal moral liability. The ineluctable corollary to democracy's dependence upon the individual as final judge of right and wrong is the command that the citizen shoulder the burden of responsibility for his judgments.

This general thesis may be brought to bear more closely on loyalty by a succinct argument. If Lincoln was right, if indeed democracy is government of, by, and for the people, who other than they can be held accountable for what the democratic government does? Nor can one blunt the thrust of the argument on the plea that a particular policy or law was a majority resolution of an issue on which he had declared with the minority. The reply is obvious and inescapable: if the majority acts immorally or imprudently it is your duty as a loyal citizen to agitate for the reversal of wrong or unwise actions. Until such agitation triumphs, you have but two choices: you may (you usually will) acquiesce in the decision, or you may take Thoreau's perilous path of civil disobedience. In either case, personal liability for your actions remains unimpaired. The philosophy of democracy, since it permits a diversity of loyalties and allows individual judgment of the wisdom and rectitude of group policies, requires in return that one realize that a loyalty freely given burdens its bestower with an untransferable weight of moral responsibility. Citizens in the democratic polity, if questioned about the justice of the government to which they have granted loyal adherence, cannot mimic Shakespeare's Bates: "That is more than we should seek after."

Recent events provide an interesting footnote to this discussion. Political philosophy wears strange masks and inhabits curious places. Practical men, disposed to disdain the seductions of its call, nonetheless fall unknowingly under its spell. Thus when the moment came for settling with some of democracy's more violent enemies after the Second World War, the ancient democratic conception of "loyalty based on reason and with attendant responsibility" was sharpened to a fine edge and used to sever branch from trunk in the authoritarian theory of loyalty. The time, as already noted, was post–World War II; the place, Nuremberg; the occasion, assigning responsibility for various war crimes. The dramatis personae were victor and vanquished. Let the Tribunal state the issue:

> It was submitted on behalf of most of these defendants [charged with violations of the laws of war, with crimes against peace, and with crimes against humanity] that in doing what they did they were acting under the orders of Hitler, and therefore cannot be held responsible for acts committed by them in carrying out these orders.[20]

And let the Tribunal speak the resolution:

> That a soldier was ordered to torture or kill in violation of the international law of war has never been recognized as a defence to such acts of brutality, though the order may be urged in mitigation of the punishment. The true test . . . is not the existence of the order, but whether moral choice was in fact possible.[21]

This is nothing other than the transformation of the democratic theory of loyalty-responsibility into binding international law. It may be true, as H. A. Smith believes, that the Nuremberg precedent amounts only to this: ". . . that the members of a Government which decides to engage in war will make their decision with the knowledge that they run the risk of being hanged at the discretion of their enemies if they do not win." [22] Even so, the fact remains that the political theory of democracy, linking personal liability with loyalty to political authority, has been written into the law of nations and used to cut down its authoritarian antithesis—that the loyal citizen lacks both the right to question authority and the duty to accept responsibility for actions taken in pursuit of loyalty. The International Military Tribunal declared that superior orders are no defense, that they are not even relevant. The only true test is "whether moral choice was in fact possible." *

CONFLICTS OF LOYALTIES

Man is both creator and creature of institutions; not of one, but of many. And to speak of institutions is to speak of loyalties. As soon as variety is admitted the possibility of conflict appears. Nor is there any easy formula for resolving these conflicts. Conflict of loyalties, then, is a perennial theme. From the distant times when Aristotle deliberated whether the good man is always the good citizen, when Socrates discussed essentially the same question from his prisoner's cell, when Sophocles dramatized the dilemma of Antigone, down to the present when men of probity debate the rightness of special test oaths of loyalty, the subject of conflicting loyalties has remained a preoccupation of Western literature and philosophy. Although the form of the problem stays constant, its content changes, and each age must seek its own formulations and resolutions.

This grand and ancient theme occupies a prominent place in political philosophy, where it usually appears under the heading "obligation." And yet, with rare exceptions, among which the outstanding is Plato's discussion in the *Crito*, the issue as stated in political philosophy is curiously abstract and artificial. The classic form of the question of obligation is: What are the grounds and limits of the subject's duty to obey political authority? This formulation inspires much subtle argument and verbal cunning, most of which is sterile because overintellectualized. Moreover, the subject of loyalty conflicts usually consumes an unduly large portion of the whole tract of loyalty. Conflict of loyalties obviously must occupy a place in any political theory and in any general discussion of loyalty. But the topic is not, or should not be, the

---

* In the interests of accuracy, it should be noted that the argument from superior orders has not been, in modern international law, a good defense against charges of violating the law of war. See Georg Schwarzenberger, *A Manual of International Law* (3d ed.; London: Stevens and Sons, 1952), p. 94, and L. C. Green, *International Law through the Cases* (New York: Frederick A. Praeger, 1951), pp. 693–697. However, the point here is that the Nuremberg Judgment goes beyond this in at least two ways: (1) it does not even consider the plea of superior orders relevant, and (2) it extends to other crimes than those comprised in the traditional and customary law of war. Moreover, the particular interest of the Nuremberg Judgment from the present point of view is its tacit recognition in theory, and incorporation into law, of the democratic theory of loyalty based on reason and with attendant responsibility.

largest share of such a discussion. So the first task is to see the matter in its proper measure.

It is true, of course, that loyalties sometimes collide. But the un-yielding fact which must stamp itself upon any vital theory of politics is that man is a social being, a being born for loyalty. From this fact any meaningful study of loyalty must take its bearings. To deal with the problems of loyalty mainly as a study in conflicting obligations is to extract only the most dramatic part and take that for the whole. Conflicts of loyalty are much discussed because they stand out, because they are interruptions of the normal pattern of affairs. But in order to place conflicting loyalties in their proper place in the discussion of loyalty, it must be stated at the outset that the subject is attractive precisely because it is exceptional and abnormal.[23]

When loyalties clash, the result is tension and indecision. But such clashes, though perhaps inevitable, are not of the essence of loyalty. What must be held always in the forefront of attention is the fact that loyalties are the clue to man's sociality. Loyalties compose the core of that common sentiment which enables men to live and work together. "Will, not force, is the basis of the state," wrote T. H. Green as the title of one of his chapters. Let it be added with Rousseau that that will is the common will, the *moi commun*, without which there can be no society and no social action. Any view which conceals that and sees conflict as the essence of loyalty ends in distortion.

One other point must be made in order to set the subject in true perspective. Discussions too often emphasize the socially destructive rather than the socially creative aspects of multiple loyalties. As formulated in political philosophy, the problem stresses the debilitating and disruptive effects of diverse loyalties. But this emphasis upon conflict does not do full justice to the positive results which can issue from the interaction of diverse loyalties. In some degree this distortion has been righted by the thinkers of the Pluralist School. They perceived that every society was in fact composed of a multiplicity of smaller societies and loyalties frequently built upon functional associations. Their lasting contribution was to insist that the only genuine freedom and the only durable social harmony emerge from a matrix in which individuals attain their highest expression through a variety of voluntary groups. They recognized that the common good can be reached by many different paths, and that diverse loyalties were the building blocks of freedom and social unity as well as the foundations of potential conflict. The Pluralists have corrected Rousseau's erroneous belief that particular wills are inherently inferior to and subversive of the general will.[24]

An individual's biography is a record of expanding loyalties—from family, to neighborhood, to school, to church, class, and nation. As one matures, his social horizons widen and he forms attachments to ever larger groups and ideals.* These later and larger loyalties are built upon and include elements from those earlier in time. Loyalty is in this sense cumulative, and the child is truly "father of the man." Yet it must not be assumed that each larger and later loyalty absorbs all those of lesser scope or earlier time, or that expansion of loyalty always takes place smoothly. The trail of the individual is strewn with shattered and abandoned loyalties. The history of the race as it has advanced into ever larger social units is punctuated with violence as group moves against group and as larger groups consolidate and consume those of lesser dimensions. What is in fact true is that one circle frequently overlaps another. And here is the root of the problem of conflicting loyalties.

It would appear that group membership and loyalty seen from the viewpoint of the individual have an inherent feature of ambivalence: loyalty is Janus-faced. The member of a group wishes and strives at one and the same time to differentiate himself not only from nonmembers, but also from the group itself. Thus, Private Jones, Infantry, differentiates himself from those who do not belong to his squad and

---

* It must be repeated, however, that often there is an inverse relation between size and distance of the object of loyalty, and intensity of loyalty: as the object grows larger and more remote, loyalty to it tends to become feebler. Sorokin reports an experiment conducted in 1928 which amply illustrates the point. Respondents, who were members of university classes in sociology, were asked how much money they would be willing to contribute to the following causes: (1) purchase of auxiliary materials for the class itself, (2) assistance for three brilliant students in the university who had been financially ruined by natural catastrophe and would be forced to drop school unless aid came their way, and (3) relief for Chinese and Russian students dying of starvation. Thus, though social distance increased from the first to the third categories, the objective importance and "emergency" character of the causes also increased. The first cause was for a mere convenience, the second to prevent a group from being forced to forego education, and the third to preserve life itself. In spite of the lesser importance of the first cause, it received more contributions from more persons than either of the other two. The second cause received second most, and the third least of all. Pitirim A. Sorokin, ed., *Explorations in Altruistic Love and Behavior* (Boston: The Beacon Press, 1950), pp. 35–38.

at the same time resists total absorption into the squad itself. He may form loyalties to a subgroup within the larger squad or he may partially identify himself with groups entirely outside the squad. In either case, he distinguishes himself from the group in which he is immediately involved.[25]

It is this "propensity," as Selznick calls it, that forms the psychological basis for conflicts of loyalty. It means that the individual is within and without a situation simultaneously. The personality is never entirely absorbed in its environment but, in some degree, always transcends it. Although all conflicts of loyalty stem from this psychological base, they can take either or both of two general forms: (1) conflict between the dictates of one object of loyalty and another quite outside it; (2) conflict within one object of loyalty.

The first category is clear. It encompasses all cases in which two or more distinct objects of loyalty clash. The root of these clashes is multiple memberships. Perhaps the examples most frequently analyzed in imaginative literature are those where loyalty to one person conflicts with loyalty to another. On a broader scale, Christopher Morley's novel *Kitty Foyle* (1939) explores fully the clash of loyalties between members of different social classes. The second category, although no more complex, is not quite so easily described and illustrated. It is meant to include those cases where an individual is rent by ambivalent conceptions of his duty to a single object of loyal attachment. Does my loyalty demand that I take this action or the other?—that is the type-question of this category of loyalty conflicts. A fecund source of this type of conflict is the varying conceptions different members or subgroups hold of the character of an organization. When members of a social unit have different images of its "organizational character," conflicts of loyalty will frequently result.*

---

* This notion of organizational character is drawn from Philip Selznick's *TVA and the Grass Roots: A Study in the Sociology of Formal Organization,* University of California Publications in Culture and Society (Berkeley and Los Angeles: University of California Press, 1949). He explains the concept as follows: "Organizations, like individuals, strive for a unified pattern of response. This integration will define in advance the general attitudes of personnel to specific problems as they arise. This means that there will be pressure within the organization . . . for unity in outlook. As unity is approximated, the character of the organization becomes defined." (P. 181.) In another place he writes: "The behavior of a faction within an organization assumes a quality of strangeness when it appears to be reckless of the basic unity of the whole group. It is the continuity of basic assumption which knits together the several administrative units. . . . When, however, a group is divided on matters of fundamental significance, the real locus

After the subject of conflict of loyalties is set in proper perspective, and some of the principal sociological and psychological factors bearing upon it are described, problems of a different order remain: the moral problems of conflicting obligations must be dealt with. To be meaningful, the discussion must take place within a defined system of normative and empirical referents. Therefore, the first job is to draw the boundaries of that system.

1) The following discussion is restricted to conflicts of obligation within democratic polities. It was remarked previously that under authoritarian and radically individualistic doctrines conflicts of loyalties raise no meaningful moral questions. Authoritarian ideologies put unqualified loyalty and obedience to the ideology and its institutional embodiments over all other ethical imperatives. Although it may or may not be valid as factual narrative, Jan Valtin reports a conversation between himself and Inspector Paul Kraus of the Gestapo which epitomizes this relationship. Kraus asks Valtin why he stayed with the Communist party long after experience had taught him to suspect it was not so pure as his original idealism had fancied it. Valtin replies:

> The Hitler Movement is built on the soldier ideal. . . . The Comintern is built upon a military discipline. Hitlerism has an ideal. Communism rejected ideas—it recognized only historical materialism. What both had in common was the soldier attitude. I was a soldier. The soldier's highest virtue is loyalty.[26]

Individualist doctrines, on the other hand, elevate the individual's loyalty to his own conscience and sense of right above all. A Thoreau, for example, who could defiantly exclaim, in his essay on *Civil Disobedience,* that a man who was right was already in a majority of one, would experience no difficulty deciding which should triumph when conscience conflicted with political authority. In his calm reply to Emerson on that famous occasion in the Concord jail there is a whole system of morality which admits of but one source and one end.

But within the liberal democratic system of political doctrine substantial ethical problems arise when loyalties conflict. Liberal democ-

---

of decision will tend to move out of the sphere of formal administrative channels. The breakdown of real unity will be reflected in administrative coördination becoming . . . a vehicle and an instrument in the unacknowledged struggle over a primary prize: the evolving character of the organization as a whole." (P. 210.) Persuasive illustration of the debilitating influence diverse interpretations of its character can exercise on an organization is provided by E. Drexel Godfrey, Jr., *The Fate of the French Non-Communist Left,* Doubleday Short Studies in Political Science (New York: Doubleday, 1955).

racy contains within itself principles that make such conflicts likely. Moreover, those same principles do not always provide unequivocal answers to the resultant ethical problems. Liberal democracy, first of all, affirms the inherent value of human personality and holds that legitimate authority must be based upon consent. Second, it maintains the principle of equality, not literal equality but equality of rights and of standing before the law. Third, the liberal democratic system accepts the technique of majority rule as the only practical and right expedient for translating into institutions and laws the doctrines of consent, of popular sovereignty, and of equality. Finally, liberal democracy encourages diversity of associations; no ban is put on the formation of voluntary groups. There is thus inherent in liberal democracy the potential for sharp moral and practical conflicts between majority and minority, with no universal formula of solution. If, for example, you posit the individual as the exclusive locus of values and at the same time agree to decide questions by counting heads, what do you do when the first principle runs up against the second? From this root dilemma between individual liberty and group authority, a dilemma inherent in liberal democratic principles, grow the fruits of conflict.*

2) The second boundary of this discussion can be drawn best by illustration. Say that the state orders a citizen into military service but his religious creed forbids such service. Here is a distinct clash between two loyalties. Discussion of the ethical problems it poses can take either of two forms. The first is to ask what formula should be followed to determine one's course of action when loyalties conflict. This is the way the problem of conflict of loyalties is usually framed.

---

* For a very different approach see Franz L. Neumann, "On the Limits of Justifiable Disobedience," in R. M. MacIver, ed., *Conflict of Loyalties*, Religion and Civilization Series, The Institute for Religious and Social Studies (New York: distributed by Harper, 1952), pp. 45–57. Neumann searches for a universal formula applicable in any political system. He holds that certain facets of human nature contain implications relevant to conflicts between citizen and state regardless of the form of the state. Neumann presents his thesis as follows: "Every doctrine of natural law is based upon the existence of man as a rational being who has an existence independent from the political society within which he lives. Only those who accept Platonism, Universalism, etc., can reject this basic truth. By speaking of man, we speak of him as being endowed with reason, for only thus can we define man (as contrasted with other forms of organic life). But if we accept the truth, then we do accept certain minims following from this proposition. These minims . . . are thus valid, regardless of the political system, valid against any political system, even against a democracy." *Ibid.*, p. 55.

But not so here. A discussion of this form must begin and end with each participant deciding for himself the order of importance of his loyalties. When two loyalties of totally different orders collide there is no universal formula by which choice between them can be made. Each must follow his own lights and answer to his own conscience. MacIver, discussing conflicts between majority and minority, puts the point clearly. When the policy of the majority seems to an individual to be destructive of the general good, he "must simply choose what seems to him the greater loyalty." MacIver continues:

> Whether he obeys, or disobeys (and takes the consequences), he cannot . . . be condemned. For his disobedience depends upon the same sense of obligation which alone justifies enforcement of the law. He disobeys in the name of the greater good, not of his own alone. The passive resister, the pacifist in time of war, the "protestant" who refuses to recant at the bidding of authority, cannot for a moment be placed in the same category as the criminal, the individual who deliberately or carelessly seeks his own ends at the cost of society. The majority is as much entitled to think the former misguided, even to coerce them where they believe their principles endanger the common welfare, as these in turn are entitled to resist. There is no solution here. The sense of right alone must guide each of the conflicting parties. Whatever the consequences, each side is right to choose what seems to it the greater value, the greater loyalty. . . . There is not one loyalty, but many, and they all spring alike from the heart of the individual, who alone must find for himself a way of reconciliation. If he is true to his own self he cannot be false to any man.[27]

But the problem can be approached from another direction, namely, by asking what canons of conduct can be logically educed from democratic principles themselves. Instead of seeking a standard by which to rank loyalties according to their "importance," we can examine liberal democratic principles for the guides they supply when loyalties clash. We can ask: What principles relevant to the solution of loyalty conflicts can be extracted from liberal democratic doctrine? This in no way assumes that any one loyalty overrides all others; it merely frames the problem so as to emphasize what the principles of democracy imply when loyalties conflict.

3) When, under the stress of rapid social change and basic ideological divisions, consensus deteriorates within a community and groups mobilize into warring factions, there is little profit in speaking of the ethical problems of conflict among loyalties. For then the received systems of moral beliefs are no longer accepted, and decisions turn not upon ethical considerations but upon calculations of power. Dis-

cussion of ethical questions presupposes a shared system of values; where that is lacking, it is idle to debate ethical niceties. So we presuppose an ongoing social order, an order in which most men are agreed upon the values of society and the meaning of social justice, and in which institutions and ideas are tolerably well adapted to material conditions. But in any working social order, even the most harmonious, conflicts of loyalties will occur. And as social organization increases in complexity so too increases the likelihood of conflicting loyalties.

The typical instances of conflicting loyalties of greatest concern to political philosophy occur when the government commands a citizen to do one thing and his private morality or the morality of his allegiance-groups commands him to do the opposite. Recent constitutional jurisprudence affords a lucid example of the type in the two cases of *Minersville School District* v. *Gobitis* and *West Virginia State Board of Education* v. *Barnette*.[28] In those cases an agency of government prescribed that all children attending the public schools of the state must salute the American flag and pledge their allegiance to it. This requirement ran counter to the beliefs held by members of a certain religious group. The issue was clear: as members of the political community the students were required to demonstrate their loyalty by pledging allegiance to the symbol of political authority, but as members of a religious community they were required to repudiate the obnoxious ritual.

Nor was there evident any of that redeeming humor which Charles Lamb achieved in his delightful essay "On Ears." He had no ear for music, Lamb regretted, and try as he might could not even manage "God Save the King." And yet, even with that baneful blemish on the character of an Englishman, no one had ever dared impugn his loyalty. But the inability of the Witnesses of Jehovah to perform the ritual act suggested their appreciation of the duties of citizenship might be something less than perfect. The Supreme Court formulated the issue as one between national unity and individual freedom. In the Minersville case Justice Frankfurter upheld the flag salute laws on the grounds that the overriding need was for national unity, that that unity was one of sentiment, and that it could be manifested and strengthened by requiring persons to engage in prescribed symbolic acts.

> The ultimate foundation of a free society is the binding tie of cohesive sentiment. Such a sentiment is fostered by all those agencies of the mind and spirit which may serve to gather up

> the traditions of a people, transmit them from generation to
> generation, and thereby create that continuity of a treasured
> common life which constitutes a civilization.[29]

Therefore, he concluded, the obligation to perform acts symbolic of
national unity transcended contrary religious scruples.

In this case the issue of conflict of loyalties was squarely posed and
bluntly answered. Frankfurter, with his usual perspicacity, saw that
the ultimate issue in all such conflicts is that of unity against diversity,
of the whole against the part. That is the way in which the problem of
obligation is nearly always posed in political philosophy. Must individual loyalties be allowed full expression, even at the risk of injury
to collective unity? Or shall the collective unity take precedence over
individual variations? Or can some compromise between the two be
effected? Frankfurter's resolution of the dilemma also followed the
usual form (as distinguished from content) employed by political
philosophers. First, the question is posed in terms of an absolute opposition between two alternatives: the law of the state commands that
the flag be saluted, whereas religious creed commands that it not
be saluted. Then it is asked which command is of superior weight,
that of the political law or that of the religious law. Next a choice
is made; one must stand and one must fall. Here it was decided that
the students' obligations as members of the political community out-
weighed their obligation as members of a religious community. In
support of that choice Justice Frankfurter appealed both to expediency and to principle; his strongest argument rested on the principle that the value of national unity—"an interest inferior to none
in the hierarchy of legal values"—transcended both mere legal obligation and loyalty to religious creed. In this respect too his resolution
followed a typical form, for conflicts of loyalty usually are settled
by recourse to another loyalty or obligation superior to those in immediate controversy.

The important point about this "either-or" solution is precisely
that it is "either-or." The triumph of one loyalty works violence on
the other. Such solutions appear more often in philosophy than in
life. When a conflict of obligations assumes the form of a legal
question, then of course the decision must be absolute, must be
"either-or." But when conflicts of loyalty burden an individual, or
press upon his relations with other persons, they usually are not
forced to the extreme. Far more frequently an effort is made to
compromise them rather than to press implacably toward a show-
down. Men will usually try to preserve something of each loyalty,

to "save the appearances," rather than to demand clarity and finality. The philosopher, of course, cannot accept such halfway solutions; it is his business to reach binding conclusions and vindicate abstract principles. But Everyman, showing perhaps a better grasp of reality than of principle, prefers to save what he can of each loyalty. Only the man who toils under the weight of an ideology will abhor compromise. Those not so burdened apply in practice an altered form of Royce's imperative: Be loyal to loyalty. Knowing that loyalty itself is a value not to be denied without pain, one will try to preserve as much as possible of all his loyalties. For when one loyalty can be saved only at the cost of another, the good of loyalty itself has suffered. No man can experience repeated destruction of very many of his deepest loyalties and still retain the courage and conviction to continue granting his loyalty to causes and groups.[*]

There are times, however, when the contrast between loyalties is harsh and destructive conflict cannot be averted. Thus it was in the Gobitis case: thus too when a man is forced to elect between one group or creed and another, although both may have great attraction for him. Then, setting aside all considerations of expediency, a choice must be made. And here all the old and troublesome problems of political obligation and civil disobedience come to the front. Is the first obligation of the citizen to his state? Is it to his own conscience? Is it to one or another of the associations to which he belongs? Or

---

[*] One research team reported this conclusion: "The workers do not accept the inevitability of conflict, nor do they accept the necessity of binding themselves to one group or the other. They accept the status of dual allegiance and, at least under normal conditions, seem to experience no internal stress as a result." (P. 1274 in first reference cited below.) Another researcher studied the same problem at one of the Swift Company plants in Chicago soon after a bitter strike. He found that even then dual allegiance was not strained for about two-thirds of the production workers. The workers refused to see loyalty to both union and company as contradictory. Thus, when union leaders urged them into a strike and posed the issue as a clear test of union versus company loyalty, the men responded by developing a dislike for their leaders but retaining their union loyalties. (Forty-seven per cent of the rank and file were unfavorable to union leaders; 27 per cent were neutral; 26 per cent approved; but 75 per cent held on to their union allegiance.) The workers distinguished between the union and its leaders and between the company and its foremen. They were loyal to both union and company as institutions. Recent studies support these points. "Dual Loyalty in Industrial Society," *The Monthly Labor Review*, LXXVI (Dec., 1953), 1276–1277. See also the perceptive discussion in Peter Drucker, *The New Society: The Anatomy of the Industrial Order* (London: William Heinemann, 1951), pp. 128–134.

can it be that none of these automatically outweighs all the others? If that be so, under what conditions should each prevail?

The theory of obligation in the democratic state is grounded in two principles. First, the citizen is presumed to be endowed with reason and conscience. Second, political authority must rest upon consent. If these two principles are admitted to be essential elements in the philosophy of democracy, then certain implications for the theory of obligation are inescapable. Although a promulgated law seldom includes a provision that obedience is optional (it may of course except specified persons from its terms), democratic theory itself must be interpreted to admit that at some times, and for some persons, the state can make no moral claim to obedience.

1) The democratic state lacks moral authority to impose duties upon any person who refuses to subscribe to democracy itself or to the particular institutional form democracy may take in one or another place. The monarchist, the anarchist, the fascist, and the many others who deny the philosophy of democracy itself can argue that the democratic state has no claim on their loyalty and no inherent moral right to impose obligations upon them. Since men who hold these views have never consented to the system of democracy, and since democratic theory insists that legitimate authority rests upon consent, it follows that the state cannot morally require obligation and loyalty from those who do not accept its tenets and who refuse their consent to the democratic system. With those classes the democratic state, consistently with its own rationale, can have recourse only to power and expediency. It can be argued, and often it is argued, that the democratic state can impose its will upon those of its citizens who refuse their consent because it is necessary for social unity or for efficiency and universality in legal administration. The chief point is that the state has no inherent moral standing to require obligation when consent is lacking. To the democrat this may seem a harsh conclusion, and one that invites disobedience and anarchy. But to fear this is to forget the first condition of effective social order, general agreement upon fundamental principles and the meaning of social justice. When that unity has splintered it is useless to fear the thrust of an argument that denies the state moral authority to impose its will upon the recalcitrant. For where generalized and voluntary loyalty to the polity is lacking, questions of morality are usually idle: the only appeal is to force and expediency. Finally, it must be remembered

that just as the person who has not consented to the system of democratic authority cannot morally be compelled by that authority, so also does he himself lack any moral basis from which to impose his own demands upon the state. In short, where voluntary consent is lacking relations between state and citizen are essentially relations of war in which both sides use the stratagems and implements of battle, and in which either may or may not grant quarter to over-powered opponents.

2) Similar considerations apply in the situation where persons may subscribe to democracy itself but insist that the political arrangements of a particular system which calls itself democratic are in fact something quite different. This, for example, might be the argument of the theoretical Marxist who must live in what he derisively calls a "bourgeois democracy." Such democracy, he taunts, is only sham democracy. Behind the façade of majoritarian principles, representative institutions, and civil liberties there lurks one inexorable fact— minority rule by a master class. But it is not necessary to read Marx in order to know that a system which appears democratic may in fact be oligarchic or contain elements of the oligarchic principle. It does not require deep study to discover that the American Congress is dominated by organized and entrenched minorities, that the electoral process often does violence to the representative principle, and that the committee system seems designed for the very purpose of baffling the translation of public opinion into public policy.[30] And by what subtle arguments can the Supreme Court with its power of judicial review be squared with the premises of democracy? At the state level, again as the most superficial study amply discloses, there are equally blatant discrepancies between democratic principle and institutional practice.

When there is a discrepancy between democratic theory and operative political institutions, and when that discrepancy is great, he who believes in democracy is under no compulsion to obey the commands of an undemocratic government. He has consented to democracy, not to some corruption thereof. He can argue that his duty of obedience ends where genuinely democratic institutions end. The citizen of the democratic state must always distinguish between loyalty to the principles of democracy and loyalty to a particular set of governmental institutions. His first duty is to principle, and when principle and practice collide, the latter must submit. Loyalty to the principles of democracy demands, in the first place, that the citizen do his utmost to assure harmony between democratic principle and practice. But if a particular set of institutions perverts democratic principle, and if it is not possible to alter those institutions by democratic techniques, then his loyalty demands that he take the road of civil disobedience.

It has been argued by some very persuasive writers, Roberto Michels and Gaetano Mosca among them, that every "democracy" is in fact an oligarchy, that the substance of power is always held by the few no matter what may be the forms of power. "Democracy," they say, can mean at best only the relatively free turnover and rejuvenation of oligarchies through easy access of new personnel into the seats of power. The writings of this "elitist" school have given political scientists and sociologists a sharpened awareness of the frequent difference between appearance and underlying reality in social life. From an earlier day when academic study of political phenomena emphasized formal analysis of law and institutions, a shift has been effected to study of the "political process" and informal maneuverings behind the headlines and the display of office. Indeed, so far has this movement gone that some fail to see, because they fail to look for, anything other than informal processes. That may be extravagant. But, *if* the fact be proven, if it be true that all government is in fact oligarchic, then it follows necessarily that the believer in democracy is under no moral compulsion to obey the commands of such undemocratic regimes. His first loyalty, again, is to principles, and where practice perverts principles his choice is clear. It makes no sense to say we must compromise with harsh reality and accept the fact that practice often falls short of perfection. The only honest answer for the democrat is that either practice must be altered, or else government has no moral claim upon his loyalty and obedience.

In the two foregoing situations, a citizen can justify political disobedience by appealing to the philosophy of democracy. In the first (the case of the disbeliever in democracy) he can argue that he never consented to the democratic system and never granted his loyalty to it. In the second (the case of the believer in democracy who maintains that the institutions of a particular regime are nondemocratic in character) he can argue that his first loyalty is to democratic principles and that when political practices subvert those principles his prime loyalty justifies disobedience to the dictates of the state. In the present writer's view, those are the only grounds upon which conflict of loyalties can validly result in civil disobedience as long as the argument for resistance starts from the democratic premises of moral individualism, consent, and majority rule. Often there will be conflicts between loyalties of different types (e.g., political and religious) in which the individual may assert that one loyalty is inherently superior to the other. One may maintain that, should there be conflict, his religious loyalties will always precede his political loyalties; but he must do so on the basis of his own value system rather than by logical argument from democratic principles.

In a recent article David Spitz suggests a third type of situation in which the democrat is morally justified in disobeying the laws.[31] He begins by positing a citizen who believes in the democratic ideology, who accepts the particular regime he lives under as being essentially democratic, and who is prepared, "on the whole," to obey the laws. "They obey not necessarily because they think that the law is right, but because they think it right to obey the law."[32] But that does not mean they are required to obey all laws. The democrat's first loyalty is to the system, not to the laws, for they are only means. And should any law threaten the principle of democracy itself the democrat "may be compelled to defend it [the democratic system] against the laws."[33]

This argument proves too much. For, in effect, it denies the principles of democracy in order to preserve democracy. Spitz argues that individuals or minorities need morally to submit only to those laws they think to be in the best interests of democracy, or at least not destructive of democracy; and yet, if democracy means anything at all, it means popular sovereignty. Popular sovereignty in turn means as a practical matter majority rule and representative government. Therefore, if a law has been passed by a legal and legitimate majority, or their representatives, then no citizen who subscribes to democracy, and who does not argue that the methods by which the law in question was passed were undemocratic, can claim personal exemption from it just because he thinks it destructive of democracy. When he subscribed to democracy he subscribed to majority rule, and to permit a minority to impose limits upon majority rule is, in effect, to substitute minority for majority rule. The principle of majority rule knows only the limits that the majority sets upon itself. Any other form of limitation is undemocratic. Of course, courts and constitutions may restrict the power and authority of majorities but that is so because, first of all, the majority has consented to the limitations and, secondly, because the majority may alter the limiting provisions when it wishes to do so. To argue that a minority may morally disobey the will of the majority whenever the minority thinks a

PART TWO

3

The Background of American Loyalty

THE HISTORY OF AMERICAN LOYALTY STILL REMAINS A relatively uncharted land. Only a few pioneers have traveled any considerable distance in those regions and returned with accounts of their discoveries. Aside from a few scattered and partial studies of American nationalism and patriotism, Curti's treatment stands as the only work of major scope dealing with the background of loyalty in America.[1] It is no criticism of that book to say that it but sketches the broadest contours of the territory and leaves most of the variations uncharted: no criticism because Professor Curti had few enough signposts to guide him. And, indeed, in more than one place he was without signposts at all.

[1] For numbered notes to chap. 3, see pp. 196–199.

THE PROBLEM DEFINED

A sense of background is indispensable if modern situations are to be understood. The size and shape of present facts and findings are less subject to distortion when projected against the screen of the past. If it be true, as Lord Bryce so often and so eloquently insisted, that it is the office of historians to provide the political analyst with empirical grist for his mill, it must be said that the historians have not discharged their obligations in this constructive contract. The political scientist, then, must prepare his own chart, even while recognizing that the risk of error is grave, and the attainment of anything better than a gross representation unlikely. It must be stipulated that the project is not one of writing a full-scale history of American loyalty, but the humbler task of sketching in boldest strokes an historical frame which can contribute to present understanding.

By and large, the American heritage of political speculation has not placed *explicit* emphasis on the factor of loyalty. It inclines, rather, to discussions of individual rights, constitutionalism, and the proper province of government. However, as the following pages will show, the tradition is by no means devoid of appreciation for the factor of loyalty. Some portions of our heritage manifest keen awareness of the meaning and importance of loyalty in politics. Thus, an immanent regard for loyalty is revealed in the dominant tone of moderation and compromise characteristic of so much native political philosophy. Great respect for loyalty is intrinsic also in the insistence upon the obligation of contract which runs as a leitmotif through our jurisprudence and ethics. Furthermore, the Americans began their career as an independent nation with a political theory pledging loyalty to government so long as it performs those obligations imposed upon it by the terms of the contract that brought it into being. These and other themes will be extracted and analyzed in subsequent pages.

Political practice and popular sentiment, as distinguished from more formal philosophy, are rich with praise for the virtue of loyalty. As a counterweight to the Brahman detachment of Emerson who, in his famous essay on "Politics," could write

> In dealing with the State we ought to remember that its institutions are not aboriginal, though they existed before we were born; that they are not superior to the citizen; that every one of them was once the act of a single man; every law and usage was a man's expedient to meet a particular case; that they all

are imitable, all alterable; we may make as good, we may make better,[2]

we have Lincoln's heartfelt pleas for loyalty to the Union, Theodore Roosevelt's strictures on the duties of citizenship and the American Way, the Constitution worship which is so much a part of the national political mythology, and many similar expressions. Perhaps the tone and some of the content of this strand of thought are suggested by the following quotations from a civics syllabus formerly used in the New York public schools for grades one through nine.

> As the work progresses, great emphasis should be laid on the value of law and order, and the importance of having a law-abiding population. The child should learn how laws are made, and his obligation to obey them. He should also learn how laws can be bettered and that he has an obligation to stand for progress.
> Care should be taken to keep constantly before the children that true patriotism consists not only in good citizenship as ordinarily defined but carries with it the obligation of making the supreme sacrifice for one's country the same as would be done for one's mother.[3]

The accurate conclusion about the role of loyalty in American thought would appear to be not that the virtue of loyalty has been neglected, but that it has been formulated and expressed by popular statesmen and orators and has established deep roots in the popular mind. This chapter then breaks into two main divisions: (1) the (relatively) formal theory of loyalty, and (2) the meanings of loyalty in the popular mind.

The recent stress on loyalty is felt by many commentators, especially those of the "Liberal" persuasion, to be antithetical to our traditions. However, in light of the interpretation offered here this emphasis is seen to be not so much a reversal of trends as an acceleration and intensification of what has always been there.[4] What is most striking and novel in the present situation is: (1) the widespread official concern with loyalty, as expressed in a plethora of investigating committees and statutory enactments, (2) the amount, duration, and intensity of popular and official attention given to the problem, and (3) a powerful tendency to equate loyalty with conformity and to brand dissent as prima facie disloyal and un-American.*

---

* Even official concern with loyalty is not entirely new, as the Alien and Sedition Acts of John Adams' Administration and the "test oath" cases during and after the Civil War attest. Compare with the third item above: "Americans have

It is noteworthy that the persistent reluctance of the political philosophers to face the problem of loyalty is still very much a part of the American scene. In the present period no political theorist has come forward to undertake a full-scale investigation of the problem in its broadest aspects. By and large, the concern of the academicians has been limited to more technical facets, such as the procedure of investigating committees and loyalty review boards, academic tenure, the legal status of test oaths, and the analysis of statutory enactments relating to loyalty and subversion. In this default, the field has been left to the politicians, the journalists, and a few scattered essayists.

THE THEORY OF LOYALTY AND DISLOYALTY

The history of American loyalty must reach back in time to a point well beyond the consolidation of the nation as an independent polity. For the documents of 1776 and 1789, which launched the young republic on its way, derived their inspiration from many lands and times. At the same time, men were asking how these foreign ideas fitted their plight as newcomers in a strange and hostile land. From the beginning the reception of foreign doctrines and institutions was not passive; nearly every importation, from Calvinism to the common law, underwent a change into "something rich and strange" after brief residence in American parts. The colonists, those who were soon to become Crèvecoeur's "the American, this New Man," did not pay servile obeisance to their imported heritage but transformed it into something distinctly their own before according it the dignity of respect and loyalty. This process began with the landing of the first sizable group of settlers on the New England coast and continues to work its magic even to our own day.

The narrative opens in England. There the revolutionary explosions of the seventeenth century struck off ideological sparks which found dry tinder in American conditions and ignited fires which, in time, consumed the framework of the old order. That old order had stern and simple conceptions of the meaning of obligation and the source of political authority. We can look to no less a personage than the

---

long been fearful of 'radicalism.' They usually do not distinguish one type from another but lump all radicals together under a label that means 'dangerous.' " And: "The tendency to coerce conformity and to resort to mob violence against the dissenters from popular opinion has been much greater in American history than men have realized or like to admit." Howard K. Beale, *Are American Teachers Free?* (New York: Charles Scribner's Sons, 1936), pp. 85, 19.

king himself for a statement of this theory of authority. In his *Trew Law Of Free Monarchies,* James I of England described kings as the "breathing images of God upon Earth," and declared that the mysteries and expressions of kingly authority were no more to be looked into than were the credentials of God Himself. "That which concernes the mysterie of the Kings power, is not lawfull to be disputed; for that is to wade into the weaknesse of Princes, and to take away the mystical reverence, that belongs unto them that sit in the Throne of God." [5] The king could do no wrong, and the subjects could do nought but yield him that "mystical reverence" which was properly his. Subjects owed their king loyalty and obedience not just because the throne was his by undisputed and ancient inheritance, but because he was as well the earthly representative of God.

This conception of the "divinity that doth hedge a king," though relatively unimportant in earlier eras, became the accepted doctrine of the monarchist and absolutist thinkers of seventeenth-century England. It was rounded out by a theory of obligation which admitted but one alternative to anarchy—total submission. This doctrine received its classic expression in the pages of Hobbes' *Leviathan,* but was also propagated by many lesser luminaries. Although Hobbes stripped from the shoulders of kings their gorgeous cloaks of divine authority and left them only secular robes, the duty to obey stood unshaken, though now it was justified by expediency alone. The king made the laws, and without him the populace was a body without a head. Thus, in 1691, William Sherlock, dignitary of the Church of England, noted that "The Church of England has been very careful to instruct her Children in their Duty to Princes; to obey their Laws, and submit to their Power, and not to resist, though very injuriously oppressed. . . ." He then moved on to conclude that ". . . all Sovereign Powers, whose Powers and Government is [*sic*] *thoroughly settled,* must be obeyed, whatever their legal Right be; for they have the Authority of God, to which our Obedience and Subjection is due, and that supersedes all further enquiries." [6]

The other side of this theory of loyalty was a theory of betrayal, of disloyalty, formulated in equally sweeping terms and expressed most fully in the English law of treason. Blackstone, that deep oracle of the laws of England, pronounced that "Natural allegiance is a debt of gratitude, which cannot be forfeited, cancelled, or altered by any change of time, place, or circumstances. . . ." He who withheld allegiance and betrayed his king was a "monster and a bane to human society." The law conceived of treason as betrayal, by thought or action, of the loyalty due from inferiors to superiors.* Treason law was a chief weapon in the struggle to establish a centralized monarchy in England during the Tudor and Stuart eras. Although the great Treason Act of 1351 [7] defined with satisfactory precision those deeds and thoughts that were of treasonous quality, it was stretched by ingenious royal judges and lawyers until, as Weyl put it, it would "fit any neck." [8] It was made to cover motive as well as action, and ranged from mere utterance of seditious words to seduction of the queen and her daughters. So flexible was the law that at one time Henry VIII could declare it treason to believe that Mary and Elizabeth were legitimate, whereas at still another time it was treason to believe them bastards. The ultimate betrayal, the conduct that constituted high treason, was a blow against the monarch himself—"When a man doth compass or imagine the death of our Lord the King, of my Lady the Queen, or of their eldest son and heir."

These doctrines of authority and obligation, with their attendant notions of loyalty and disloyalty, were doomed to a short and sickly existence in America. Royal governors soon discovered that the more frequently the doctrines were asserted, the more vigorously they were countered by new principles whose impact shattered imperial authority. The English themselves provided the colonists with their sturdiest weapons in the ideological contest that preceded the military struggle for independence. From the pages of Harrington, Sydney, and Locke came all the basic ideas underlying the American Revolution. John Locke, who granted that ". . . civil government is the

---

* At this time, feudal concepts were still heavily stamped on the law. The word "allegiance" derives from the French *a* (to), plus the French *liege* (meaning literally fief-holding, and by extension, having the right to receive obedience and service). In Old French a *ligeance* meant the jurisdiction or territory of a liege lord. In archaic English it meant allegiance. Webster's Unabridged states that the meaning of "allegiance" also was influenced by the Latin *ligare* (to bind), and by *lex, legis* (law). The close connection between the ideas of loyalty and legality is revealed by the derivation of the word "loyal." It is a combined form of the Old French *leial* and the Latin *legalis*. "Loyal" is an obsolete synonym for "lawful," "legitimate." The concept of allegiance, being feudal, was also personal, and implied a relation of inferior-superior in the feudal hierarchy. In the course of time, during which the feudal order disintegrated, it was applied only to the king and not to intervening lords. But something of the ancient notions still lives on in the law. For illustrations, see Calvin's Case 7 Co. Rep. 1a (1608); and *Joyce* v. *Director of Public Prosecutions*, A.C. 347 (1946). Both cases are reprinted in part in L. C. Green, *International Law through the Cases* (New York: Frederick A. Praeger, 1951), pp. 460–467, 471–478.

proper remedy for the inconveniences of the state of nature . . . ," could also assert that since man was born free and rational there was nothing ". . . able to put him into subjection to any earthly power but only on his own consent. . . ." He found it equally easy to maintain that government might be ". . . directed to no other end but the peace, safety, and public good of the people." It followed that if the governors, by "a long string of abuses, prevarications and artifices . . . ," acted contrary to their trust and put themselves into a state of war against the governed, then "everyone has a right to defend himself and to resist the aggressor." [9]

After milder measures failed, this theory of obligation was eagerly embraced by the revolutionary colonials and became the official philosophy of the age. Thomas Jefferson, who wrote it into the Declaration of 1776 in language as majestic as any ever penned, could say with modesty and accuracy that he created no new doctrines but merely stated the consensus of his time and party. The Declaration rests on the basic premise that faith and loyalty are owing only to a government founded on contract and consent, and working for the common interest. The American theory of loyalty smashed the ancient English notions and built anew on consent rather than tradition, on individual judgment rather than forced conformance. This conception of loyalty had great impact on subsequent developments and is a living force even in the present day. It must be said, however, that in our time it has encountered an increasingly critical attack.*

---

* One of the most sensitive indicators of this shift in opinion is the Supreme Court. It appears that the right of revolution, the core of the early American conception of loyalty, and once official doctrine of the land, is now repudiated by the Court on the argument that the existing order provides techniques of peaceful change and is therefore justified in adopting measures for its own defense against projected violence. Note the following quotation from a recent case: "Whatever theoretical merit there may be to the argument that there is a 'right' to rebellion against dictatorial governments is without force where the existing structure of the government provides for peaceful and orderly change. We reject any principle of governmental helplessness in the face of preparation for revolution, which principle, carried to its logical conclusion, must lead to anarchy. No one could conceive that it is not within the power of government to prohibit acts intended to overthrow the Government by force and violence." *Dennis* v. *United States,* 341 U.S. 501 (1950). Of course, the Communists, against whom this salvo was directed, maintain that American democracy is sham democracy, giving the populace only the forms, but never the substance, of power. Moreover, the Communist Control Act of 1954, "outlawing" the party, cuts the ground from under the Court's assumption that processes for "peaceful and orderly change" are available to all.

We can now reverse the coin of loyalty and observe its other side, disloyalty. The American conception of treason, deemed sufficiently important by the fathers of the Republic to merit inclusion in the supreme law of the land, in some ways rests upon English ideas. But in other ways it subjects the English tradition to profound modifications. The importance of the law of treason in the early American mind stemmed from two factors: (1) those who signed the Declaration and nearly all who endorsed the Constitution were clearly traitors under English law; (2) these same men were deeply devoted to human freedom and poignantly aware of the oppressions that attend arbitrary political authority. Jefferson summarized both sentiments when he wrote that ". . . the unsuccessful strugglers against tyranny have been the chief martyrs of treason laws in all countries." These men well knew the brutal purposes to which the law of treason had been bent in eradicating political and religious dissenters in England and on the Continent. To that cruel history they did not propose to add further chapters from American experience.

The first step was to strip away the many accretions which had fastened to the law of treason through the course of centuries and lay bare the kernel of the idea. Treason was restricted to public acts and had no relevance to private betrayal.* It applied only to deeds and not thoughts. It had nothing to do with the betrayal of social superiors by their inferiors. It ran only against betrayal of a sovereign government and not against one or another official. After these encrustations were removed, the essence of treason was seen to be just as it had been in the statute of 1351: "If a man do levy war against our Lord the King in his realm, or be adherent to the King's enemies in his realm, giving them aid and comfort in the realm, or elsewhere, and thereof be provably attainted of open deed. . . ."

It would be superficial analysis, though, to conclude that this is the sole meaning of disloyalty in American political thought. If the ideas of the Declaration are coupled with those in the Constitution and its Preamble, it becomes clear that the only legitimate loyalty is loyalty to the free society and its government. Refusal to obey a government that has itself betrayed the trust reposed in it by the citizenry is not disloyalty; it is the duty of the conscientious citizen. This is

---

* Under the English practice treason was tightly bound up with private betrayal. Thus, betrayal of husband by wife was petit treason and, if the betrayal ran far enough, was punishable by death. Similar reasoning was applied to serfs who showed disloyalty to their lords and broke the web of allegiance and protection which held the feudal order together.

to say that there is a theory of *just* government contained in the Declaration and the Preamble and never lost sight of in later times; only this kind of government—the responsible agent of a free society —merits loyalty. When government fails in the attainment of certain ends, when it becomes actually destructive of them, it no longer commands allegiance. Resistance then becomes moral duty. Thus did Jefferson boldly proclaim: "Resistance to tyrants is obedience to God." Legal obligation of course remains. "Treason against the United States," reads the Constitution, "shall consist only in levying war against them, or in adhering to their enemies, giving them aid and comfort." It says nothing of the quality or type of government against which the treason is perpetrated. Nor should this paradoxical result excite astonishment: the American political tradition has never made the facile equation of legality with morality.

Thus far the concept of loyalty is seen to contain two elements: (1) a precise legal definition of disloyalty, and (2) a positive theory holding that loyalty is owed only to the just government. These two constituents still compose the core of what might be called the formal theory of American loyalty. The doctrine can be stated in precise language and would appear to be clear enough. Yet, this attractive simplicity is deceptive: there are two complicating factors.

The first is the recurrence of statutes that expand and complicate the concept. There have been, and there are now, federal and state enactments that proscribe the profession of specified beliefs and the performance of certain acts on the dubious assumption that loyalty can be legislated into being by prohibiting disloyal acts and thoughts. Indeed, for a while one state believed, and a majority of the federal Supreme Court agreed, that loyalty could be brought into existence by requiring the performance of a specified ritual act. The Court, at least, thought better of this after a couple of years.[10] The notorious Alien and Sedition Acts of the Adams Administration and the equally well-known "Smith Act" of 1940 provide the best illustrations on the federal level of the attempt to legislate loyalty by forbidding conduct considered to be its opposite. On the state level, ample illustrations are afforded by the ill-famed Civil War test oaths, by the criminal syndicalism laws of the post–World War I period, and by the more recent rash of legislation concerning communism and subversion.*

---

* The states have shown high exuberance in legislating on these subjects in the recent period. At the end of 1950 there were over 300 state laws aimed at communism and subversion. See Walter Gelhorn, ed., *The States and Subversion* (Ithaca: Cornell University Press, 1952), p. 359. All such laws are conveniently

These and similar statutes, because of their number and elasticity, have complicated and confused the original concept of loyalty. Certainly, loyalty now means far more than its constitutional definition. One of the more melancholy features of the current period is the difficulty of specifying the content of this "far more." But that is for later consideration.

The second complicating factor is really an extension of the first. Simply stated, it is this: as a result of the proliferation of laws regulating loyal and disloyal conduct, the meaning of "just government" cannot be identified easily and precisely. Lacking such identification, the kind or extent of loyalty owing to government is not readily ascertained. Is the so-called Smith Act wise legislation? Unwise? Or, as the Communists insist, is it a slave law? If the latter, surely government has broken the terms of the political compact and no longer merits loyal adherence. "Resistance to tyrants is obedience to God." What of the wisdom and rectitude of laws excluding certain parties from access to the ballot? Again, if unjust, the same conclusion must follow. But note that the important consideration here is the complexity of the issues; on these questions honest and informed men may differ. And, what is more likely, they may confess inability to reach

----

classified and abstracted in Appendixes A and B of that book. These state efforts range from the ludicrous to the grotesque in tone and content. Thus, the legislators of the state of New York in their wisdom once considered painting public school buses red, white, and blue—apparently hoping the colors would cast a patriotic light which might brighten the shady teachings of the schools. Sometimes the laws are more somber. Michigan in 1950 authorized imprisonment for life for writing or speaking subversive words. One year later Tennessee made the death sentence a possibility in cases of unlawful advocacy. (*Ibid.*, pp. 368–369.) Governor Shivers of Texas announced recently that he plans to place before the next session of the state legislature a measure prescribing the death penalty for proven Communists. Gelhorn reports that in 1950, fifteen states barred from the ballot groups that advocate overthrow of the government by force and violence, or are foreign controlled. (*Ibid.*, p. 373.) Note that this was the same year in which the Supreme Court in the Dennis case denied the right to rebellion on the ground that the ". . . existing structure of the government provides for peaceful and orderly change." For additional illustrations of state action, see William B. Prendergast, "State Legislatures and Communism: The Current Scene," *American Political Science Review*, XLIV (Sept., 1950), 556–574. Prendergast's conclusions are interesting: "In none of the states which enacted anti-subversive laws in 1949 was any need for the legislation demonstrated." (P. 571.) "Proponents of the anti-subversive laws here discussed failed to name a single Communist employed by their state in 1949. They failed to cite a single dangerous act recently perpetrated by Communists within their states." (P. 572.)

any conclusion whatever. There are just too many factors, too many implications, too many subtleties; judgment is baffled. This new problem adds the second complicating factor to the original core of the American doctrine of loyalty.

Precise legal formulation of disloyalty, and prescription of the type of government worthy of the citizen's obedience, were but two of the approaches to the loyalty problem in early American thought. Equally important was the wish to preserve provinces of action and belief that were politically irrelevant—neither loyal nor disloyal, but simply outside the realm of political concerns. Those who penned the Declaration and the Constitution were determined to save spacious areas for what the French call *le vie privée,* areas in which the citizen might pursue his own ends with no insinuation that the limited support he might give the state constituted disloyalty or treason.

This "right of privacy" in its most general formulation means the right to be let alone. Its philosophic justification in the United States has rested almost invariably on a natural rights premise, and the courts have been moved to protect it by an "innate feeling of natural justice." The concept builds upon the notions of limited government, human free will, and the dignity of personality. As one of the older cases reads, it is "a recognition of the dignity of solitude, of the majesty of man's free will and the power to mold his own destiny, and of the sacred and inviolate nature of one's innermost life."

Under early American conditions it was enough that this concept of individual privacy remained only a part of the mores and of popular philosophy. But under modern conditions the interests it encloses can be secured only with increasing difficulty. The result has been a movement to translate the doctrine into legal terms, and the history of this trend provides a fascinating example of the adaptation of traditional philosophic and moral conceptions to modern needs through the medium of law. The movement gained its animus from a creative essay in the *Harvard Law Review* of 1890. The authors expanded this thesis:

> The intensity and complexity of life . . . have rendered necessary some retreat from the world, and man, under the refining influence of culture, has become more sensitive to publicity, so that solitude and privacy have become more essential to the individual; but modern enterprise and invention have, through invasions upon his privacy, subjected him to mental pain and distress far greater than could be inflicted by mere bodily injury.[11]

From this source, the doctrine gradually worked its way into law. The first American case to discuss specifically the philosophic basis, the social need, and methods to enforce the right appeared in 1905.[12] Today, eighteen states recognize it at common law and three safeguard it by statute. Only two have rejected it outright.

Thus far the movement to import a right of privacy into the law of the land has succeeded only in state jurisdictions. But expressions of a desire to see the doctrine become law appear with increasing frequency in federal jurisprudence. Also, it seems, the Supreme Court is beginning to regard the doctrine with an approving eye. Mark the contrast between these two dicta on the subject.

> Neither the Fourteenth Amendment nor any other provision of the Constitution . . . confer[s] any right of privacy on either persons or corporations.[13]

> The security of one's privacy against arbitrary intrusion by the police . . . is basic to a free society. It is therefore implicit in the concept of ordered liberty and as such enforceable against the States through the Due Process Clause.[14]

Finally, the importance of the concept of *la vie privée* is attested to by its frequent service as a *ratio decidendi* in cases of search and seizure. The idea would appear to underlie the whole Fourth Amendment immunity from unreasonable searches and seizures and has been mingled inextricably with due process thinking in the same area. Perhaps the best example is found in a dissent by Brandeis. He argues that the Fourth Amendment must be enlarged to meet present conditions; he then adds:

> The makers of the our Constitution undertook to secure conditions favorable to the pursuit of happiness. They recognized the significance of man's spiritual nature, of his feelings and of his intellect. They knew that only part of the pain, pleasure and satisfactions of life are to be found in material things. They sought to protect Americans in their beliefs, their thoughts, their emotions and their sensations. They conferred, as against the Government, the right to be let alone—the most comprehensive of rights and the right most valued by civilized men. To protect that right, every unjustifiable intrusion by the Government upon the privacy of the individual . . . must be deemed a violation of the Fourth Amendment.[15]

· We find then that the concept of individual privacy retains a valued role in American political and legal philosophy. It delimits areas of thought and conduct upon which the state may not trespass.

It restricts the scope of loyalty to government to a narrowly circumscribed province and insists that the criteria of loyalty and disloyalty are irrelevant in many realms. In effect, the American tradition holds that thought and actions may be loyal, disloyal, or simply nonloyal. All behavior cannot be compressed into the first two categories. There is a third division of conduct—a large one—which has no relevance to the state, and which the state may not claim to judge or regulate. Here lies the basic distinction between political loyalty in limited and in totalitarian regimes. This distinction Americans have never been willing to relinquish; were it surrendered, it would effect fundamental revisions in the American theory of loyalty.

The account presented thus far traces only a few major developments in the growth of the American concept of loyalty. There are others equal in substantive importance. One of them consists in the gradual fragmentation of a comprehensive, undifferentiated loyalty to church, to state, and to society into compartmentalized loyalties separated one from another. For that story we must turn to the early Puritan society of New England.

From its earliest beginnings within the body of the Anglican Church, Puritanism was both a religious and a political phenomenon. The English Puritans were caught up in that great seventeenth-century transition from the economics of feudalism to those of capitalism, and from the politics of divine right monarchy to those of parliamentary government. Although these early reformers announced their only intention as being the removal of all residues of Romanism from Anglican doctrine and practice, James I spoke truly when he declared at the opening of Parliament in 1604 that the real difficulties with the Puritans stemmed from the fact that they were ". . . ever discontented with the present government and impatient to suffer any superiority, which made their sect unable to be suffered in any well-governed commonwealth." [16]

Let it not be inferred from the dictum of James that the Puritans proposed anarchy; they hoped rather to organize their own order in which economics and politics might be made instruments in the service of religion. The earliest Puritan pioneers in America were bound closely together by profound loyalties to a common creed which comprehended all facets of life and thought. As Perry said, these early colonists ". . . were a church, a joint-stock company, and a state, all in one." [17] There is drama and fascination in the historical pageant which saw the iron determination of the colonists overcome the hardships of land and climate: through will and work they fashioned a theocratic society which flourished for some four decades, only to be destroyed from within by the same doctrinal fanaticism and contentious temper that had first built it. The history of loyalty in the Puritan period was disintegrative in pattern. It moved from a comprehensive and undifferentiated union of sentiments binding the individual as with an endless chain to church, state, and society, over to a system wherein the one is linked by separate chains of loyalty to distinct institutions and ideals. The Puritan saw this life as an arena in which the forces of man's natural depravity locked in grim struggle with the saving powers of divine grace for the prize of the human soul. In this conflict his master goal was the attainment of purity through stern discipline and strictest obedience to the dictates of the true religion. Since there was but one such true religion, he saw no argument against bringing the full weight of the state to bear against those who demonstrated their imperfect comprehension of it by such wanton actions as heresy, idolatry, or schism; disobedience, idleness, or intemperate living. It was written down in John Calvin's *Institutes* that "No polity can be successfully established unless piety be its first care." In short, Puritanism was theocratic in essence.

At its inception, the New England theocracy was full and absolute. But changing events and shifting currents of thought were soon to modify, and then to destroy it. Puritan theology supported the sovereignty of God and His spokesmen, the Visible Saints of the Congregation. It also admitted the congregational polity, which contained an implicit element of consent. However, as the formidable Cotton was quick to emphasize, this by no means meant democracy in civil or church affairs. First of all, the Visible Saints did not include the whole community. Secondly, elected officials were responsible to God and their consciences for the conduct of office. Still, the theocracy was an uneasy compromise between a theology which upheld the full dominion of God, and a theory of organization in both religious and civil corporations which stressed consent.

In religious life this compromise was effected through the devious subterfuge of the halfway covenant. The form the compromise took in political life was to uphold the consent of the governed as essential to the legitimate exercise of political authority. But that consent, after all, could be granted only to the government which God sets over the people and through which He speaks in the voice of the magistrates. The doctrine may sound oversubtle to the modern ear and should therefore be elaborated.

> The people consent to the Puritan government erected by their suffrages; but they can after all only consent to a divine government chosen in Christ. The Lord thus frames the people to a willing and voluntary subjection to the magistrates whom He has appointed through the people's suffrages; and the law of God, by virtue of the people's choice, becomes incarnate in the Christian State. The state still has a seed of divinity in it, and the magistrates rule by a right as divine as that of a feudal king; but God, by virtue of the many covenants he has made with his chosen people, has come to rule by the consent of His governed, and will hold His people personally liable for any breach of the divine contract.[18]

This all-encompassing loyalty could endure only so long as the theology conferring on God and His Elect full authority to decree the content of Christian truth and duty stood above dispute. But Puritanism was conceived in a spirit of faction and dissent. Also, it had inherited the original Protestant doctrines of the Inner Light and the Priesthood of all Believers. The "stewards of theocracy," in Parrington's telling description, forever must be contending against "enthusiasms" of one and another kind, ranging from a sinister witchcraft on the one side, to the passionate and pious excesses of an Anne Hutchinson on the other.[19]

Subsequent generations have selected one of those enthusiasts as the hero who did most to harass and obstruct the totalitarianism of theocratic loyalty. Roger Williams is a figure of mighty size in the American tradition; around him have grown an epic and a cult lauding him as one of the first and greatest proponents of democracy in America. Parrington, for example, could describe his work and character only with the aid of the sublime imagery of the *Song of Songs.*

> With this spirit of Christian fellowship, warm and human and lovable, there was joined an eager mysticism—a yearning for intimate personal union with Christ as symbolized in the parable of the vine and branches, a union as close as that of the bride and her husband. . . . But when he went out into the broad ways of Carolinian England, seeking the rose of Sharon and the lily of the valley, he discovered only abominations. The lover was tempted by false kisses; the Golden Image was set up in the high places. . . . And so as a Christian mystic Roger Williams became a Separatist, and set his mind upon the new world as a land where the lover might dwell with his bride.[20]

For our purpose it suffices to say that Williams expounded the now so simple—but then so explosive—doctrine that civic and political loyalty do not entail uniformity of religious loyalty. Roger Williams fragmented the original undifferentiated loyalty of Puritanism into distinct spheres and declared each to be of equal merit. To Nathaniel Ward's thesis ". . . that there is no Rule given by God for any State to give an affirmative Toleration to any false Religion, or Opinion whatsoever . . . ," [21] he countered that ". . . an enforced uniformity of religion throughout a nation or civil state, confounds the civil and religious . . . and denies the principles of Christianity and civility. . . ." [22] Williams' distinction between political and religious loyalty is clarified in his discussion of the place of religious associations within the body of civil society.

> The church, or company of worshippers, whether true or false, is like unto a body or college of physicians in a city . . . which companies may hold their courts, keep their records, hold disputations, and in matters concerning their society may dissent, divide, break in factions . . . and yet the peace of the city not be in the least measure impaired or disturbed; because the essence or being of the city, and so the well being and peace thereof, is essentially distinct from these particular societies. . . . The city was before them, and stands absolute and entire when such a corporation or society is taken down. [23]

These were among the first expressions of the spirit of toleration of diversity in the American clime. Similar statements were to increase in scope and number until they culminated in formal reception as part of the grand design of government in the nascent Republic. The crux of the matter is that in America loyalties are different in kind, but of equal independence and validity. Hence we can permit a wide variety of religious, political, cultural, institutional, and territorial— the list is not exhaustive—loyalties and hold these differences to be the stuff of which common strength and union are made. This line of thinking merged with the previously described concept of political loyalty to form the core of the theory of loyalty in American life. We learn from it that loyalty in America is pluralist rather than unitarian.

Undue stress should not be given to the efforts of individual thinkers and reformers in bringing about toleration of religious diversity in particular and the pluralist philosophy of loyalty in general. The main factor in this development was simply the proliferation of religious and other bodies. First in the colonies, and then in the states, men were met with such a welter of clamorous and contentious sects and societies that toleration seemed the only practical policy.

In early days only a very few writers, among them Williams and Jefferson, argued for toleration as a matter of principle. Not until later, after conditions had made toleration a necessity and long practice had made it part of the climate of opinion, did publicists and popularizers happily discover it to be the natural unfolding of the seed of American liberty and one of the brightest glories of the American experiment.[24]

The Puritan experiment offers further instruction. It was the first of a long line of efforts to construct utopian communities entirely isolated from the larger environment. In these "closed societies," all of life followed a prescribed pattern and, most importantly, all loyalties were consolidated into one integral whole. Without exception, they failed. The reasons for failure were usually twofold: (1) it was impossible to insulate the group against outside pressures, and (2) tensions and factionalism destroyed the order from within. Both forces were operative in the Puritan theocracy as well as in most subsequent attempts.

The failure of these closed societies elucidates the difficulties and dangers of trying to make all the members of a community accept a single comprehensive package of loyalties. Their internal history shows the utility of multiple loyalties serving as conduits through which social tensions may be tapped and drawn off without destructive impact on the whole social order. Men, it seems, are a long time learning this lesson; yet, it is the whole moral of the pluralist tradition of loyalty in America.[25]

As is not infrequently the case, it required a foreigner to first elucidate certain facets of American life which, by reason of their very familiarity, eluded native observers. Alexis de Tocqueville, with his remarkable insight and unerring sense of the significant, journeyed to the New World ostensibly to study penal conditions. While here he was impressed by many other features of American life more worthy of his attentions. In his analysis of American democracy he included a treatment of the role of private voluntary associations which, though embellished by later writers, still stands as the classic introduction to the subject.[26]

Tocqueville is most illuminating in his discussion of the relations among democracy, liberty, and private associations. In a striking phrase, he described the art of association as the "mother of action," and noted that associated activity not only reduced the burdens of the state but also taught the citizens how to combine and set themselves under a common discipline to achieve common ends. In this school, where men learn the general theory of association, they simultaneously explore the arts of obedience and coöperation. "Freedom of association in political matters," he insisted, "is favorable to the prosperity and even to the tranquility of the community." [27] He observed that Americans employed certain governmental practices in their voluntary associations which made them an excellent school of democracy. Concerning the type and quality of participation in voluntary associations, he wrote: "The independence of each individual is formally recognized; the tendency of the members of the association points, as it does in the body of the community, toward the same end, but they are not obliged to follow the same track. No one abjures the exercise of his reason and his free will; but every one exerts that reason and that will for the benefit of a common undertaking." [28] Tocqueville believed that the quickest way to dry up these springs of private voluntary thought and action was to impose restrictions on the right of political (as distinguished from intellectual, religious, social, and so forth) association. For when men are taught that only some and not other associations are permissible, they soon become suspicious of the principle of association itself. "In this state of doubt men abstain from them altogether, and a sort of public opinion passes current, that tends to cause any association whatsoever to be regarded as a bold and almost an illicit enterprise." [29]

These passages could serve as an introduction to the political theory of pluralism had that theory not assumed, under the ministrations of its best-known advocates, the form of a reaction against the legal doctrine of absolute state sovereignty, and had it not been confused with a curious metaphysic of the "real personality" of corporations. American writers have not pressed this far: John Marshall told us very early that corporations were "artificial creatures of the law." What Tocqueville was saying at base, however, was that American society was pluralistic in essence. Subsequent commentators have generally substantiated his conclusion. This urge to form associations, and the luxuriant variety of private societies which is its creature, still play a leading role in American life.*

---

* That the practice still persists is affirmed by an anecdote reported by an observer of modern suburban culture. Referring to this joining tendency, he writes: "Nearly everyone belongs to organizations and, generally speaking, tries to be actively involved. Group activity is fervently believed to be good for all, 'something you should do.' A minister, for example, told me that while canvassing a neighborhood, he once encountered a man who declared he was an atheist. With-

The implications of this national pattern of voluntary social action for the theory of loyalty are plain. Theory and practice join to assert that within very broad limits men are free to proffer their loyalties to particular bodies without incurring suspicion of disloyalty to the larger community. Membership in private bodies is under no cloud, as it was, for example, in all but a few "coördinated" organizations in the Fascist states of Italy and Germany. There is no *Loi Chapelier* of loyalty in the United States. This doctrine, made law by the provisions of the First Amendment, merges with the previously noted belief in the existence of areas of activity which are politically irrelevant to support three theses: (1) that loyalty in America must be voluntarily given, (2) that it is subject to revision or revocation at the will of the individual, and (3) that a diversity of private loyalties is not incompatible with loyalty to the whole community and the general interest. The theory holds that loyalty to the political community is the final product of the loyalties bestowed on more limited associations and ideals, that the general good is advanced by many men moving along many paths but all in the same general direction. It is plainly Adam Smith's vision of the invisible hand gently manipulating diversity toward harmony. The American theory of loyalty erects into a position of philosophic dignity that ". . . charming . . . variety and disorder . . . ," that condition of freedom and equality in democracy where even ". . . the horses and asses have a way of marching along with all the rights and dignities of freemen; and . . . will run at anybody who comes in their way if he does not leave the road clear for them: and [where] all things are just ready to burst with liberty." [30] What was deeply offensive to the aristocratic sensibilities of Plato—his penchant was for Nocturnal Councils and boards of censorship in the arts—the American embraces and incorporates into his panel of popular virtues.

This tradition of voluntary bestowal of loyalty on private associations forms another of the strands in the design of American loyalty. It should be noted here, briefly, that the tradition shows signs of strain and change. There are some current practices, for example the preparation of lists of organizations officially declared "subversive," [31] and the nascent tendency toward public regulation of political associations on the ground that their activities spill over into the public domain,[32] which appear to run in direct opposition to it.

---

out batting an eye, the minister responded, 'Well, you should have a club. I'll see if I can't find some others and get you all together.' " Harry Henderson, "Rugged American Collectivism," *Harper's Magazine,* CCVII (Dec., 1953), 81.

There are others, such as the reception in constitutional law of the principle of group libel, which seem to grant it an even firmer position in American life.[33] But, since the immediate task is only to prepare a context for discussion of current issues, those matters are best left for systematic consideration in another place.

Thus far, five lines of development in the background of loyalty have been traced: (1) the evolution of the concepts of treason and disloyalty, (2) the relations between loyalty and a theory of just government, (3) the notion of limited government with its corollary provision for areas of activity beyond the categories of loyalty and disloyalty, (4) the separation of political loyalty from other loyalties, and (5) the growth of a concept of pluralistic loyalty. To these another must now be added. When that is done, we should have before us the main dimensions of the background of the (relatively) formal and explicit concept of loyalty in America. The final factor alluded to is individualism. So much has been written on this topic that it is doubtful whether there are any novelties yet undiscovered. The purpose of this section, however, is not to rehearse well-known facts nor to investigate the subject systematically and at great length. It is, rather, to suggest a few of the implications that the dogma of individualism holds for the philosophy of loyalty.

Throughout much of the course of American history the slogan "individualism" comprised a moral doctrine, a climate of opinion, and an economic and political condition. Certain writers have found an equally strong tradition of "collectivism" in the national life, but it is questionable whether that label contributes to accurate identification of the phenomenon it purports to describe—joint action through voluntary groups.[34] And at least one writer maintains that when inspected closely the myth of individualism dissolves into a deep-felt fear of centralized authority.[35] Perhaps this thesis is not without considerable basis in evidence.

First, then, American individualism rested on moral foundations. The Whigs of the Glorious Revolution and the *Philosophes* of the Age of Reason had taught Americans that the law guaranteeing the individual natural and inalienable rights was written into the very constitution of the universe. Adam Smith introduced the argument that both science and ethics required the full extension of individualism into economic affairs. For somewhat later generations, Bentham and Mill explained that the doctrine of individualism was anchored in utility as in morality: indeed, the two were one. Still later, native

American Romantics and Transcendentalists—Whitman, Emerson, Thoreau—elaborated a theory of moral personality which elevated the individual above all law and convention if they conflicted with the commands of conscience. "A man who is right," announced Thoreau, "is already in a majority of one." Emerson's famous essay on "Self-Reliance" abounds in epigrammatic expression of the same sentiment.

> Whoso would be a man, must be a nonconformist.
> Nothing is at last sacred but the integrity of your own mind.
> No law can be sacred to me but that of my own nature.
> What I must do is all that concerns me, not what the people think.

In the late nineteenth and early twentieth centuries the doctrine was reinforced in science and ethics by the application of Darwinian tenets to social affairs.

Secondly, American individualism was a climate of opinion. Individualism is a phrase that epitomizes the dominant psychological frame of reference of an entire age. The legion of spokesmen for the view only articulated the deepest convictions of all but a minute and melancholy minority. Ralph Henry Gabriel considers the idea of the free individual one of the two basic articles of the popular democratic faith of nineteenth-century America. The other was the notion of the moral order. Referring to the former doctrine, Gabriel writes: "It contained a theory of liberty and of the relation of the individual to the State which he ultimately governed. The doctrine was derived from that of the moral order. The path which led from the one to the other was a philosophy of progress." [36]

American individualism, finally, was an economic and political condition. To harness the natural environment required strong men; rich prizes accrued to the determined and the cunning. Vast spaces and sparse population put a premium on individual initiative and self-reliance. Until the third quarter of the nineteenth century the economy was still one in which the relation between one's talents and his material position was easily discernible. Even when large corporate enterprise had effectively erased this connection in most instances, the ideal of the self-reliant and independent enterpriser continued to dominate the popular mind.*

---

* One essential qualification of this discussion of the nature and importance of American individualism must be made. Gunnar Myrdal points out that ". . . in retrospect the American becomes rather pronouncedly a hero-worshipper," and, ". . . the other side of this picture is, of course, the relative inertia and inarticulateness of the masses in America." His point is that the individualism of the

The developments outlined above had two major general consequences. First of all, they spawned social philosophies which
canonized *laissez faire* as the national creed and awarded the places
of power to its high priests. It was at a rather late date in our
national history that Justice Holmes had to remind his fellows of the
robe that the Fourteenth Amendment did not enact Mr. Herbert
Spencer's *Social Statics* into the law of the land. Only after im-
measurable human suffering and immense physical waste already
had been done were men willing to concede the legitimacy of extensive public regulation of private economic activity. The issue,
needless to say, still generates intense heat.

As a second major consequence, individualism and liberty became
virtually synonymous both in the popular mind and in political theory.
The free man was the man who could move toward his own ends
by his own modes of action; if one's means and ends ignored fair
and humane treatment of others—well, theirs was the right of re-
taliation. Individualism in the American clime was often aggressive
and socially irresponsible.* But no way could be found by which
this capacity might be limited in the public interest, for that was
to encroach upon the freedom of individuals. The state was only to
oversee the melee of competing wills as a tolerant umpire might
regulate an athletic contest; its purpose was not the positive one
of promoting justice and protecting the weak, but the negative one
of assuring that all contestants conformed approximately to a few
rules of the game. It was forgotten that in politics, unlike other
popular sports, the contestants make their own rules as the balance
of power shifts and the game turns now in one direction, now in
another.

W. J. Cash, in his penetrating study of the Southern mind, probed
the connections among environmental conditions, the growth of individualism, and attitudes toward political authority. His analysis

---

few is complemented by a "passivity of the masses" in political and social activities. See his informative discussion of these points in *An American Dilemma*
(New York: Harper, 1944), pp. 709–719.

* Who can doubt that these words of Emerson, again from "Self-Reliance," express the temper of much of this individualism: "The nonchalance of boys who are
sure of a dinner, and would disdain as much as a lord to do or say ought to con-
ciliate one, is the healthy attitude of human nature"? Or take the following: "I
shun father and mother and wife and brother when my genius calls me. I would
write on the lintels of the door-post, Whim. . . . Expect me not to show cause
why I seek or why I exclude company. Then again, do not tell me . . . of my
obligation to put all poor men in good situations. Are they *my* poor?"

might be partially reproduced here as a model of its type. He emphasizes that in the South, as elsewhere, individualism reached a high development. Indeed, he asserts, Southern individualism was even more intense than its Northern and Western counterparts. The argument first traces the influences which environmental conditions exerted on the growth of individualism:

> . . . the frontier had loosened his [the Southerner's] bonds as completely as it is possible to imagine them being loosed for man in a social state. The thin distribution of the population over vast reaches of country, the virtual absence of distinctions, and of law and government save in their most rudimentary stages, the fact that at every turn a man was thrown back wholly upon his own resources—all these combined to give his native individualism the widest scope and to spur it on to headlong growth.

To this he adds the thesis that the growth of the plantation system was also a sharp spur urging the Southerner on toward individualism. Given these things, the result was foreordained:

> Inevitably, then, the dominant trait of this mind was an intense individualism—in its way, perhaps the most intense individualism the world has seen since the Italian Renaissance and its men of "terrible fury,"

and this individualism was of a peculiar stamp:

> . . . the individualism of the plantation world would be one which, like that of the backcountry before it, would be far too much concerned with bald, immediate, unsupported assertion of the ego, which placed too great stress on the inviolability of personal whim, and which was full of the chip-on-shoulder swagger and brag of a boy—one, in brief, of which the essence was the boast, voiced or not, on the part of every Southerner, that he would knock hell out of whoever dared to cross him.

Finally, Cash spells out the implications of this bluff "personalism" in the realm of popular political thinking:

> The upshot of this is obvious. It made powerfully against the development of law and government beyond the limits imposed by the tradition of the old backcountry. There was in that tradition, of course, a decided feeling that some measure of law and government was necessary. . . . But against this was the fact that the tradition contained also, and as its ruling element, an intense distrust of, and, indeed, downright aversion to, any actual exercise of authority beyond the barest minimum essential to the existence of the social organism. This feeling,

common to the American backcountryman in general, had, in truth, reached its apogee in the Southern coon-hunter.[37]

What extrapolations relevant to the background of American loyalty can be made from this brief survey of individualism? The main one, of course, is that individual opposition to political authority could always be anchored in solid doctrinal grounds. First the natural law in various forms, then the Transcendental doctrine of the moral individual, and later Social Darwinism were enlisted in this program. The result, in Emerson's apt phrase, was that the individual became a "higher power" than his government. In matters of faith and morals, as it were, the individual was subject only to the imperatives of his own conscience. His loyalty to governing authority or to political creed could not be coerced but must be offered freely and could be extinguished at will. These ideas were conducive to the growth of a spirit of criticism toward political authority. It was felt that only a government that acted morally was worthy of loyalty. And the private person was final judge of that moral rectitude; his was a higher power.

Moreover, it is important to understand that individualism of the nineteenth-century stamp was inherently hostile to the growth of loyalty to political institutions. The strong, capable, resourceful individual appreciates and respects other men, not abstract and distant conceptions and institutions. Government was remote, in the first place, and men, getting little from it, owed little to it. Secondly, the individualist naturally thinks of government not in terms of some metaphysical State, but in terms of men—men like himself, with his strengths, his weaknesses, his ambitions. In this climate of opinion political authority cannot don the cloak of dignity and evoke loyalty through its majestic symbolism and haughty superiority. As William Graham Sumner explained in his tart essay on *What the Social Classes Owe to Each Other,* government is just some of us temporarily ruling all of us. Finally, it was general opinion that men who turned to government for a career were most probably weak and defective characters to begin with, and therefore hardly commanding the respect of real men. Given these factors, it can be seen that individualism militated against the development of political loyalties.

The present century has witnessed a rising tide of assaults against all three bastions of traditional American individualism and a consequent weakening of the ideology itself. This is perhaps one of the trends underlying current discussions concerning the nature of loyalty. For, as individualist doctrines descend, and the ideologies of collectivism ascend, it becomes ever more difficult for the (recalcitrant) individual to find social support for conduct and beliefs suggestive of limited loyalty to political authority. There is a marked decline of belief in the doctrine of moral personality, at least in its more extreme formulations, and men are now wondering whether the older doctrines of loyalty voluntarily given only to a morally deserving political authority and creed are without flaw. There is, furthermore, a clear tendency to demand loyalty to a particular doctrine and to impose sanctions against the wayward. The cry that "all stand and be counted," that all make public professions of faith and allegiance, is a telling indication of this shift in mental climate. Here again we find that the older tradition of American loyalty is no longer fully accepted and firmly held. Apparently, the present period is one of transition; new doctrines and practices are emerging to replace or modify the old.

GROWTH OF POPULAR LOYALTY

Even the briefest history of loyalty must include more than the theoretical and formal facets of the subject. It covers too those amorphous and richly emotional popular displays collected under such rubrics as patriotism and nationalism. The history of loyalty in this sense is nearly as broad as the history of the evolution of the American character, and, as yet, remains unwritten. Since the purpose is to bring present conditions into sharper focus, it is enough to mark only the historical highlights.

In order to circumscribe the field of inquiry, it is useful to begin with a definition of the kind of phenomena to be treated. In this context, loyalty becomes virtually synonymous with patriotism, which is, in Professor Curti's succinct definition, ". . . love of country, pride in it, and readiness to make sacrifices for what is considered its best interest." [38] If this be thought inadequate, a fuller formulation should provide assistance:

> Patriotism is usually assumed to be a broadly functioning loyalty to the general totality of country, with that totality construed as including the physical basis of country in its land, the governmental institutions of the country, its other institutions of social life, its mores, its technology, its past history, its literature, its art—in short, all of the basis for, and all of the superstructure of the culture built up within its borders. [39]

Since the growth of loyalty to strange lands and ways is the product of a long time rather than the fruit of a brief season, the only profound loyalties that could flourish in early colonial days were attached to mother country or to religious creed. This original loyalty to imported creed or motherland became, in the course of time, divided in its objects of regard between the old and the new. It might be called an Anglo-American loyalty. On the very eve of the Revolution most colonists were reluctant to abandon their English attachments. Even at the late date when the Continental Congress appointed Washington commander of the colonial troops in the impending struggle against England, it protested that it did not mean "to dissolve that union which has so long and so happily subsisted between us." And even after independence had been declared, but not yet achieved, there was little to be loyal to ". . . but a consummation devoutly to be wished for." [40]

Although British obduracy contributed generously to the growth of loyalty to the American cause by supplying a list of grievances, and giving American pamphleteers plenty of targets at which to level their broadsides, the Revolution itself was fought by a deeply divided populace. Some estimates place the number of Loyalists as high as one-third of the total population. This imperfect sense of nationhood was evident in the early use of the word "country" to designate one's state or local area rather than the country as a whole. When a Virginian or a Pennsylvanian referred to his "country," he meant Virginia or Pennsylvania rather than America. Even in the Convention of 1787 there was a pervasive vagueness in the use of the concept "nation." * These matters must not be given undue stress, however, because there was surely in the convention a supreme awareness of certain "national" interests, and the Constitution there drafted was to serve as a symbol around which much of the loyalty of later generations was to rally.

During this early period of American loyalty, when its growth was slow, halting, and unconscious, there were discernible the beginnings of thought patterns which appeared frequently in later historical stages. Professor Curti extracts from contemporary letters, pamphlets,

---

* See Merle Curti, *The Roots of American Loyalty* (New York: Columbia University Press, 1946), pp. 21, 27–28. Merrill Jensen, discussing this period, writes: "The 'nationalism' of the individual state is a factor too often overlooked. It was loyalty to one's country that moved men, whether radical or conservative, and one's country was the state in which one lived, not the thirteen more or less united states along the Atlantic Coast." *The Articles of Confederation; An Interpretation of the Social-Constitutional History of the American Revolution, 1774–1781* (Madison: University of Wisconsin Press, 1948), p. 163.

and speeches numerous expressions of the core ideas of pride in the natural beauty and magnificence of the land, the gradual broadening of attachment to ever larger units, the idea of a people favored by a special relation to the Deity and with a unique mission and destiny, and an oft-expressed irritation with the pretensions to superiority of other nations—especially England. Philip Freneau's short verse voiced this latter idea with force, if not with poetic delicacy, when he queried:

> Can we never be thought to have learning or grace
> Unless it be brought from that horrible place
> Where tyranny reigns with her impudent face? [41]

Many of these sentiments were spoken by Washington in his classic "Farewell Address," in which he reminded the nation of its unity and charted the propitious course of future progress. Although much of his speech was concerned with the distressing rise of factions in the country and "the baneful effects of the spirit of party, generally," Washington also urged his countrymen to remember the numerous loyalties cementing them into one whole:

> The name of American, which belongs to you, in your national capacity, must always exalt the just pride of patriotism, more than any appellation derived from local discriminations. With slight shades of difference, you have the same religion, manners, habits, and political principles. You have in a common cause fought and triumphed together; the independence and liberty you possess are the work of joint counsels, and joint efforts, of common dangers, sufferings, and successes.

In his peroration the first President cautioned his compatriots to be forever on the alert "against the insidious wiles of foreign influence," and reminded them that America had a distinct opportunity and destiny within the society of nations. Here appeared one of the earliest examples of that theme of standoffishness which was to play such a spectacular part in the drama of American loyalty and patriotism. As everybody knows, it became the prime constituent of a foreign policy which blended a clear appreciation of the material advantages to be derived from distance, with a prim but rather fuzzy-minded conviction that that same distance might protect American virtue against the blandishments—the insidious wiles—of degenerate Europe. Tocqueville, with the perspicacity we have come to take for granted, recorded the prevalence of this kind of thinking.

> The Anglo-Americans are not only united together by these common opinions [he speaks of political and religious, moral

and philosophical opinions] but they are separated from all other nations by a common feeling of pride. For the last fifty years no pains have been spared to convince the inhabitants . . . that they constitute the only religious, enlightened, and free people. They perceive that . . . their own democratic institutions succeed, while those of other countries fail; hence they conceive an overweening opinion of their superiority, and they are not very remote from believing themselves to belong to a distinct race of mankind.[42]

After full weight is given these burgeoning sentiments of national loyalty, the scale must be returned to true balance by adding to it the persistence of sectional and local loyalties. Although loyalty to place has been less important in America than in Europe, by no means has it been entirely absent. Indeed, the Civil War revealed for all to see that national feeling could not override sectional interests and loyalties fostered by distinct social systems in North and South. The clash of values could not be arbitrated within a frame of shared national loyalties; it had to be worked out in bloodshed and hardship. But the growth of really rich and abiding local loyalties always has been countered by the phenomenal spatial mobility of the American. We are a rootless people. Our highways bear a vast traffic serpentining back and forth across the land, pausing now here, now there. Our cities swell with persons recently arrived from the rural provinces. A characteristic figure in American writing is the hero who goes from town or country to the city in search of fortune only to find the city a lonely place and himself a man who left part of himself elsewhere. Moreover, since the Civil War, the convergence of an emotional need for unity after the disruptions of civil strife, and a developing economic system that was blurring old boundaries and welding the country into a single unit, resulted in the steady weakening of sectional loyalties and the continuing evolution of a firm loyalty to nation. The organic nation was emerging; its call was strong, its prophets many.[43]

Let us pause here long enough to underline this point. With growing national sentiment, a corresponding change was effected in the symbols Americans revered as the expression of their unique character and faith. "Perhaps," suggests Gabriel, "the most striking phenomenon in the post-Appomattox history of the democratic faith is the evolution of its symbolism. It has paced evenly with the intensification of the sentiment of American nationalism."[44] That change was the change from Washington and the Declaration to Lincoln and the Constitution. Changing symbols reflected an underlying transformation of sentiment: from natural rights and revolution, liberty and localism, over to stability, order, and nationalism. Not that the older symbols stand repudiated—not at all—but that, although their forms remain, their content has been subtly altered. No longer is Washington pictured in the popular mind as the very human, the struggling and despairing, the valiant and hopeful man who inspired and cajoled the scraggly colonials through discouragement to victory. He is now portrayed as the remote and austere, the stern and majestic, but benign, Father of His Country. Similarly has it been with the Declaration. Democracy, after all, is now the old order, defiantly opposed to the revolutionary onslaughts of fascism and communism: having witnessed the triumphant revolutions of Lenin, Mussolini, and Hitler, Americans are not disposed to regard the natural right of revolution with the same admiration as did Jefferson.

The Constitution is now the Ark of the Covenant, and its protector, the mighty Lincoln, is suffused with the holy glow radiating from it. Worship of the Constitution is part and parcel of emergent nationalism. In the Constitution we celebrate the glory of our nationality, and against it we measure the imperfections of other peoples and systems. Americans intone endlessly and fervently with Gladstone that the Constitution is ". . . the most wonderful work ever struck off at a given time by the hand and the purpose of man." *
In that wonderful work are contained all the articles of the Higher Law. Moreover, we have a Body of Elders to safeguard the Higher Law against impious hands. He who would violate the Covenant must first deal with the Supreme Court; to do that is to hazard the awesome fate of the Roosevelts, Theodore and Franklin, when they offered their "modest proposals" for Court reform. Let this rhapsody evoke the religious tone of Constitutional fetishism.

> Our great and sacred Constitution, serene and inviolable, stretches its beneficent powers over our land—over its lakes and rivers and forests, over every mother's son of us, like the

---

* The author might be permitted to report a personal experience which points up this uncritical adulation better than any declaratory statement could. In a discussion section of the introductory course in American Government, the author asked his class to be prepared to discuss in the next class meeting the "principal defects of the Constitution as an instrument of government under modern conditions." The students dutifully recorded the assignment. But at the end of the hour, one of them, a graduate student in psychology, said plaintively to the author: "You know, your assignment shocked me. My first reaction was one of hostility. I never imagined there could be anything *wrong* with the Constitution."

outstretched arm of God himself [*sic*] . . . the people of the
United States, creating the first constitutional government ever
created, created also a judiciary . . . the people ordained and
established one Supreme Court—the most rational, considerate,
discerning, veracious, impersonal power—the most candid, un-
affected, conscientious, incorruptible power—a power unique in
the history of the world. . . . O Marvellous Constitution! Magic
Parchment! Transforming word! Maker, Monitor, Guardian of
Mankind! Thou hast gathered to thy impartial bosom the peoples of the earth, Columbia, and called them equal. . . . I
would fight for every line in the Constitution as I would fight
for every star in the flag.[45]

The same exercise could be rehearsed with the Lincoln cult. But
that the reader should be spared. After the heady apostrophes of
Estabrook, it is time to descend from the sublime and summarize, in
language drab but precise, the capital point. American loyalty, as an
aspect of American nationalism, has moved from devotion to liberty
and localism over to order and nationalism. Simultaneously, the
symbols of loyalty have undergone attendant change from the Declaration and the early historical Washington to the Constitution and
the idealized image of Lincoln. In this transformation—as nowhere
else—lies a trenchant history of the growth of American loyalty.

An exciting chapter in the evolution of loyalty is written around
the transformation of immigrants into Americans. This chapter shows
a fascinating and intricate interplay—recorded fully in W. I. Thomas
and Florian Znaniecki's ground-breaking study of *The Polish Peasant
in Europe and America* [46]—between an experience and culture that
wrought sweeping changes in the diverse foreign types who have
become Americans by adoption and assimilation, and a culture and
experience that, in turn, were modified by the incoming hordes.
America has made the immigrants; the immigrants have made America.
The national culture has been enriched by the gifts of some dozens of
peoples, but those gifts have been accepted selectively and bent to
purposes other than those their bestowers had imagined. The American environment has had a leveling and smoothing effect on its new
citizens, placing them in a common mold of culture and experience
and releasing them as products with basically similar qualities.

This still continuing process has not been without its conflicts
and its critics. The country has known numerous nativist societies
which identified their own background of biology and belief with
loyalty and Americanism. In earlier periods it was the Irish who bore

the brunt of this sort of patriotism; later it was the Italians and the East European peoples. All three groups had in common the fact that their religion was Catholic, and this proved a fecund source of conflict in a country that frequently inclined to equate Protestantism with patriotism. That this narrow conception of Americanism persists is demonstrated by the vehement assault against the presidential candidacy of Alfred Smith, revolving around the theme that the first loyalty of the Catholic was to the Roman Pope rather than to the American Constitution. According to a popular anecdote of the period, Smith, after conceding defeat, addressed to the Supreme Pontiff a terse telegram—"Unpack." Some ethnic groups, notably those of oriental extraction, have yet to be absorbed into the mainstream of American life. In the shock of Pearl Harbor, this nation could regard whole thousands of her people as potentially disloyal and remove them to prisons—euphemistically called Relocation Centers—where their presumed malevolence might be curbed by the mailed hand of the state. In the twentieth century, foreigners coming to these shores often have been suspected as carriers of virulent ideological germs. Socialism, anarchism, and communism alike are seared with the brand of foreignism.* President Harding's Commissioner of Education articulated a prevalent sentiment when he spoke with unmistakable emphasis:

> There is altogether too much preaching of these damnable doctrines of Bolshevism, Anarchy, Communism, and Socialism, in this country today. If I had it in my power I would not only imprison, but would expatriate all advocates of these dangerous un-American doctrines. I would even execute every one of them—and do it joyfully.[47]

---

* That there was considerable truth in the charge cannot be denied. With all its inaccuracies and inconsistencies, Benjamin Gitlow, *I Confess* (New York: E. P. Dutton, 1940), pp. 21, 57, shows beyond doubt that ". . . in 1918 the bulk of the membership of the American Socialist Party was made up of the foreign born." His reports on the 1919 Chicago Convention of the Socialist party, where the Right and Left Wings split irrevocably, and the Left Wing itself splintered into three factions, bear out this point: "Before the Chicago Convention the Left Wing had approximately sixty thousand members. Most of them were foreign born, belonging to the foreign-language-speaking federations of the Socialist Party. About a tenth— roughly six thousand members—were either American-born or belonged to the English-speaking branches. . . . After the Chicago Convention both communist parties were even more foreign-born in their complexion than the Left Wing had been. . . . What stands out as a result of the Chicago experience is the Russian character of the movement."

In Americanizing the foreign-born, great emphasis was placed on the public schools as the chief agency of character formation. The American public mind has always had high hopes for "Education," and our leading pedagogues, from Jefferson to Dewey, have insisted that the schools be used as training grounds for democracy. Many men have tried to outline the nature of the new republican education; most apparently agreed with Dr. Benjamin Rush who argued that it was possible, given formal instruction of the right sort, "to convert men into Republican machines." [48] The modern counterparts of Jefferson, Rush, and Franklin are still grappling with this problem in educational engineering.

There runs throughout this use of the school as an agency of Americanization a dual tradition, one side of which sees loyalty as the final product of freedom and diversity expressed within a growing and creative community, whereas the other tends to see loyalty as the fruit of restriction, conformity, and the inculcation of received principles. [49] The two parts of this heritage stand in open opposition to each other and the issue is not yet resolved.

POPULAR LOYALTY; THE DUAL TRADITION

This issue evokes themes whose implications should be spelled out in fuller terms. "Americanism," "Americanization," "foreignism"—these hastily sketched ideas are pregnant with consequences for the meaning of the popular conception of loyalty. Moreover, while exploring them we may be able to weave into a coherent design some of the loose strands in this historical survey. What follows is interpretive and suggestive, not descriptive and final.

Pulsing through our national history, as theme and countertheme, are two distinct conceptions of popular loyalty, of Americanism. They were intimated when we spoke of the two conceptions of the role of the public school and the meaning of Americanization. But their ramifications go beyond that. If one examines the ideas of patriotism held by those whom Alan Barth calls the Americanists, and whom Sidney Hook calls the cultural vigilantes, he soon finds that they have no explicit and stable content. The values judged "American" are usually unspecified except by contrast with what is "un-American." Allied terms, such as "the American Way" and "one hundred per cent American," inherit the same malady. Their meanings can be discerned only by noting what their users, from the Native American party of the 1850's to the American Legion and Pro-America groups of today, regard as un-American.

First of all, it is clear that "un-American" denotes ideas advocated and conduct followed by persons not born in the United States or not assimilated into the typical behavior patterns. It means much more. Historically, the concept applied to the immigrant and the alien but it has been stretched far beyond that scope. To be "American" in this broader usage is not merely to be by birth or naturalization a citizen of the United States. It requires a complex of additional innate or acquired traits: traits of color, race, national origin, number of generations in America, education, habits of work and leisure, and correct political and social views. According as one possesses these assets in one or another degree, he is located along the scale of Americanism. This subtle measuring device permanently bars some types from ever attaining the acme of Americanism. Likewise, anyone whose position on the scale is inferior to the speaker's may be labeled "un-American." The chief utility of this device is its flexibility; the units of measurement can be changed to fit the convenience of the user.

Contrast this with the idea of Americanism upon which the Republic was founded and from which its noblest ideals have sprung. Benevolent Deity had bestowed upon Americans a unique and grand opportunity to create a new society—pure, and protected from the decadence of Europe. The American mission was to show a doubting world that the "model republic," in Rossiter's phrase, could work, that men did not need the ancient trio of king, priest, and aristocrat to direct their affairs.[50] This model republic, a legitimate child of the Enlightenment, sprang from certain natural and immutable principles, principles made incarnate in the Declaration, the Constitution, and the Bill of Rights. Whoever subscribed to them became eligible for membership in the republic. Corollary to this notion was a steadfast faith in the power of education and environment to mold character into valued forms. There was no fear of foreigners; they would easily and soon become Americans. America was the hope of the world—or so believed Americans—and those who escaped to her sheltering bosom showed by their very flight how they detested the ways of tyranny and yearned for the ways of freedom. This act of affirmation, plus brief residence in the new republic, sufficed to shape Americans out of even the most unlikely types.

> . . . the idea of American nationality was original; a nation dedicated to certain political principles voluntarily accepted and practiced in an asylum provided by Divine Providence from a tyrannous and corrupt Europe. Inherent in this conception was the element of choice, affirmation, will; and so long as this element remained an essential feature of the idea of Ameri-

canism the immigrant was regarded, not as a political outcast, but as a continuing sign that the great experiment was renewing itself.[51]

Here are the two main opposing conceptions of what it means to be a loyal American. Until around 1880, the second held firm sway.* The loyalties that bound people together and made them Americans were still rooted in the old revolutionary dreams. Thus, two visitors to the United States in the mid-century period, Charles Latrobe and Francis Grund, thought the Americans possessed hardly any nationality at all in the European sense. To Latrobe, their only distinctive traits were a hatred of monarchy, an unbounded admiration for republicanism, and an excessive sensitivity to foreign criticism. Grund believed that the strongest ties among the populace were a universal hope of personal improvement and an unshakeable faith in the promise of American institutions.[52] Between 1830 and 1850, although the beginnings of nationalism could be discerned, sectional loyalty ascended. But after the Civil War, with the Southern power destroyed, the wave of nationalism began to surge full swell. The Supreme Court spoke the sentiments of the victorious North when it declared that the United States was an "indestructible union of indestructible states." "The union of the States," pronounced the Court, "was never a purely artificial and arbitrary relation. . . . It began among the Colonies and grew out of a common origin, mutual sympathies, kindred principles, similar interests, and geographical relations." [53] This radical shift in sentiment from the prewar idea of the nation as based on contract and consent to the concept of the nation as a true organic growth received full expression from the pen of Francis Lieber, professor of political science at Columbia University.

By the 1880's the growth of organic nationalism had outstripped the original concept of the model republic. This nationalism preceded the doctrines of one hundred per cent Americanism and of un-Americanism.[54] The 1875 population was nearly one-fifth foreign-born. In 1880 just under 800,000 more immigrants entered the country. For the most part, these newcomers derived not from the older English, German, Scotch, and Irish stocks, but were newer and more "foreign" types from

---

* It is necessary to make certain qualifications. The doctrine was not applied to the Negro. On the northeastern seaboard and the tidewater there were strong vestiges of aristocratic control. Some newcomers who remained in the Eastern cities, especially the Irish, bore the brunt of racialism and religious intolerance. This culminated in the nativist movement of the 1850's, which Horace Greeley dubbed the "Know Nothing Party."

Southern and Eastern Europe. Most brought scant resources of capital, skill, or education. Many were driven to America not by a desire to escape oppression but to share in the fabulous material wealth of the New World. They peopled the slums of the cities, and became industrial workers employed at mean rates with but little hope of gaining independence. No longer was the immigrant transformed into the sturdy frontiersman and homesteader.

Under this impact antiforeignism increased in volume. Anti-Catholicism, prejudice against the newcomers for retaining their own in-group structures, the feeling that the foreign hordes glutted the labor market, fear that the immigrants were importing radical ideologies—these sentiments shaped the views of native Americans. For almost the first time doubts were widespread concerning the possibility of turning these peoples into Americans. Nativist groups more passionately asserted superiority over the foreigner. True Americanism necessitated more than brief residence in these lands; it required strict conformance to the codes and values of the native-born.

This new emphasis was a natural product of indigenous conditions. America was founded on explicit repudiation of tradition, dogma, and reverence for ancient institutions.* Without symbols of identification around which all might rally and manifest their membership in the same community, it became necessary, in order to mold a common character, to exact conformance to codes of thought and behavior.

The luxuriant flowering of private associations is probably in large part a result of this dearth of community symbols and traditions. Life was so fluid, so diverse, so impermanent that the individual had to

---

* Americans too easily underestimate the compelling force such symbols, especially if they can be personified, can exert in the life of the community. An appreciation of that force may be gained from the majesty and poetry of these words from the Dedication of the King James Bible: "Great and manifold were the blessings, most dread Sovereign, which Almighty God, the Father of all mercies, bestowed upon us the people of *England,* when first he sent Your Majesty's Royal Person to rule and reign over us. For whereas it was the expectation of many, who wished not well unto our *Sion,* that upon the setting of that bright *Occidental Star, Queen Elizabeth* of most happy memory, some thick and palpable clouds of darkness would so have over-shadowed this Land, that men should have been in doubt which way they were to walk; and that it should hardly be known, who was to direct the unsettled State; the appearance of Your Majesty, as of the Sun in his strength, instantly dispelled those supposed and surmised mists, and gave unto all that were well affected exceeding cause of comfort; especially when we beheld the Government established in Your Highness, and Your hopeful seed, by an undoubted Title, and this also accompanied with peace and tranquility at home and abroad."

satisfy his need for belonging through some group membership in the vast area between the immediate family unit and the remote nation. This compulsion to belong has resulted in exaggerated conformity, a phenomenon emphasized by many foreign observers of the American scene.[55] Being very much aware of the heterogeneous ethnic, cultural, and religious groups around him, the American often tends to assert his Americanism by joining patriotic organizations which can provide a sense of belonging to an in-group and of being superior to the out-groups. But this conformity to an in-group orthodoxy must exist within an environmental context which is incredibly complex and heterodox. Exaggeration is the result. The real need here is to achieve security and a sense of sameness with one's fellows. That need cannot be satisfied by self-conscious and fervently patriotic in-group sentiments when, in fact, the enveloping environment is composed of so many disparate types of men and groups. All it achieves is to exacerbate the tensions and differences between in-group and out-groups. This stems from the nearly universal tendency of in-group members to believe in their superiority to the outs and to universalize their own standards of orthodoxy in belief and conduct. The point is basic to an understanding of the first type of loyalty (or Americanism) described in this section. Perhaps the following paragraph will provide fuller appreciation of it.

> It is hardly surprising that the superficial nature of this conformity should induce an uneasiness on the part of the insecure both about their own orthodoxy and about the real intentions of strangers whose conventional handshake and necktie do not conceal an alien skin colour or speech pattern. The contradiction between the idealized standard and the reality, with its disparate racial, ethnic, religious, economic, and class groupings, has engendered a fear that beneath the surface of American society there may lie a dangerously explosive condition which the individual can neither fully understand nor control. This fear finds an outlet in intolerance for the exceptional which by the logic of conformity must be rejected as foreign and "un-American." When Senator McCarthy preaches anti-communism he touches this secret nerve of fear.[56]

This brief sketch of the popular meanings of loyalty and Americanism has indicated two opposing traditions. The first, which is essentially rational, dedicated to certain principles, pluralistic, and extranational, has been complemented in the course of time by an idea of Americanism wholly unlike it in tone and content. This latter strand is irrational, nationalistic, and conformist. The first views America as an uncompleted process; the latter views it as a finished and organic being. In the "great debate" over loyalty these two conceptions define the central positions of the contending forces.

It must be noted finally in this sketch of popular loyalty that there appears to be a narrowing of the boundaries within which diversity of thought and action may take place without fear of the stigma of disloyalty or un-Americanism. The modern citizen is astounded at the extent to which open opposition to official policy and accepted ideas were tolerated without the taint of disloyalty in the wars fought by the United States prior to the 1914–1918 conflict. The wars of 1812, 1848, and 1898 were fought by a nation deeply divided on the fundamental issue of the legitimacy of the war itself. It is indisputable that the Civil War saw extensive suppressions of seditious speech and literature and the application of executive power to quell opposition to adopted policies; but a Lincoln could still at the height of the crisis retain the equanimity and humor to transport a Vallandigham to the South, where he properly belonged, rather than to execute him for treason, which he doubtless deserved. This temper altered markedly after the First World War when the might of the federal government could be exerted against such a harmless and pathetic creature as Benjamin Gitlow for indulging in pamphleteering and orating which, as Professor Chaffee observed, if they could incite to violence at all, would incite it not against the war effort but against Benjamin Gitlow. This same hardening of temper, this narrowing of the limits of diversity, this tendency to equate radicalism with disloyalty, is observable in our own era in the plethora of legislative committees laboring to root out the forces of un-Americanism, the indiscriminate application of test oaths to many sections of the population, the construction of loyalty programs, the formation of numerous vigilante groups to protect the nation from those who would sap its strength and defile its purity, and attempts to create an *index expurgatorius* of proscribed authors and lecturers. There is truth in Chafee's judgment that "we are drawing the American party line and questioning all deviations from it." [57]

But at this point the past flows into the present. And since the present is the focus of this study, these matters merit more systematic attention. For the purpose of this section was only to paint broadly the historical backdrop before which modern scenes are enacted. That backdrop is definitely complex and manifold; the treatment given it here merely touches the surface. The hope of this section was to aid present understanding—to strike a mood and develop major themes—

not to undertake an exhaustive historical study. Perhaps, to change the figure, a few of the main threads in the fabric of American loyalty have been separated from the tangle of event and circumstance and made to serve as strings of Ariadne for guidance through the labyrinthine ways of loyalty.

4

The Modern Issue

PREVIOUS SECTIONS OF THIS STUDY HAVE SHOWN THAT THE problem of loyalty is not novel but has roots deep in the American past. The modern period, however, has distinctive features which set it off from earlier periods and justify its treatment as a unit. That is what is proposed here. And, logically, the place to begin is with a study of the causes behind the current stress on loyalty.

Causes? Perhaps the word is misleading. More accurately stated, the problem is: What are the factors that have generated the current stress on loyalty? This formulation suggests a search for mutual dependence and correlation rather than linear cause and effect. The reality which the social analyst must deal with is not the straightforward mechanical universe dear to the mind of the eighteenth century, but the pluralistic universe of William James, the reality that is a "booming, buzzing confusion," as he so vigorously described it. What is needed to reduce this confusion to order is a broad perspective capable of placing political phenomena within a dynamic existential field, and a delicate touch for the subtle interactions of events.

The argument that is to follow builds on the procedural assumption, stated above, that social forces are interrelated. Analysis opens with a brief statement of the process of social change, moves on to fill in the details of this schema with empirical data, and finally concludes with certain larger implications of the problem of the factors conditioning the current stress on loyalty. It might be well to state at the outset the dominant thesis which the investigation aims to establish: In modern America, certain social-economic, political, and ideological changes of large scope, high complexity, and rapid movement have generated a number of tensions or insecurities within the social order which have resulted in a plea (or demand) for increased collective unity and conformity. The cry for loyalty is a cry for a closing of the ranks in the face of the unknown and the dangerous.

THE ANATOMY OF SOCIAL CHANGE

In order to fix a point of departure, let us look at the problem from a special angle. Society—a number of men standing in ordered relations to each other—is a great conspiracy against change. If a collection of men is to be anything more than a transitory "coming-together," if men are to live and work side-by-side for more than a passing moment, then some pattern must be given to their interactions: leaders must be selected to guide the group in common endeavors; laws must be written to arbitrate conflicts of will; agencies must be developed to care for and instruct the young in the ways of the group; methods of producing the material necessities must be devised; defenses against external hostility must be constructed. In short, the group must develop institutions and persons must be assigned to roles in them. It is this that is meant when we speak of social structure.[1]

If one may employ a metaphor, institutions are the skeleton of social structure. They are stable and recurrent patterns of action and sentiment around which the life and work of the group move and through which it wrests existence from the environment.[2] This is not to suggest that institutions are rigid and unchanging—even cursory examination reveals otherwise—but only that they are relatively fixed and enduring, and that their inherent tendency is toward rigidity. The individual is linked to institutions through his performance of social roles.

---

[1] For numbered notes to chap. 4, see pp. 199–203.

And, from this standpoint, an institution is really an organized system of roles.

Institutions through time build up a tradition, an ideology, a set of interests, and a customary way of perceiving their environment. Each of these factors introduces an element of stability. They combine to form an "institutional character." Edmond Taylor has analyzed in detail how an institution develops a typical character type and an ideology which may distort perception and resist change.[3] He observed that when British civil servants first came to India they had no collective view of the Indian situation. But, over time, the activities involved in being a civil servant developed an ideology within the group which eventually distorted perception and blinded most officials to the grossest facets of reality. He noted too how new members entering the Indian Service were quickly integrated into this pattern. This occupational ideology created a certain blindness in perception and led to great misunderstanding between the civil servant and the Indian, and to British resistance against patently needed change. Talcott Parsons, analyzing the role of "vested interests" as sources of resistance to change, writes:

> It is inherent in the nature of an institutional system that it should create, and is in part supported by, a complex system of vested interests. . . .
> Among "interests" in general those which may be called "vested" are distinguished by the fact that they are oriented to the maintenance of objects of interest which have already become established. This means that . . . the status and situations and their perquisites to which such interests are attached already involve some element of legitimacy. . . . To . . . deprive a person or a group of something in which they enjoy a vested interest thus involves not only imposing the frustrations attendant to the deprivation as such but also . . . outrages the moral sentiments surrounding the claim of legitimacy. The resistance of the people or groups affected is thus strengthened by their sense of injustice.[4]

If it is remembered that institutions are basic components of social structure, that they circumscribe individual conduct, and that they are inherently conservative—if these things are kept in mind—then the statement that "society is a great conspiracy against change" takes on concrete meaning.

Although it is clear that men live in a world they perceive and structure in definite patterns, it is equally plain that this world is ever changing. When environmental change occurs, social institutions and ideas also must change if they are to continue in existence. There must always be, in man and society, adaptation to new situations. But adaptation is not achieved easily; it is not easy to see vested interests overturned, nor to discard familiar ways of thinking and acting. It is in fact, for most men and most societies, an imperative heavy with peril and travail. Every change, however small, confronts us with a challenge. But since change by its very nature poses a novel challenge it can never be faced with full equanimity and confidence. Adaptation to altered social conditions does not offer the sort of challenge-response situation that confronts, say, the prize fighter. He may never have met this opponent now entering the ring, but he has met others and he has undergone rigorous training to meet this one. Knowing his training was thorough, he is confident in his ability to engage the opponent and deal him blow for blow. But social change, because it poses conditions entirely new, can never be trained for; there is no academy where men and societies may take instruction in the art of coping with problems that are new, or, perhaps, not yet recognized and formulated. Lacking this, we lack confidence. To use Kierkegaard's phrase, we move in the quandaries of change with "fear and trembling."

To say that confidence is lacking is only another way of saying there is insecurity. And there is no doubt that ours is an age of insecurity. W. H. Auden has pronounced it the "Age of Anxiety." The usually optimistic James B. Conant observes that modern man is "deeply troubled." [5] Harold D. Lasswell even says we are living in a "world crisis of insecurity that may last for a generation." [*] When we are insecure it is necessary to find some way of reducing that insecurity. The first way, as will be noted, is to cling more tightly to the old order. But if the factors inducing insecurity are great enough, at some point—and who can locate it with mathematical exactitude?—it becomes apparent that accepted categories of thought and action no longer avail to interpret the altered scene. Here is the point of crisis, the point where men must prove their mettle and where fateful decisions must

---

[*] "Propaganda and Mass Insecurity," in Alfred H. Stanton and Stewart E. Perry, eds., *Personality and Political Crisis* (Glencoe: Free Press, 1951), p. 23. The concept of mass insecurity used here is that expounded by Lasswell: "Social investigators speak of mass insecurity as comprising all apprehensions about the self which are widely shared, whether these apprehensions can be traced to an adequate provocation in the environment or whether they come from lack of harmony within the individual psyche. Apprehensions are often sustained by anxieties superimposed upon uncertainty. Mass insecurity is pooled uncertainty and sustained anxieties." (*Ibid.*, pp. 16–17.)

be taken. Professor Toynbee observes relentlessly that nineteen of twenty-one recorded "civilizations" have failed to respond adequately to their peculiar crisis and have either ossified or expired.

Before that point is reached additional symptoms appear, again traceable to want of confidence in the face of change. A frequent first result of change threatening old institutions and definitions is to make us want to hold tighter to what we already have. All classes answer the query, "whether 'tis better to keep the ills we have than flee to others that we know not of," with an emphatic endorsement of the *status quo.*[6] In the face of threatened change, before the unknown and therefore the dangerous, present ills appear no ills at all. Familiar ways of acting and existent categories of thought are embraced with a passion which blinds the eye to their blemishes. Thus, on the level of the folk saying there echoes the plaintive sigh for the "good old days." In the books of Chilam Balam, written down after the Spanish conquest of Yucatán, there runs a tragic lament for the bygone days when the old order stood intact, when life was secure and meaningful. It is a lament sounded by many other men and times.

> Then everything was good. Then they adhered to the dictates of their reason. There was no sin; in the holy faith their lives were passed. There was then no sickness; they had then no aching bones. . . . At that time the course of humanity was orderly.[7]

Closer home, the history of the immediate pre-Sumter South demonstrates how far a society can go toward intensifying and idealizing its attachment to what it already has when confronted with threats to its being.[8] From about 1830 to Sumter, the South was under mounting pressure to adjust to changing social conditions and reform her systems of economy and society. The Southern reaction was to hold more tightly to the old order. Around her "peculiar institution" there developed dogmatic theories of sociology, economics, and politics. Critics were silenced or banished; criticism became synonymous with treason, loyalty with conformity. Needing confidence, the South tried to secure it by grasping with fingers of steel the anchor of the old, the known, the tried. In such times, what is wanted is not the clear eye and bold spirit of the critic, but the myopic vision and narcotic slumber of the conformist.

Many other historical illustrations could be provided. One of the best is offered by Nibley's study of the Roman loyalty problem between the victory of Constantine and the Vandal sack of A.D. 450, a period when Rome was suffering her "time of troubles." Nibley con-

siders three aspects of the Roman attempt to assure loyalty in a time
of great change and stress. They are: "(1) the attempt to excite loyalty
by appealing to the traditions of Western civilization while emphasiz-
ing a world-wide culture-polarization, (2) the attempt to solve the
problem of divided loyalty by lumping all things together in a 'one-
package loyalty,' and (3) the attempt of certain large and important
interest groups to use the new loyalty as a club against old opponents,
thereby effectively wrecking the whole program." [9] One cannot fail
to see the parallels between the events of that ancient period and those
of our own day.

Thus it is that social change, if great enough, stimulates a demand
for loyalty. Men feel the need for banding together more tightly to
defend themselves against the new and the dangerous. Part of this
banding together is an insistence that all accept the ideology of the
group and swear their allegiance to it. The ideology itself becomes
formalized and rigid, its articles are spelled out in detail and deviation
from them is punished harshly. The group assumes a posture of hostility against those of its members who propose revisions in the creed.
In a word, a demand for loyalty arises, and loyalty becomes synonymous with conformity.

Reaction to change may, of course, take other forms. It may take the
form of trying actively to secede from the situation. There are even
extreme cases where withdrawal goes so far that the will to live is lost,
and the society "turns its face to the wall" and dies.[10] Or, withdrawal
may be accomplished through fantasy. It may be the kind of action
dramatized in Existentialist doctrine—mere busyness, mere *divertisse-
ment,* mere keeping-on-the-go to evade the real issues. Frequently it
will assume the form of revivalist and nativist movements, as it appears
to be doing now with the Mau Mau of Kenya. It may be a valiant effort
to identify and overcome the root problems. But, as likely as any of
the foregoing, action make take the shape of searching for an "accursed group" upon which to lay present ills.[11] Here, perhaps, is part
of the explanation behind the current anti-Communist furor in the
United States. America is unprecedentedly uneasy. Behind it all there
must be some malevolent power. That power, it is easy to believe, is
the Communist. The phenomenon of the accursed group is as old as
human society itself and its psychology is simplicity itself. It is not
fanciful to suggest, even in this day of the laboratory, that much of
man's history is dominated by a belief in the existence of a society of
demons and spirits beyond the confines of our own terrestrial sphere.
Indeed, to doubt it would be to call in question the testimony of most

historians and anthropologists—to say nothing of the theologians, who might be deemed biased witnesses. It is very easy to soothe your own malaise and scourge the opposition by identifying your enemy with the powers of darkness. Once that identification has been effectively established, the *status quo,* and policies in defense of it, are equated with virtue and right. Opposition becomes synonymous with evil. When that stage is reached, society becomes a seething ferment of plots and counterplots. Reason abdicates. The job of the politician and the thinker is not to seek solutions for concrete problems but to wield the lash of right against the legions of error.

But it is not necessary to press this far. It is not suggested that this language portrays faithfully the state of contemporary American society. Analysis of the course of social change intentionally has been pushed beyond the true measure of factual conditions in order to have a standard by which to measure reality. With this model it is easier to estimate the level of development and probable future movement of present tendencies. It is only suggested that the current stress on loyalty-conformity is a result of social change, and that that social change partakes of the characteristics that have been drawn here in exaggerated strokes. Now to fill in some of the details of the schema.*

NEW CONDITIONS AND THE OLD ORDER

The nineteenth century in America was an era of expanding freedom: in philosophy, politics, economics, and literature new roads were opened to travel. Yet this freedom—and this may be the secret of its success—was curbed by a traditional and scarcely questioned set of institutions and moral ideas. Americans had received from the Age of Reason a rich bequest, a bequest including faith in liberty, intelligence, and progress. Protestant Christianity supplied them with a panel of

---

* This sketch of the process of social change rests on the premise that men and societies in general resist change. It should be noted that under certain conditions the reverse is true. The following passage suggests some of these conditions. "For men to plunge headlong into an undertaking of vast change, they must be intensely discontented yet not destitute, and they must have the feeling that by the possession of some potent doctrine, infallible leader or some new technique they have access to a source of irresistible power. They must also have an extravagant conception of the prospects and potentialities of the future. Finally, they must be wholly ignorant of the difficulties involved in their vast undertaking." Eric Hoffer, *The True Believer: Thoughts on the Nature of Mass Movements* (New York: Harper, 1951), p. 11. For a brief but systematic and well-rounded treatment of the entire process of social change, see Hans Gerth and C. Wright Mills, *Character and Social Structure* (New York: Harcourt, Brace, 1952), pp. 375–405.

moral precepts, covering a range from the largest social questions to the details of personal conduct. Among its articles were the gospel of work and belief in individual conscience. Moreover, their English descent gave them a code of fair play in everyday affairs and an ancient common law studded with moral precepts and extolling the virtues of property and independence. The patriarchal family, the village community, and religious institutions all enforced a code which held in check a freedom that otherwise would have been quite without bounds. Riesman is correct in his description of the typical character structure of that era as being one of "inner-direction," meaning that personality is controlled from within and kept on course by an internalized code derived from the elders which acts as a built-in "gyroscope." *

By the end of the second decade of the present century the American people were reaping the harvest of changes which had begun sixty or so years before, and which, once set in motion, had expanded at a constantly accelerating pace. Behind these changes were two main forces: (1) immigration, and (2) industrialization.

1) Between the years 1890 and 1914, a staggering twenty-two million foreigners came to this country. More than two-thirds of them came from Latin and Slavic Europe, where they had lived largely under feudal conditions of poverty, ignorance, and servitude. They had not come from lands where the ideals of democracy, individualism, and progress reigned. They were isolated from the dominant sections of American society by barriers of language, religion, and education. All these things meant problems of assimilation very different in quality and scope than Americans heretofore had known.

The prodigious fact is that the immigrants were assimilated. That they were is a monument to American ingenuity and diligence. But not for a moment should we forget that the task was accomplished at

---

* David Riesman, with Nathan Glazer and Reuel Denney, *The Lonely Crowd: A Study of the Changing American Character* (Doubleday Anchor ed., abr.; Garden City: Doubleday, 1953). Riesman writes: "In Western history the society that emerged with the Renaissance and Reformation and that is only now vanishing serves to illustrate the type of society in which inner-direction is the principal mode of securing conformity. Such a society is characterized by increased personal mobility, by a rapid accumulation of capital (teamed with devastating technological shifts), and by an almost constant expansion. . . . The greater choices this society gives—and the greater initiatives it demands in order to cope with its novel problems—are handled by character types who can manage to live socially without strict and self-evident tradition-direction. These are the inner-directed types." (Pp. 29–30.)

considerable expense to indigenous patterns of thought and behavior. Before this mass immigration, assimilation had been a largely spontaneous process carried out by the immigrant himself with the aid, possibly, of his neighbor, his fellow-immigrant, and his small local community. Earlier immigrants tended to move into the lands of the West where, individually or with a few others, they carved out lives in emulation of established patterns. Soon they became, as it were, more American than the Americans.

But the new immigrants came in hordes to the cities, there to work in the factories or to perform the most menial jobs. Assimilation became a national problem and great administrative and educational systems were erected to cope with it. The public schools, especially, were made agencies of Americanization; there the immigrant learned that conformity to accepted standards was the price of his admission to full social status. Parental authority weakened because the older generation was more closely tied to its traditional ways and the younger found it easier to adjust to novelty. The key to success was conformity to standards of a peer group rather than to family standards.

2) The second driving engine was mechanization. In a relatively few short years that complex of forces called the industrial revolution altered both land and people beyond the recognition of early nineteenth-century citizens. The generation that fought with Grant at Appomattox turned from field to factory both in the military and in the economic sense. The generation that fought with Pershing on the fields of France was the first to experience fully the way of life that was the end product of the industrial revolution. A huge and rich territory, a continental market, and contributions of European capital and technical skill combined with the native ethic of work and progress to produce large-scale industry. The immigrants provided a body of labor willing to perform rough and tiresome work, and an inexhaustible market for cheap, standardized goods. By 1920, industrialism and urbanism had triumphed; the ways of handicraft and family farm no longer set the style in economy and society.

Outward changes of such magnitude were not without devastating effects on the quality of inner experience. Venerable institutions, especially family and church, were twisted into strange shapes. Respected habits of thought, notably the doctrines of the moral individual and the higher law as the sources of ethical canons, were attenuated and weakened. These were great transitions, not to be made painlessly. To adopt Lenin's figure, at each turn the rushing locomotive of history cast off those whose grip was slack. The Roaring Twenties saw not only unprecedented prosperity but also the Lost Generation. Many young artists and writers, appalled by the tragedy of the First World War and sickened by the wanton ugliness of machine civilization, sought other values to live by. America was repudiated by many of her most sensitive sons and daughters. They found no new positive system of values, but they could not live with those already there. They were spiritually homeless. This was, it can be seen in retrospect, a clear manifestation of the crisis of values foretold by Nietzsche.

The Lost Generation was only a rather noisy expression of a process which had been going on more quietly for some time. Social change had swept across the nineteenth-century pattern of life; a new material environment tore great chunks from the moral codes which had held liberty in check and kept men united in a sense of community. Also, the institutional supports of this code were undermined. But although the traditional codes were weakened, and their institutional foundations undermined, the new order could offer no acceptable replacements. Men were now required to live in a social environment for which they were poorly equipped.

The point is fundamental to an appreciation of the factors behind the current stress on loyalty. Therefore, it requires elaboration. Perhaps some of its implications can be clarified through brief examination of the transformations that have overtaken one basic social institution and the impact this in turn has had on life. For this purpose one could select no better example than the family, both for its importance in shaping character, and because of its sensitivity to changes in the enveloping environment.

"As it has become more and more contractual," writes Sorokin, "the family of the last few decades has grown ever more unstable, until it has reached the point of actual disintegration." [12] The modern family of which Sorokin writes has undergone sweeping changes in its structure and functions as compared with its predecessor of as recent a time as the nineteenth century. It has been reduced in size, impoverished in function, and weakened in prestige.[13] No longer is the family unit a largely self-sustained economic organism. Since children no longer are economic assets, family size decreases. The family has lost its valued place at the center of religious, social, economic, and recreational life. These functions are now performed by specialized commercial institutions in which persons interact not as valued members of an intimate and organic primary unit, but as pale "card-holding" members of vast and impersonal collectives. For the family holidays, the games and readings during the long evenings, the sense of participation in an ongoing community process, we substitute the motion-picture theater, the dance hall, organized sports which one observes but in which he does not participate, and the job as hired hand in the line of mass production. As a result of these transformations, the family falls in prestige as a social institution, loses its sense of tradition and continuity and, perhaps above all, loses its integrity and privacy from the surrounding environment.

If this impressionistic portrait of the modern family is an accurate symbolization of reality, is there not possible truth in this prophetic warning?

> The Western family is rapidly approaching its third violent crisis. The climax will be reached before the end of this century. It will be reflected in extremely high rates of all the symptoms of family decay—divorce, childlessness, disloyalty of family members to each other, and the unwillingness of many persons to burden themselves with families.[14]

Indeed, what is there in the present aspect of affairs that permits us to expect otherwise? The family as a social unit must now endure in an environment that denies it all the essential elements which must be present if a "culture" is to grow from humans in interaction.[15] For a culture to develop from human association, certain conditions must be assured. There must exist close and continuing relations among enough individuals to allow for some variety and specialization of function. The group should be rooted in a fixed territory, for this contributes to continuity and the growth of tradition and permits a culture to emerge which is adapted to its environment. Moreover, the territory itself becomes an object for sentiments binding the group together. Finally, the group should be sufficiently isolated so that an indigenous culture, rather than a mere reflection of what lies beyond, may emerge.[16] In America the family lacks all these conditions in one or another degree. The result is inability of the family unit to develop a culture that invests its members with durable common sentiments and values. No longer does the individual repose in the bosom of a warm and secure family life, a life which has shaped him and to which he admits deep obligation. A previously cited article puts the point succinctly: "Despite the 'moral idealization' of the family, a few dollars and the absence of protest will sever almost any family unit on the grounds of any one of many real or fictitious allegations." [17]

The first result of the breakdown of traditional family culture is a certain brand of freedom. Modern society offers the individual a multitude of alternative values and ways of behavior. Riesman's conformity based on inner-direction is giving way to conformity resting on the need for getting along in a world of near-strangers and deriving its content from newspapers, motion pictures, radio, and magazines. Norms derived from these sources are, in the anthropologist's language, "profane" rather than "sacred," superficial and ephemeral rather than deeply rooted and enduring. In this situation, one is, in a sense, free. He may choose among many socially sanctioned alternatives; even nonsocially sanctioned behavior is punished less severely than formerly.

But in a deeper sense this new-found freedom is spurious. It is a freedom that permits one to choose but that omits to offer adequate basis to judge of the relative desirability of alternatives. Without moral map and compass, the individual wanders aimlessly through a labyrinth which, no matter what his turnings, leads to no satisfaction and security. His freedom to choose is futile, and his choices amount to little more than a series of wanderings.* This freedom is more than futile. It is also dangerous and frightening. Mere freedom of action is no freedom at all; it is really an invitation to fear and despair. If freedom is not to be a synonym for insecurity, it must be a freedom within freely accepted but clearly defined limits. If the individual has acquired no moral compass—no sound basis for judgment—he easily falls prey to any temptations which happen along in the course of his odyssey. Let Redfield clarify these points and summarize the position of the argument:

> We may ask, to what extent can the individual ever really be free? To live in society at all is to accept a series of limitations upon action. Those whose personality [sic] has not been shaped by intimate attachments appear not only less human but also more vulnerable. Our complex civilization requires, it seems, a balance between the detachment which makes for adaptability—a detachment aided by the processes of mechanization—and that inward attachment which gives some fixed values and creates some sort of moral order for the individual in spite of rapid changes in the environment.[18]

---

* Hoffer, *op. cit.*, p. 30, points out some of the ramifications of freedom which frequently are overlooked: "Freedom aggravates at least as much as it alleviates frustration. Freedom of choice places the whole blame of failure on the shoulders of the individual. And as freedom encourages a multiplicity of attempts, it unavoidably multiplies failure and frustration. Freedom alleviates frustration by making available the palliatives of action, movement, change, and protest. . . . Unless a man has the talents to make something of himself, freedom is an irksome burden. Of what avail is freedom to choose if the self be ineffectual?"

To return, then, to this use of the family to illustrate the effects on personality and society stemming from the disruption of traditional institutions, it is clear what the conclusion must be. We know that ethical codes rest not merely upon rational judgment. They stand ultimately upon emotional attachments which are best formed in the intimacy of the family circle. It was an appreciation of this principle that led Montesquieu to recommend that if you wish the children of a nation to acquire love and devotion for their country and its laws, there is one sure way to do it—see that their fathers have this love.[19] Decay of familial institutions, unless adequate substitutes are provided, means decay in moral stability and a weakening of the entire social fabric. Machine civilization, with its mass production, specialization, and impersonality, has weakened the family but has supplied no adequate substitute for the moral and spiritual functions the family formerly performed. The results are often specious freedom and loneliness for the individual, with a consequent urge toward conformity based upon other-directedness.

The analysis is easily broadened to comprehend more than the family. This institution was selected for emphasis primarily because of its substantive importance, and not because it offers the only source of evidence. Other institutions could have been substituted. For example, religious institutions have suffered ill under the modern environment. A recent commentator has some words on the temper of contemporary religion which merit extensive quotation:

> To get an adequate sense of what religion means to Americans one must not listen to the sermons of the clergy but must observe the behavior of the laymen. The layman is not as articulate in stating his faith as are the preachers . . . , but he shows his common sense [*sic!*] continually in supporting religion that is not militant. The average churchman is chastened. . . . He is not dominated by religious faith; he expects his religious faith to conform to his secular conscience. Such civilized conformism, if I may so term it, is a fairly recent achievement. . . . The average, statistically normative church-goer does not expect his devotions to *change* his ideals but to *support* them. He does not welcome a gospel which exaggerates the conflict between the spiritual and the temporal. He expects a Sabbath service to be an integral part of a day of recreation; and if it fails to be an "up-lift" so much the worse for the service. . . .
> There is a noticeable difference between the kind of loyalty to a church which prevails today and the faith in the redemp-

tive power of the church which used to prevail. Churches continue to be supported as much if not more than ever. . . . But
in order to get this support the churches must be content with
less attendance, more "social services," and in general a more
responsible performance of religious institutions in the context
of our other institutions and humanities. Whether they believe
in it or not, American churches are expressions of American
culture; they can not expect to dominate much of the lives
of most Americans, for very few Americans are *religiosi*. . . .
This means that religion is not a separate kind of faith, but an
aspect of "animal faith" that has been civilized.[20]

A host of social scientists and literary figures join in swelling chorus
on the theme that the individual in this new society is lonely and insecure. Modern literature repeats the ideas of uprootedness and isolation in many books and plays. Maurice Barrès, author of *Les Déracinés*
(1922), is the spiritual forefather of much of this. His germinal concept
was that modern life has ripped men from their warm communal existence in the embrace of traditional institutions but has provided no
substitutes. Other writers cry that competition and the cash-nexus
comprise the only ethic this new life has to offer.[21] Rebecca West mod-
ernizes Barrès' hypothesis and uses it to identify the source from which
the "rank and file" of fascism were recruited. This rank and file, she
writes, came from ". . . the mindless, traditionless, possessionless
urban populations that are the children of the machine. Those have
wholly lost their sense of process."[22] For such types, West goes on to
say, life is lived on the very brink of meaninglessness; to fill this void
they will clutch at any straw. Nowhere is the theme more dramatically
expressed than in the "dreadful freedom" and the "absurdity" of the
Existentialist.

John Dewey, although instinctively shunning the histrionics of the
Existentialists, articulates their thought all the same. Twenty-five years
ago Dewey addressed himself to the salvation of the "lost individual"
in modern society. The human being, he wrote then, has lost his moor-
ings and his bearings; he can neither rest securely nor move confi-
dently.

The significant thing is that the loyalties which once held individuals, which gave them support, direction, and unity of outlook
on life, have well-nigh disappeared. In consequence, individuals
are confused and bewildered. It would be difficult to find in history an epoch as lacking in solid and assured objects of belief
and approved ends of action as is the present. Stability of individuality is dependent upon stable objects to which allegiance
firmly attaches itself. There are, of course, those who are still

fundamentalist in religious and social creed. But their very clamor is evidence that the tide is set against them. For the others, traditional objects of loyalty have become hollow or are openly repudiated, and they drift without sure anchorage. Individuals vibrate between a past that is intellectually too empty to give stability and a present that is too diversely crowded and chaotic to afford balance or direction to ideas and emotion.[23]

Sociologists, meanwhile, insist that mere physical crowding in the cities has not produced adequate emotional substitutes for the different closeness of the functional family, the farm, and the village neighborhood.[24] Intricate specialization of the economy, combined with large-scale organization, has destroyed the firm bonds of tradition and custom which bound the artisan of a former day to a sense of membership with others of his craft and gave him a pride of workmanship; very different from today's factory hand was the farmer's hired hand or the master craftsman's apprentice of yesteryear. The factory system has debased work into a hollow exercise performed only for cash reward. The modern factory worker feels himself to be an unimportant part in a vast machine which is not of his making, and which is quite beyond his understanding.* The middle classes have lost their independence and are lackeys of a system that holds their destiny in its grasp but that deigns not to consult them in making decisions.[25]

---

* Confirmation comes from many quarters. The pilot study was the famous Hawthorne experiment. It was found there that the most basic deprivations the workers felt were absence of attention and recognition from management and lack of a sense of the significance of their work. Production and morale rose directly with increased attention and recognition gained by the worker even when the physical environment was made harsher and more unpleasant. In the passionately grateful response of the emotionally starved workers to the interest shown in them by the experimenters lies a tragic comment on the bleakness of modern factory life: somebody broke through the system and saw them as *men,* listened with respect and sympathy to their views, wanted to help with their problems. Their response was eager; it was human. F. J. Roethlisberger and William J. Dickson, *Management and the Worker* (Cambridge: Harvard University Press, 1950), esp. pp. 379–551. Peter Drucker's major judgment on the human adequacy of industrial society is worth quotation: "The modern corporation as a child of laissez-faire economics and of the market society is based on a creed whose greatest weakness is the inability to see the need for status and function of the individual in society." After summarizing the relevant evidence he concludes: "The realization of human dignity, the achievement of status and function would thus emerge as the major unanswered question of industrial society." *Concept of the Corporation* (New York: John Day Co., 1946), p. 152. Catholic social doctrine devotes considerable attention to this problem. See especially the encyclicals *Rerum Novarum* (1891), and *Quadragesimo Anno* (1931).

All these themes—spiritual uprootedness, individual isolation and loneliness, declining sense of values, impotence before blind and powerful forces—recur in contemporary psychological, sociological, and imaginative writing. They mirror the pressures bearing on individual life. Their sources lie deep in the massive transformations occurring in social structure—urbanization, growth of gargantuan industrial enterprise, decay of the functional family, compartmentalization of life, destruction of primary ties in an impersonal and mechanized world, substitution of mass culture diffused through mass media for customary patterns of belief and conduct. These causes have been operative for a considerable period. They are ubiquitous and mighty; their impact on human life is profoundly disturbing. A recent study illustrates the points.[26] Lowenthal and Guterman assert that the successful "agitator" rests his appeal on an "emotional substratum" of popular sentiment which has five components: distrust, dependence, exclusion, anxiety, and disillusionment. "Are these," they ask, "merely fleeting, insubstantial, purely accidental and personal emotions blown up by the agitator into genuine complaints or are they themselves a constant rooted in the social structure? The answer seems unavoidable: These feelings cannot be dismissed as either accidental or imposed, they are basic to modern society. Distrust, dependence, exclusion, anxiety, and disillusionment blend together to form a fundamental condition of modern life: malaise." [27] They continue:

> This malaise reflects the stresses imposed on the individual by the profound transformations taking place in our economic and social structure. . . . These objective causes have been operating for a long time with steadily increasing intensity. They are ubiquitous and apparently permanent, yet they are difficult to grasp because they are only indirectly related to specific hardships or frustrations. Their accumulated psychological effect is something akin to a chronic disturbance, an habitual and not clearly defined malaise which seems to acquire a life of its own and which the victim cannot trace to any known source.[28]

Etched against this background of basic insecurities are other factors which add to the rising feeling that "the times are out of joint." War and depression have destroyed the lives of millions and left even more millions with a pervading fear that modern social organization is irrational and malevolent. America's international position has become one where the old policies of security through isolation just do not make sense. But what policies do? The threat of atomic war looms in the background of contemporary life like an ominous storm cloud whose torrents might be unleashed at any moment. There is but scant time for thought, and there may be no time to rectify mistakes once made; in this situation, where the issues are crucial, there is a feeling that we cannot afford the luxury of error. Added to this is a thorough suspicion of the stability of the economy. Will 1929 be repeated? More poignantly than any statistics, the depth of this distrust is indicated by the fact that we have resorted to a sort of word magic in an attempt to dispel the evil. There is little talk of depression; rather, much is heard of recession, adjustment, leveling off, slight decline. By abolishing the word, perhaps the thing will be exorcised. The reality itself is such a "fearful indescribability," to borrow one of Carlyle's astonishing phrases, that men must find euphemisms to describe it.

If one doubts that insecurity is widespread in American society, and that men are beginning to question the validity of received values and institutions, he need only scan the pages of any of a dozen mass-distributed "slick" and not-so-slick periodicals. There he will find a plenitude of very suave and effective attempts to sell the traditional version of American capitalism and democracy to the common man. Much of the advertising sponsored by the giants of American industry has a markedly "ideological" tone: it seeks to demonstrate the virtues of a "system," and to show how everybody has a stake in the system, rather than to "plug" a particular product. But the clamor is too loud; such efforts disclose lack of confidence more than they reveal the cunning of American advertising. In spite of our fabulous wealth, our herculean strength, our official optimism, these displays confess an uneasiness about the stability and acceptability of the present system. Businessmen and politicians unite to laud the free enterprise system and to declare its proven superiority over all rivals. Yet, at the same time, they appear to regard collectivism as so virulent that the populace must be inoculated against it by progressively larger dosages of propaganda.

THREE DIAGNOSES OF THE PRESENT CONDITION

At this point, the argument can turn to some of the broader aspects of the phenomena so far considered. The general thesis offered, remember, is that social and economic changes have resulted in insecurity and that the current loyalty drive is a response to this powerful chord of popular thinking. It might be useful to spell out just what is meant by this "chord of popular thinking." The problem could be approached by sampling the voluminous records of the opinion pollsters. But that would be both laborious and inconclusive. It is proposed here to adopt a different approach, one that has the merit of simplicity and is open to no more objections than the polling device.

Within the past thirty years or so a large literature has appeared purporting to describe systematically the general "state of the masses." This writing, though based upon the findings of sociology and psychology, does not let the subject rest there but moves on to assert conclusions of a broader, more philosophic nature. From this material three books were selected that would be of use to the present problem. The books chosen were selected not because they support all the arguments in this essay, but because of their high reputation, and because they contribute to the problem from three different points of view. Their germinal themes will be presented briefly and their relevance to the problem of the causes underlying the loyalty stress will be shown. The volumes are Erich Fromm's *Escape from Freedom,*[29] David Riesman's *The Lonely Crowd,*[30] and Sebastian de Grazia's *The Political Community.*[31]

Fromm's major thesis is that modern man has been cast adrift on a lonely sea of freedom, without the reference points of traditional morals and institutions. Without guides, he is alone and lost, forlorn and frightened. He strives to overcome his malaise and gain security through a number of techniques, by diverting himself with work and play, or by "making contacts" with others. Eventually, however, these devices may fail and he may try to overcome his impotence and escape his insupportable freedom by fusing with something more powerful. He overreacts and loses all freedom. He becomes a cog in some mass machine.

Fromm thinks the trouble lies in the inherent nature of modern society—its bigness, impersonality, mobility, and aggressiveness. This society has destroyed the old web of custom, tradition, authoritative institutions, and primary groups which formerly enclosed the individual. Modern industrial civilization has freed man, but his new-found freedom is "empty"; he yearns for comfort and content.

De Grazia agrees with Fromm that modern man is in search of community. He argues that community is found through participation in shared belief-systems and attachment to revered rulers. When there is a conflict among rulers or belief-systems within a society the result is *anomie*—lawlessness. In its rudimentary form this engenders uncertainty and conflict in the life of individual and collectivity. In its acute stage, *anomie* results in personal or collective breakdowns such as suicide or orgiastic mass movements. He goes on to insist that modern society is characterized by sharp and pervasive conflicts within belief-systems, and deals particularly with the conflict between religious and economic directives.[32] It follows that *anomie*, in its simple forms, is endemic in modern industrial society. It frequently builds up to the acute stage where it is discharged in violence.

Riesman adds new dimensions to the analysis. His thesis is that modern society is producing a type of character which is "other-directed" and almost passionately eager to conform to the standards of those around him. Yet with all his yearning for popularity, conformity, adjustment, this pathetic creature is doomed by the conditions of life to remain a lonely member of the crowd. Those conditions again are found in the large-scale impersonal life of the city. The individual has lost the "inner-direction" that formerly came from close family ties and the authoritative morality he absorbed in the process of social conditioning. In his search for new guides he becomes conformist and automaton-like in conduct. Freedom is gone and adjustment—"getting along"—is the watchword.

The amount of agreement among the three volumes is remarkable. All agree that modern man is lonely, that the desire for freedom is giving way to the urge for security, that individuality and diversity are surrendering to conformity and uniformity, and that the eager pursuit of these new goals is not producing much satisfaction. In a word, all agree that man is avidly in quest of community, and that the more he seeks, the less he finds. This is the modern *mal du siècle*.

In terms of the analysis presented here of the factors underlying the current stress on loyalty, these conclusions all point to the increasing urge toward conformity in American life. These urges come from the deepest wellsprings of life and are not to be blocked easily. In terms of the balance between liberty and authority, individuality and conformity, it means that the second terms of each pair are being emphasized. The current stress on loyalty is but one manifestation of these general tendencies and cannot be understood apart from the existential field this analysis has tried to outline. Evidence supporting the conclusion comes from many places and is highly complex, but it is hoped that at least the major items have not escaped notice.

THE CRISIS OF VALUES

One aspect of the pattern is of enough importance to merit particular attention before moving on. Many of the disjunctions and tensions in modern American life focus in their impact on the role and nature of values. Perhaps the result could be summarized under a heading mentioned on a previous page—the crisis of values. The new order of the machine has destroyed, or is now destroying, older institutions and values but as yet has created no satisfactory replacements. The results are everywhere about us, in the academy as in the market place, and they are not hard to read. We have explored some of these results in practical affairs and it may be instructive now to peer into the cloisters of the academicians and see what forms the crisis assumes there. Once inside, we observe a sight not uncommon in those precincts: There are many jarring factions each with its own version of the gospel, each distinguished from others by nuances of tone and content, but all agreed upon the prime dogmatic article—there is no method known by which moral propositions may be validated (here Hume is often mentioned); therefore you must concede that all values are of equal value. In a word, outside of those who ground their values in authoritative religion, nearly all accept the relativist position in one or another form. This modern crisis of values expresses itself in more than one way. Perhaps a few should be pointed out to suggest some of the chief possibilities. It should be clear here that the referent includes both theory and practice, both the academy and the market place.

1) Some plead for a return to the traditional sources of morality and right conduct. These "traditionalists" insist that since our error lies in repudiating the ancient sources of authoritative principles our salvation lies in returning to them. Frequently, recourse is made to the doctrines of Christianity. This position is defended in a recent textbook in political philosophy. The argument is straightforward. "The sickness of the modern world," according to this diagnosis, "is the sickness of moral confusion, intellectual anarchy, and spiritual despair." The causes of the malady are twofold: alienation from God and repudiation of the reason He has granted man. "Having alienated himself from God, having discredited the reason with which he was endowed by God, . . . modern man oscillates between extravagant optimism and hopeless despair." The remedy is not far to seek: ". . . the insights of the Christian faith provide the best insights we have into the nature of man and of the crisis in which we find ourselves. . . . Only through a return to faith in God, as God revealed Himself to man in Jesus Christ, can modern man and his society find redemption from the tyranny of evil." [33]

2) Others stand at the opposite end of the spectrum. With a certain quiet courage, or sometimes a defiant bravado, they face the void alone and without the crutch of tradition or external authority. To man's petty comings and goings, his small hopes and faiths, the universe is quite indifferent. Any truth or beauty is but the fragile product of

imagination; that is its source and its only justification. But that is good and sufficient justification. This position might be defined as "personalism." The motto of its members might be: "I keep my countenance, I remain self-possessed." Let Bertrand Russell evoke the mood and suggest the content of the doctrine.

> Brief and powerless is Man's life; on him and all his race the slow, sure doom falls pitiless and dark. Blind to good and evil, reckless of destruction, omnipotent matter rolls on its relentless way; for Man, condemned today to lose his dearest, tomorrow himself to pass through the gate of darkness, it remains only to cherish, ere yet the blow falls, the lofty thoughts that ennoble his little day; disdaining the coward terrors of the slave of Fate, to worship at the shrine that his own hands have built; undismayed by the empire of chance, to preserve a mind free from the wanton tyranny that rules his outward life; proudly defiant of the irresistible forces that tolerate, for a moment, his knowledge and his condemnation, to sustain alone, a weary but unyielding Atlas, the world that his own ideals have fashioned despite the trampling march of unconscious power.[34]

3) A third reaction to the crisis of values is that of "fanatic nihilism." This is the way that leads from despair through moral anarchy and thence to total order. The engine of movement is *action*. There is no idea or value that cannot be changed when expediency demands. Sorel had this in mind when he spoke of the energizing role of myths. Hermann Rauschning, using this concept to characterize the whole National Socialist movement, described it as the revolution of nihilism. The Spaniard José Ortega y Gasset, whose work is in many ways an elaboration of this theme, explains an essential element of the doctrine:

> Under the species of Syndicalism and Fascism there appears for the first time in Europe a type of man who does not want to give reasons or to be right, but simply shows himself resolved to impose his opinions. This is the new thing: the right not to be reasonable, the "reason of unreason." [35]

4) There are, as everyone knows who has studied the history of ideas, dominant styles of thinking characteristic of an era and a particular group. Probably the theory of values most in fashion today among social scientists is something called "cultural relativism." A diligent student could trace its roots at least back to the time when the Sophists taught that there was one law in Athens, another in Syracuse: Which, then, is the law of nature? Montaigne too expressed the essence of the doctrine when he wrote that "the laws of conscience, which we pre-

tend to be derived from nature, proceed from custom." In our day this notion, particularly as propagated by the cultural anthropologists, is in wide currency; it is, indeed, almost doctrine. One anthropologist who has discussed the idea at length may be heard as spokesman for the general position.[36]

Cultural relativism means that each culture develops its own values, and that values can be understood and appreciated only in terms of their specific cultural context: all values are culture-bound. Herskovitz puts it this way: "Judgments are based on experience, and experience is interpreted by each individual in terms of his own enculturation." [37] But then the argument takes another step: it asserts that we should strive to appreciate and accept as equally good all values. Herskovitz again: "Cultural relativism is a *philosophy* which, in recognizing the values set up by every society to guide its own life, lays stress on the dignity inherent in every body of custom, and on the need for tolerance of conventions even though they may differ from one's own. . . . Emphasis on the worth of many ways of life, not one, is an affirmation of the values of each culture." [38]

It is not the purpose here to criticize, but one curious feature of this argument should be noted. It begins with a statement of fact, i.e., values are culture-bound. It moves on to an affirmation of values, i.e., we should respect all values. "But," as Professor Redfield makes clear, "there is no true 'therefore' between these two parts. It cannot be proved, from the proposition that values are relative, that we ought to respect all systems of values. We might just as well hate them all." [39]

5) A fifth response to the crisis is the way of professing the ancient morals and values, while at the same time "watering down" their content until their essence and integrity are lost. To hold fast to the form when the substance has fled—that is the technique of watering down. A recent commentator, analyzing factors behind the sometimes astonishing success of the outrages of Senator Joseph McCarthy, employs this idea as partial explanation.

> He has made a profession out of disclosing that as Americans we do not believe what we profess to believe. . . . One by one, in Tocqueville's hushed phrase, we "noiselessly secede" from the positions of the Paines, the Thoreaus, the Parkers, the Altgelds of our prior history. To cite Tocqueville again, "the majority have ceased to believe what they believed before, but they still affect to believe, and this empty phantom of public opinion is strong enough to chill innovators and to keep them silent and at a respectful distance." [40]

Henry Steele Commager elucidates another implication of this watering down of the content of values:

> It seems fair to say that while the moral standards of the nine-
> teenth century persisted almost unchanged into the twentieth,
> moral practices changed sharply, and that though the standards
> persisted the institutions that had sustained them and the sanc-
> tions that had enforced them lost influence and authority.[41]

John Dewey has put this idea in somewhat different words, words
which suggest that while watering down is apparent, enough of the
old values and moral notions remains embedded in the modern mind
to cause much anxiety and confusion. He is here really documenting
de Grazia's notion of simple *anomie*. We are between the new and the
old, Dewey explains in the following passages, and therefore doomed
to the discomforts of both and the pleasures of neither.

> It is becoming a commonplace to say that in thought and feeling,
> or at least in the language in which they are expressed, we are
> living in some bygone century, . . . although physically and
> externally we belong to the twentieth century. In such a contra-
> dictory condition, it is not surprising that a report of American
> life, such as is contained, for example, in "Middletown," should
> frequently refer to a "bewildered" or "confused" state of mind as
> characteristic of us.

He continues:

> The tragedy of the "lost individual" is due to the fact that while
> individuals are now caught up into a vast complex of associa-
> tions, there is no harmonious and coherent reflection of the im-
> port of these connections into the imaginative and emotional out-
> look on life. This fact is of course due in turn to the absence of
> harmony within the state of society.[42]

It is the present writer's belief that watering down is the typical
response of today to the crisis of values. Most citizens are ignorant of
the complex arguments of the academicians. The response of the
"average man" has taken the form of vitiating and impoverishing the
values that have nourished the life of the Republic. This is, perhaps,
one of the chief factors behind the stress on loyalty. An effort will be
made to show that there has been a watering down of the values of
individualism and liberty—that men still pronounce the words but lack
firm faith in or knowledge of their substance—and a consequent emphasis on values urging toward conformity and community. But that
can be left for later. Before moving on, we should get some rough

measure of the extent to which watering down has occurred. Perhaps a measure of the chasm Commager describes between moral standards and "moral" practice is afforded by the following opinion poll.[43] A group of respondents were asked this question: "Do you believe in Freedom of Speech?" The replies were as follows: 2 per cent—don't know; 97 per cent—yes; 1 per cent—no. Those who answered "yes" were then asked: "Do you believe in it to the extent of allowing Fascists and Communists to hold meetings and express their views in the community?" On this question the percentage of "yes" answers dropped to twenty-three. Virtually all others indicated they did not believe in free speech to the extent of granting it to those with whom they disagreed. The case speaks for itself. If, as Justice Holmes held, freedom of speech means freedom for those who profess even the most despised of doctrines, then most of the American people have watered down the content of the value until only its form remains.

Given this kind of evidence, there is force in the disquieting dictum of the President's Committee on Civil Rights. The committee found much that was shocking and more that was shameful in the recent record of American civil liberties. Furthermore, the committee reluctantly concluded, "The pervasive gap between our aims and what we actually do is creating a kind of moral dry rot which eats away at the emotional and rational bases of democratic beliefs." [44]

This report, one of the most intelligent and provocative public documents of our time, and concerned with issues vital to the future of the Republic, met with little interest outside the thin ranks of professional students and the handful of others actively concerned with civil liberties. The American Civil Liberties Union designates correspondents in nearly every state in the Union to report on the condition of civil liberties in their district. They reported, a year after the study of the President's committee was issued, that it had aroused little public response. Forty-four of seventy-five reported it had evoked no interest in their area; twenty-eight thought it had, but that most people regarded it as being concerned with a strictly Southern problem.[45] This public indifference to individual liberties is itself disturbing evidence of the movement away from belief in civil rights. In 1789 the Constitution could not be ratified until the Bill of Rights was accepted; in 1948, people were simply indifferent to it. The existence of this gap between profession and action is, as the President's committee reported, creating a "kind of moral dry rot" which debases values and reduces them to mere rationalizations for whatever ends we wish to pursue.

All the ideals in the world won't feed us.
Although they give our crimes a certain air.[46]

ALIENATION AND THE NEED FOR COMMUNITY

In the foregoing pages the fundamental conditions influencing the current emphasis on loyalty have been outlined. The chapter opened with a rough statement of the thesis. Then, in order to fix a framework, the processes of social change were sketched. That done, an excursion was made into the late nineteenth and early twentieth centuries. That excursion was just long enough to permit the suggestion that a new material order had transformed the old. It was necessary to examine those "larger forces moving obscurely in the background," to use a famous phrase, in order to set the problem in proper context. After that, three diagnoses of the present stance of events were presented. Finally, it was shown how these tendencies had culminated in the crisis of values. There matters rest.

Now the development enters another phase. The problem remains the same—analysis of the factors underlying the current emphasis on loyalty—but the focus changes. The job now is to organize the material so far presented more tightly around a dominant theme which can gather into one fold many implications of the data still lying where they were scattered. That theme is alienation. All the tendencies and developments presented to this point revolve around one hub, alienation of individuals from society. Furthermore, the current emphasis on loyalty-conformity is directly related to this phenomenon of alienation. The following pages elaborate these ideas.*

The great historical movement, called variously the Age of Liberalism, or of Progress, or of Enlightenment, which began in the city-

---

* Throughout the following discussion the word "alienation" has been substituted for the term *anomie*. The concept of *anomie* was used by Durkheim to describe a society in which the norms were disintegrating and community was weakening. Alienation was preferred here because it emphasizes individual or group detachment from the bonds of community. One of the best modern discussions of *anomie* is Robert K. Merton, "Social Structure and Anomie," in Ruth Nanda Anshen, ed., *The Family: Its Function and Destiny* (New York: Harper, 1948), pp. 226–258. Whereas Merton attributes *anomie* rather narrowly to capitalist competitiveness, the present writer prefers to see it as the result of large and rapid social change and of culture clash within society. See also the discussion in R. M. MacIver, *The Ramparts We Guard* (New York: Macmillan, 1950), pp. 84–95.

states of Renaissance Italy and rose to a brilliant zenith in the late eighteenth century, is now on the wane. Even as it achieved its greatest triumphs and its finest systematic expression, the conditions that had given it life and nourishment, and that it in turn was meant to interpret, were undergoing radical change. John Stuart Mill, perhaps the last great spokesman of Liberalism, lived long enough, as his *Autobiography* soberly confesses, to fear that all was not maturing in the event as it should have according to the terms of the doctrine. So his intellectual energies, as with most of those who succeeded him in the Liberal line, were divided between reaffirming and revising the old ways of thought and feeling. A Herbert Spencer, for example, could believe that beneficent forces were urging toward progress at such a rapid pace that women soon might even be persuaded to give up the barbarities of cosmetics. However, at the same time, his hymns to science and freedom were characterized by a strained and querulous tone which revealed that his faith was not entirely secure. He lacked the serenity that comes with the unshakeable conviction that one is firmly astride the wave of the future.

The Liberal ideal, of course, is not dead. But men now utter it with far less confidence than they used to. Moreover, although the official political ideology is still costumed and displayed in the familiar symbols, its inner spirit has undergone sharp change. In the early nineteenth century, when Liberalism seemed to be sweeping away inexorably the rubbish of the past and the evils of the present, its spokesmen were almost arrogantly confident that theirs was the voice of the future. Liberal democracy would triumph, and its triumph would work good for all men everywhere. Thus could Jeremy Bentham solemnly advertise himself as a sort of political adviser and constitution writer extraordinary for whatever benighted people had not yet followed the light to reform and progress.

There was the heart of the matter: It was necessary only to show men the light and they would themselves then hurry forward to the heights where splendid vistas of liberty and democracy lay spread before their delighted view. Liberalism assumed that men were rational and that, given political rights, they would come to appreciate and use them to achieve their own best ends. Great indeed was the rejoicing when it was learned that if each acted to gain his own ends the general interest also would be advanced. Under the influence of this doctrine the franchise was broadened, education extended, and freedom of speech, assembly, and petition granted to all citizens. Given these rights and privileges men would naturally, it was held, engage eagerly and intelligently in the political life of the community.

It was a noble and generous conception; its later critics have not done it justice. Liberalism is usually criticized as having had an overintellectualized view of human nature. It is true that Liberalism inherited many facile and overly optimistic assumptions about the nature of man from its Rationalist ancestors. And it is also true, as Oakeshott has pointed out, that modern history is ". . . littered with the projects of the politics of rationalism." [47] But the criticism, although valid, is misleading. The failure of Liberalism was no greater than the failure of any other social philosophy; that is, Liberalism was formulated under special conditions and meant to apply only to them. Its fate was that of other social philosophies; that is, it was extended into provinces beyond its original setting. Most of the early Liberals, such as Locke and Montesquieu, took as their model of human nature the aristocratic type. This holds true even for Jefferson, Bentham, and the two Mills, although theirs was an aristocracy of talent rather than of blood or position. Secondly, Liberalism was formulated in, and meant to apply to, social and political conditions of relative simplicity and small scale. Population was small, the economic order was basically handicraft or small-factory production, and government was simple and close to the people.

But Liberalism became democracy and social simplicity became complexity. A doctrine that was meant to apply only to small bodies of people under special circumstances was extended to huge masses living under entirely different social, economic, and political conditions. The great Liberal theorists unanimously insisted that if the individual was to function as a rational, intelligent, and active citizen, he must reside in a community that affords leisure to discuss and think out questions with his fellows, and that permits unlimited access to accurate political information and intelligent opinion. As mass democracy has developed, these conditions have not been met. Walter Lippmann's classic *Public Opinion* demonstrated with an irrefutable cogency just how far modern social organization falls short of providing these prerequisites to intelligent and active citizenship. Between individuals and the events of politics there is a vast gap, a gap which broadens as society becomes larger and more complex. The mass media of communication are the only bridge across this divide. But the mass media present a picture of politics that is banal, distorted, and bowdlerized. The consequence is that the citizen's mental processes are warped; he cannot function in the political realm as Liberalism intended he should because the conditions Liberalism stipulated have not been fulfilled.

That is but part of the full story. Liberalism assumed that men, given the right and the opportunity, would strive to become informed and energetic participants in the political process. The facts have been quite different. Thus far, we have tried to show that facilities of communication have not been adequate to their task. The problem goes deeper than that. In his study of loyalty, Josiah Royce repeatedly referred to the "self-alienated social mind." What he meant is not always clear, but from a number of passages the conclusion emerges that Royce, in 1908, was groping toward one of the chief facts of social and political life in the United States—alienation of the self from social process. "We as a nation, I fear," he wrote, "have been forgetting loyalty. We have been neglecting to cultivate it in our social order. We have been making light of it. We have not been training ourselves for it. Hence we, indeed, often sadly miss it in our social environment." [48] This is Royce's principal thesis. On first reading, it appears as though he were saying that lack of loyalty is due to conscious choice, a view which is fortified when he says we have fixed our vision on personal material success and too seldom show individuals the meaning of social loyalty. The results are evident—and disastrous. "Narrow loyalties, side by side with irrational forms of individualism and with a cynical contempt for all loyalty,—these are what we too often see in the life of our country." [49]

Royce also knew that the problem had other roots as well. Quoting Hegel, he explains that our social consciousness has become "estranged from itself." Social structure has become so vast and complex that individuals are unable to see the unity of social life. Social power is organized in mysterious and frightening ways; power seems foreign, unintelligible, arbitrary. The vast organizations that determine man's destinies seem as impersonal and impervious to human sentiment as the forces of nature. All one knows of the meaning of power is that he must submit to it when necessary. The result is that the individual tends to withdraw into a privatized world and seek his own ends in his own ways. Men have become estranged from their own social order because social organization is so vast, so complex, so unintelligible, and so arbitrary that they no longer understand their relation to the ongoing collective process. The depersonalization and insecurity of modern life, stemming from all the factors analyzed in the preceding pages, have culminated in self-estrangement. People become alienated from social process when they can not see their social unity in familiar and understandable terms. "The smoke of our civilization hides the very heavens that used to be so near, and the stars to which we were once loyal." [50]

This is the conclusion toward which the ideas and empirical data presented earlier in this chapter pointed. The new order has greatly weakened, sometimes even destroyed, traditional institutions and moral codes. Familiar categories of meaning and traditional community ties no longer seem adequate. Without these supports, the individual finds it increasingly difficult to locate his position in the social process and understand his bonds of community with his fellows. Social process seems ever more abstract, separated from the self, and difficult to understand and control. As a result, there develops a tendency toward alienation of the self from society.[51]

The fact is that in mid-century America the Liberal model of the politically alert and involved citizen does not correspond with the facts. The salient feature of modern political life is not involvement in, but abstention from, politics. Political scientists have not given this problem the attention it merits, perhaps because most of them still operate under the Liberal ideology and thus fail to see the problem in its true proportions. There are very few studies of alienation (which political scientists often call indifference or apathy) in current political literature.[52] Those that exist usually confront us with evidence showing the meager turnout of voters on election day.[53] That evidence is valuable and important, but it deals merely with surface manifestations. The basic problem is one of attitudes: in the Lazarsfeld study over two-thirds of those who failed to vote stated before the presidential election that they did not intend to vote.[54] With them there was no question of sickness, or of failing to meet the formal voting requirements, or of the other factors political scientists often employ to explain nonvoting. They were indifferent, or sometimes actively hostile, toward the electoral process. Very little progress has been made toward understanding just why there is this massive indifference.[55]

Moreover, the extent of political alienation goes far beyond nonvoting and other overt forms of nonparticipation in the political process. The salient feature of American politics is widespread public indifference, negativism, inaction. This conclusion rests on a general sense of our present condition more than on any precise indicators. But those indicators are useful. When it is known that nearly half the people fail to vote in national elections, and very many more than half in state and local elections, it is clear that ours is as much a government by default as by choice. But when we know further that well over half of those who do vote do so because it is family tradition, as much a part of their heritage as their genetic structure, then it becomes plain that most voting is a ritual act, with little personal involvement or choice, and with few expectations of much moment. More decisive, however, for the position here taken (that alienation is the dominant feature of American politics) is a sense of our general social condition. Political events seem to be somehow unreal, detached from the self and its interests, incomprehensible. The individual is a spectator at a spectacle he does not understand, cannot control, and feels little involvement in; his life is privatized, his attitude toward politics blasé and indifferent. Rousseau's warning inevitably comes to mind: "As soon as any man says of the affairs of the State *What does it matter to me?* the State may be given up for lost." [56]

No one questions the fact of formal democracy; that is not even at issue. The important point is that democracy is more formal than felt. Government is something apart from us, something we know of only as symbols and slogans, and something which now and then presses its impersonal force upon our lives. But it is not ours, not something we are involved in and responsible for. It is very doubtful whether many Americans now perceive their relation to government in the plain and homely terms of William Graham Sumner. Government, said Sumner, is just some of us temporarily ruling all of us. That formulation may have been too simple even when it was written, but that is irrelevant. It voiced a prevailing attitude which was the very epitome of the liberal democratic theory of the proper relation between citizen and government.

In a time of sweeping social change, and when alienation is a widespread mentality, an urge toward conformity is to be expected. The current emphasis on loyalty-conformity is directly related to the sweeping social changes outlined in previous pages and the alienation of individuals from society which has been their salient result. These tensions express themselves in a plea (or demand) for increased social unity and cohesion. It is this demand that underlies the current public interest in loyalty. The cry for loyalty is essentially a cry for certainty and stability in the face of uncertainty and change. It is an attempt to strengthen the bonds of community by creating a surface uniformity of belief and feeling. For, when a group is faced with great social change, when old ideas and beliefs no longer serve adequately, when alienation is a typical experience, then there is a sort of vacuum in the minds of men.

But nature abhors a vacuum in the minds of men quite as thoroughly as she does elsewhere. If our ideas and beliefs are not the natural and spontaneous products of our collective life-experience, if as a result there is insecurity and tension, then an apparent consensus will be achieved by artificial and forced methods. Here is the fundamental condition behind the powerful drive toward imposing conformity on American thought and opinion. The present loyalty stress is but one manifestation of this basic condition. Many writers have been introduced in evidence to support the thesis that our modern collective values and typical character structure are not in harmony with the social conditions in which they must move. The result, according to the terms of this thesis, is a frantic effort to heal the rupture by external agencies, to obtain, by artificial means, a consensus which has not emerged naturally. Our minds are being actively manipulated toward a conformity which might dull the stabs and pangs of social change, alienation, and the crisis of values.

Genuine loyalty, however, is not the same thing as a surface uniformity of belief and feeling. It grows only from shared experience and interactions. It is the fruit of a sense of sharing in a rich and meaningful common cause. The youthful members of the "gangs" studied by Thrasher and Whyte felt a loyalty toward their gang which was rich in content and high in tone because their group experiences were meaningful, were valuable, and were shared. And Ernie Pyle, who appreciated the outlook of the combat soldier perhaps better than any other journalist of his time, also knew this to be true. The "G.I.'s," he reported in *Brave Men,* endured the agonies of danger and death not because of devotion to distant and abstract causes, but because of deep and abiding loyalty toward their comrades in arms.

> Then darkness enveloped the whole American armada. Not a pinpoint of light showed from those hundreds of ships as they surged on through the night toward their destiny, carrying across the ageless and indifferent sea tens of thousands of young men, fighting for . . . for . . . well, at least for each other.[57]

Loyalty cannot be imposed when the conditions that nourish it are absent. Therefore, an attempt to strengthen the bonds of community by imposing a surface uniformity of thought, and equating that conformity with loyalty, is a false solution to the problem. It confuses likes and unlikes. It deals with symptoms rather than with causes.

ALTERNATIVE SOLUTIONS

It is a chief contention of this essay that the current emphasis on loyalty cannot be understood apart from this broad context of popular sentiment and need. Still, explanations have been offered which ignore or minimize the factors here considered important. So, before leaving this topic, a word, albeit a critical one, should be said about them.

Two alternative explanations of the loyalty problem hold widest sway today. The first might be called the "devil theory." Its major thesis is that the whole thing is an effort on the part of the dominant conservative elites, allied with a few unscrupulous politicians, to suppress the opposition and maintain their own power. The second asserts that the concern with loyalty is due entirely, or predominantly, to the state of relations between the United States and Russia. It can be called the "foreign agent theory." Both go too far on too little evidence.

1) Undoubtedly, the loyalty theme has been exploited by some politicians and some representatives of the conservative elites. But to attribute it all to their machinations would be superficial. The important point is that the slogan of loyalty has struck profound chords of popular thought and feeling. It is a fact, written repeatedly in opinion polls and at the polling booth, that much of the public agrees with the efforts of the loyalty investigators in House and Senate.* The national political figures whose names are synonymous with the struggle against the disloyal and the nonconformist have

---

* On several occasions the Gallup Poll asked this question of a representative sample of Americans: "What is your opinion of Senator McCarthy?" The results were as follows:

	Favorable opinion	Unfavorable opinion	No opinion
August 1951	15%	22%	63%
April 1953	19	22	59
June 1953	35	30	35
August 1953	34	42	24
January 1954	50	29	21
March 1954	46	36	18

SOURCE: *U.S. News and World Report* (March 19, 1954), 20.

struck upon a popular theme and only within this context can their successes be understood.

Perhaps the most accurate statement of their role is that they have channeled the insecurities reviewed above into a concern over disloyalty and subversion in high places. That this has been done sometimes for partisan advantage is indisputable—but that, after all, is part of the workings of the democratic process.* Additional factors in the current situation have made their work easier and intensified the concern over questions of loyalty. The first is the desire to find a scapegoat on which to lay present ills.[58] The second is the presence of an anti-intellectualism that tends to identify criticism and nonloyalty (or loyal opposition) with disloyalty. Both these factors are widespread in popular thinking and both have been skillfully exploited for partisan ends.

a) The Communists make a perfect scapegoat: they are few in number, associated with foreign ways, suspected of possessing miraculous and sinister powers, and their destruction would do no grave material damage to the functioning social system. Furthermore, there is enough objective proof of their malevolent designs and subversive conduct to supply the necessary basis for identifying them as the perpetrators of evils not yet discovered. This gives them supreme value as a scapegoat and makes it effective to point to them as the source of our problems.

The current assault against communism is, it need hardly be said, extraordinarily loud and far-reaching. Yet we know that the party itself is minute in size and, today at least, in influence. President Eisenhower has assured us that the party numbers only about 25,000 adherents; Mr. J. Edgar Hoover has assured us that the Federal Bureau of Investigation knows who they are, where they are, and what they are doing. Congress has cast the party beyond the pale of the law. Moreover, Communist doctrine has very little appeal for Americans; as Justice Douglas remarked in the Dennis case, Com-

---

* Evidence suggestive of the extent and sophistication of this political exploitation of the loyalty theme is provided by a former (Democratic) member of the House of Representatives. Clinton D. McKinnon writes: "During the four years I spent as a member of Congress, I became acquainted with many Republican legislators. In the quiet conversations of the cloak-room or office, I have yet to find a responsible Republican who believed our government was endangered by Communists. But on the political platform it was different. Charges of subversion and communism made strong medicine, and they were used for political effect." Los Angeles *Daily News*, Feb. 15, 1954, p. 10.

munists in the United States are "the miserable merchants of unwanted ideas." Given these conditions, the Red Menace would appear to be virtually no menace at all. But efforts to destroy this pale and feeble being continue unabated. A dispassionate observer must conclude that there is a ludicrous disproportion between all these excursions and alarms and the danger toward which they are directed. To understand this passion we must look for causes other than the inherent threat posed by the Communist party.

The first, as has been said already, is that the Communists are a perfect scapegoat. We may unload all our guilts and problems on their condemned backs and offer them up as sacrifices on the altar of national unity without irreparable damage to the country. Our anxieties, our tensions, our fears of all the "things that go bump in the night"—in the phrase of the witch-hunters of yore—are thus directed and dissipated. Also, the political fortunes of some politicians are advanced. But the Communists strike fear into the hearts of Americans for other reasons as well. It is, in fact, due to these other reasons that they form such an ideal scapegoat. The reasons alluded to are two: first, the Communists have become the unhappy heirs of certain indigenous historical legacies; secondly, there are not enough of them.

Americans are a heterogeneous people; our society is an amalgam of diverse groups, creeds, and traditions. In addition, we as a nation often have been beset with problems created by disaffection and disloyalty.[59] The Revolution had its Loyalists, the Civil War its Copperheads, the First World War its suspect German-Americans. Americans, briefly, have sustained the tribulations of divided national and ideological loyalties. As a result, the nation has a tradition of harsh treatment of those who appear to put some other interest above the national interest. And as the tide of nationalism swells, treatment of dissenters becomes increasingly severe. In our period the Communists, officially and popularly identified as agents of a foreign power, bear the concentrated wrath of this legacy. It is interesting to mark the contrast here between Britain and the United States.

> "Un-British," in the context of a community as cohesive as Britain, is a term of contempt; "Un-American" has always smacked of treason. The Communist Party inherits the fear and hatred with which Americans have generally regarded people who appear to put their loyalty to some other nation above their loyalty to the United States.[60]

The Communists are feared and subject to the persecutions that flow from fear in part because, secondly, they are so few in number.

The point here is not that we need more Communists—indeed not—but simply that the Communist as an individual, living human being is something quite beyond the experience of most citizens. The Communist known to the citizen is not a thing of flesh and blood at all; not his neighbor, his business associate, his fellow-worker. Since the Communist is beyond personal ken, it is very easy to think in terms of "all Communists," to conceive them in abstract and stereotyped terms. We know there are many shades of Republicans and Democrats, Christians and Jews, businessmen and workers, because we live in the midst of such types, have intimate contacts with them, and perceive them as individuals with diverse qualities and defects.

Not so with the Communists. There just are not enough of them to go around among the population and permit folk to live with them, work with them, play with them. They are not, in a word, palpable. So we think of Communists in the abstract, as a stereotype. And, given this, it is a simple task to paint them with the brush of evil, to portray them one and all as dedicated, professional revolutionaries with but one design and will—violent destruction of all that the rest of us hold dear. The stereotype fits Lenin's image of the ideal Bolshevik, but Lenin, being one of them and knowing others, knew full well that most of them would be quite useless on capitalism's *Dies Irae*. His image of the average Communist, since it was based upon direct experience, was accurate. The American, knowing nothing of Communists personally, finds it natural to imagine them all stamped in the same mold. Even professional students, who ought to know better, have fallen into the same error. It is becoming commonplace to see studies of communism and Communists based almost entirely upon party documents. The technique here is to quote from party manuals or documents and then proceed to generalize about the "nature of communism." [61]

This point is made clear by contrast with countries where Communists are far more numerous than in the United States. In those countries it is elementary wisdom to distinguish among types and grades of Communists. France will serve to illustrate the point. Thus, Pierre Bertaux, former chief of the French *Sûreté Nationale*, a position that teaches one much about Communists, and a role not occupied by Romantics, is reported by an American journalist to have said the following:

> You Americans are wrong in trying to force your methods on our country. You believe in theology, in sorcery, in witchcraft. For you, communism is a sin, and the Communists are witches to be

burned. The fact is they are very simple, ordinary people. For fifteen years the Communists have pulled to their ranks the finest young people of France. . . . They, the young men of communism, are the truest victims, and the job is not to persecute them, but to liberate them.[62]

b) As for the factor of anti-intellectualism, it should be remembered that the intelligentsia have long been an object of humor and derision in American folkways. We have contributed generously to the rich literature of the fuzzy-minded intellectual—the egghead—who dreams his dreams and spins his schemes from the privileged sanctuary of the ivory tower. This class has never set the tone of American life and often has found itself in opposition to the trends of the times. The 1930's, for example, saw a large-scale defection of the intelligentsia from the enthroned economic ideology. A good many flirted with radical, sometimes Marxist, panaceas for the nation's maladies. This defection has never been forgotten or forgiven and lies behind many of the attacks against academics today. The classes that supply the money to run the schools feel betrayed when this money supports men who assault the very system that pays them. It was the schools that furnished the *Ideologues* of the New Deal and they have not been forgiven that sin either. Alistair Cooke was right in interpreting the trial of Alger Hiss as symbolic of the trial of a whole generation and way of thought.[63] There was throughout that trial an implicit but powerful urge to equate the personal figure of Hiss with the New Deal and try it through him. Both lost. The new Administration is even now busy cleansing the government service of the remaining representatives of the type.* In this way, as well as through such auxiliary devices as teachers' oaths, it is being made

---

* Discussing personnel changes made in the federal bureaucracy by the Eisenhower Administration, a recent analyst emphasizes this point: "In general—and nothing is altogether general in this highly varied picture—suspicion is directed primarily at the type of personnel so prominent in the past 20 years, the 'planners,' the 'idea men,' the people who translated vague policy objectives into substantive proposals, the intellectuals who kept contriving new ventures and new paths to explore. These people—'egg heads' is now the accepted term—are not in good standing; they will depart or be quiescent. In so far as substitutions are being made, the tendency is to seek the efficiency engineer or the management expert—by and large men whose interests or talents differ from those of their predecessors." As a footnote, the same writer adds: "The Undersecretary of the Interior publicly boasted that he had booted out 'a group of Ph.D's from Harvard and Columbia' whom he found on his staff." Herman Miles Somers, "The Federal Bureaucracy and the Change of Administration," *American Political Science Review*, XLVIII (March, 1954), 146.

clear that what is wanted at the present time is not criticism but conformity.

This phenomenon of anti-intellectualism takes another form, alienation of the intellectual from American life. The theme defies precise documentation; it appears in a thousand ungainly shapes in contemporary literature, educational discussion, and shoptalk among writers and artists. Julien Benda may insist that the "clerk" must be detached from the society in which he moves in order to perform his role of confronting the masses, who are immersed in the squalid trivialities of material life, with a vision of the man whose kingdom is not of this world but who lives for ideals and abstract principles. There may even be truth in his judgment that, thanks to the "clerks," ". . . humanity did evil for two thousand years but honored good." And, even further, it may be true that the "clerk" who has become socially accepted has sold out his high calling for the tinsel of public praise: ". . . the clerk who is praised by the laymen is a traitor to his office." [64] But this fact remains: that is a hard and lonely course to follow. Most intellectuals, like other men, want to feel themselves a part of the functioning community life, with a valued role to perform and with recognition commensurate to that role.

The American intellectual classes do not occupy such a position in the national life. The larger social system has repudiated them and they, in turn, counter in kind. We admire not the clerk who devotes his life to great literature, or philosophy, or painting, but the sensible technician who can make things run, and teach our children practical skills. The current stress on loyalty is directly related to this repudiation and alienation of the intellectual. The evidence is overwhelming; it comes from the rooms where loyalty hearings are conducted, from the chambers of governmental investigative bodies, from the halls where oaths are being imposed upon teachers and professors. But let us rest content with a passage from a previously cited foreign writer, who suggests some of the ramifications of this relation in speaking of the factors behind the current drive against Communist and other "heretical" ideas:

> One must not neglect, either, the profound alienation of "intellectuals" from the rest of Americans, much deeper than it is in Britain. Intelligent and sensitive Americans tend to be repelled by the commercial, pragmatic, militantly "low brow" cast of American life. Some of them become Communists or fellow-travellers, not out of admiration of Russia, but from antagonism to America. For their part, many of the more primitive type of Americans seem to think that intelligence is a half-way post to

communism. The intelligent person doubts and questions, even takes an interest in "foreign" ideas; these are danger signs. Hence much of Mr. Acheson's unpopularity arises from his obvious intelligence and good breeding, which excites anger and suspicion —"This pompous diplomat in striped pants, with a phony British accent," as Senator McCarthy expressed it.[65]

Much of the attractiveness of the devil theory, perhaps, stems from an extravagant view of the efficacy of propaganda in manipulating the mind of the masses. Today much is heard of the power of the propagandist to achieve almost anything he will with his clever techniques and cunning appreciation of the role of symbols in behavior. Yet this art, like all others, has limits. Take, for illustration, the totalitarian dictatorships. When all is said that can be said concerning the power of propaganda in Nazi Germany, Fascist Italy, and Communist Russia, the fact remains that these systems depended on the systematic use of brutality for their strength. Indeed, could they have employed verbal persuasion rather than brute power to gain their ends—even their internal ends—they would not have become such barbarous things. The following passage suggests some of the limits of propaganda.

> The truth seems to be that propaganda on its own cannot force its way into unwilling minds; neither can it inculcate something wholly new; nor can it keep people persuaded once they have ceased to believe. It penetrates only into minds already open, and rather than instill opinion it articulates and justifies opinions already present in the minds of its recipients. The gifted propagandist brings to a boil ideas and passions already simmering in the minds of his hearers. He echoes their innermost feelings. Where opinion is not coerced, people can be made to believe only in what they already "know." [66]

2) The foreign power theory suffers from the same defect as the devil theory, that is, it tries to explain too much with too little evidence. The point of view taken here is that the current interest in loyalty is influenced greatly, but not caused exclusively, or even predominantly, by the state of American-Russian relations. The inadequacy of the foreign power theory becomes clear in the light of the following test. If one were to construct a graph depicting fluctuations in the amount of tension between the United States and the Soviet Union for the period since 1918, and then compare it with a similar graph showing fluctuations in the amount of domestic concern with loyalty and conformity, he would find no constant and direct correlation between them. He would find that the two do not

vary concomitantly but sometimes appear to fluctuate quite independently of each other. For example, during the period 1932–1945 relations with the Soviet Union were generally good and, except for 1938–1939, showed steady improvement. The policies of Russia during that period could not be said to represent a threat to the United States. Yet, during the same time the concern with loyalty grew steadily greater. If there was any correlation between the two, it would appear to have been negative. The reasonable conclusion seems to be that relations with Russia are but one, albeit very important, factor among many influencing the situation. Those other factors can be appreciated better with the assistance of the "field" analysis employed here than by an approach that searches for linear cause-and-effect connections. That is the only superiority to which this analysis lays claim.

This attempted analysis of the factors underlying the current public concern with loyalty should have shown, if nothing else, the complexity of the problem. No claim is made that the analysis "explains" all the issues in a way that compels agreement and renders alternative explanations indefensible. It is doubtful whether social science has the tools for such proof as that in any but the most simple cases. When the operative factors are many, the field broad, and the time span long, we usually must rest content with "reasonable" and self-consistent analyses and cannot hope for conclusive explanations. But that is no excuse for refusing to play the game; if the social scientist spoke only when he was sure of his analysis, when he could muster irrefutable proof of its validity, much wisdom would be lost in the deep silence which would descend over the halls of learning, and most of our major social problems would go untreated. "Certainty," said Justice Holmes, "generally is an illusion, and repose is not the destiny of man."

5

Emergent Concepts of Loyalty

IN THE PREVIOUS CHAPTER SOME OF THE PHENOMENA underlying the current stress on loyalty were appraised. With that preparation, it is possible to examine current situations in a more realistic setting.

Not all current situations, however. No reasonably brief essay could hope to accomplish a full narrative of even the salient facts and events of loyalty today. Again there are problems of selection. If choices are made wisely the destination of understanding the principal features of the current problem should be reached with the least motion squandered in the exploration of misleading byways. In what follows many aspects of the current loyalty situation will be surveyed from a philosophic and synthetic perspective. But the main objective will be to discover what conceptions of loyalty are now current. If they can be identified much of the rest will fall into pattern.

This choice can be defended on two grounds. Firstly, and very simply, one expects a study in political ideas to deal with ideas. Secondly, an analysis of emergent concepts of loyalty will contribute most toward appreciation of the essential character of the present-day loyalty problem. A great jurist has told us that the most important part of the law is the philosophy behind it. So too with loyalty. All the studies of loyalty-board procedures, or of the antics of congressional loyalty-hunters, or of the impact of loyalty programs in schools and factories do not get at the central issues. The critical question is the conception of loyalty operative in a specified context. If that is known the other things will be found to follow. For, after all, there is a relation of ends to means here. Ideas are plans of action. They contain within themselves implications about the means needed to effect them. To work from means to ends is reverse procedure, for, in reality, the relation goes the other way.

A student who wanted to discover what political concepts are emergent or dominant in a society could collect his data from a number of sources and in a variety of ways. He might, for example, adopt the technique of the opinion pollster. Or, he might study the attitudes of significant organized groups as articulated in their published statements. But for the problem in hand a better approach is possible. For some time now the federal government has been testing the loyalty of its employees. Many states have followed suit. The men who direct and staff the federal program are not political philosophers. They are administrators; they start with given facts and concepts and conclude with specific decisions. In addition, the top loyalty boards have tried to secure members of various occupational backgrounds in order to achieve an approximation of popular thinking. Here, then, is a rich source of data concerning the emergent concepts of loyalty in America.

BACKGROUND OF THE LOYALTY PROGRAM

Before 1939 applicants for employment in the federal civil service were assumed to be loyal. In fact, probes into the political opinions and activities of applicants were forbidden as beyond the proper scope of government's interest. A civil service rule of 1884 makes this very clear.

> No question in any form or application or in any examination shall be framed so as to elicit information concerning the political or religious opinions or affiliations of any applicant, nor shall any

inquiry be made concerning such opinions, or affiliations, and all disclosures thereof shall be discountenanced.

But in 1939 there appeared a drop of what was soon to swell into a sizable stream of legislation designed to wash the civil service of impure elements and, later, to cleanse the public mind of whatever stains of disloyalty might therein reside. Section 9–A of the Political Activities Act of 1939 (known as the Hatch Act) forbade any federal employee to hold membership in any party or organization that advocated the overthrow of our constitutional form of government.[1] The Civil Service Commission rose to meet this new demand and announced, in June of 1940, that it would not certify for employment any person found to be a member of the Communist party, the German Bund, or any other Communist or Nazi group.[2] Two years later the commission announced a standard of judgment which was destined to a long and dubious career. It declared that an applicant would be disqualified when there was "a reasonable doubt as to his loyalty to the Government of the United States."[3] The commission solved the problem of the status of Communists when it classified them as "potentially disloyal" and hence unemployable under the reasonable doubt standard. Commissioner Fleming testified before Congress to his belief that

> A member of the Communist Party or a follower of the Communist Party line has clearly indicated that his primary loyalty is to a foreign political group owing its allegiance to a foreign government, and that there is therefore a strong presumption in favor of his willingness to take steps designed to overthrow our Constitutional form of Government if directed to do so.[4]

The Emergency Relief Appropriation Act for fiscal 1941 included restrictive measures which became standard in numerous subsequent acts.

> Sec. 15(f) No alien, no Communist, and no member of any Nazi Bund Organization shall be given employment or continued in employment on any work project prosecuted under the appropriations contained in this joint resolution and no part of the money contained in this joint resolution shall be available to pay any person who has not made or who does not make affidavit as to United States citizenship and to the effect that he is not a Communist and not a member of any Nazi Bund Organization. . . .
> Sec. 17(b) No portion of the appropriation made under this joint resolution shall be used to pay any compensation to any

---

[1] For numbered notes to chap. 5, see pp. 203–207.

person who advocates, or is a member of an organization that advocates, the overthrow of the Government of the United States.[5]

In 1940 and 1941 Congress authorized the secretaries of War, Navy, and State to remove summarily any person who, in the opinion of the Secretary, constituted a risk to national security.[6] The military agencies operated under these measures until they were superseded by comprehensive legislation of 1950.[7] So far as can be determined, the laws of 1940 and 1941 contained the first formal recognition of a distinction between loyalty and security. It is apparent, however, that from the beginning spokesmen in favor of loyalty legislation usually argued their stand on the premise that disloyal persons were by definition security risks.[8] Concluding this line of legislation designed to combat the threat of infiltration in wartime, President Roosevelt decreed in 1942 that one of the grounds for exclusion or expulsion from the civil service was reasonable doubt as to the loyalty of the person in question.

During the wartime period two executive commissions were established to study and report on the loyalty program. In April of 1942 the Attorney General appointed an interdepartmental committee to look into the cases that had originated under the Hatch Act. The committee's purview was limited to inquiries concerning organizational membership or personal advocacy of revolution. It investigated complaints against 4,579 employees, of whom 36 were dismissed.[9] Concluding its labors, the committee reported that the record showed that "the futility and harmful character of a broad personal inquiry have been too amply demonstrated. . . ." Moreover, the committee continued, "the objective test of membership in a Communist front organization is thoroughly unsatisfactory as a measure of loyalty." [10] This report met an angry reception in Congress and attacks against the presumed or suspected disloyalty of employees in the executive branch continued. President Roosevelt, hoping to quiet the clamor, promulgated an Executive Order establishing another interdepartmental committee to consider the entire problem of "subversive activity." It concluded, with its predecessor, that the only acceptable definition of subversive conduct was the one prescribed in Section 9-A of the Hatch Act. It added a few more names to the list of organizations proscribed under the Hatch Act and recommended standards of judgment and procedure in deciding loyalty cases. This committee functioned rather listlessly until it was superseded in March of 1947.[11] Thus, from 1939 on, a general but sometimes haphazard loyalty program was in operation.[12] From its inception, the program was hampered by ambiguity, vacillation, and indecision. In the last analysis, the difficulty reduced to this: no authority had ever (or has yet) taken the time and trouble to define the meaning of loyalty, prescribe reliable criteria for determining its presence or absence in a particular human container, and elaborate the relations between loyalty and security. One committee did make an effort to define it by a sort of negative technique, that is, by declaring the meaning of "subversive activity." Perhaps it can be argued that one whose disloyalty was far-reaching and intense might try to subvert the nation and its institutions. So the definition at least merits reproduction. Furthermore, it should be preserved as a rare specimen; there are few enough definitions in this field.

> Subversive activity in this country derives from conduct intentionally destructive of or inimical to the government of the United States—that which seeks to undermine its institutions, or to distort its functions, or to impede its projects, or to lessen its efforts, the ultimate end being to overthrow it all. Such activity may be open and direct as by effort to overthrow, or subtle and indirect as by sabotage.[13]

The clumsiness of this tool for the eradication of subversives was revealed very early when it was applied against three men who, by any reasonable standards, would appear harmless and ordinary citizens. The strongest evidence adduced against Robert Lovett was that he had joined many organizations which the Dies Committee thought were "fellow traveling." [14] Goodwin Watson, it appeared, had been so bold as to express in writing certain views he held concerning defects in the profit system. William Dodd, Jr., had permitted his apartment to be used for a cocktail party for Harry Bridges. The incident became a *cause célèbre* when the alleged subversives took the issue to law. An incensed Supreme Court found that Congress had inflicted punishment by means of a bill of attainder.[15]

Is it unfair to ask, if we are going to talk of subversives, and if we use the definition announced above, just where was the subversion here? Was it in the three accused? Or could it have been in a Congress that violated the prohibition against bills of attainder in its eagerness to remove three men from the federal payroll? Surely, such action must "undermine" or "distort" American institutions as much as does permitting Harry Bridges to drink cocktails in your apartment.

Other than this definition of subversive activity, the only formal criteria evolved during this era were those of the Hatch Act—membership in organizations that advocated forceful overthrow of constitutional government, and personal advocacy of the same. The real standard, then, was the guilt-by-association doctrine propounded by the Dies Committee and incorporated in the 1940 Smith Act. The basic problem, then as now, was the so-called front organization. How can front organizations be determined? What weight should be given to membership in them as evidence of potential disloyalty? How measure the scope and significance of an individual's involvement? How discover the motives he had for joining and the extent of his knowledge of the nature and ends of the organization? These problems were never solved, and the Attorney General's committee reluctantly concluded, as was previously noted, that the test was "thoroughly unsatisfactory" as an index of loyalty.

But, as is inevitable in these matters, a definition of sorts emerged in practice. Agents of the Federal Bureau of Investigation and investigators hired by the Civil Service Commission had to have some standards of relevancy, some lines of guidance, if they were not to dissipate their energies in random activity. What kinds of questions, what criteria, did these men employ in their probings into individual cases? Here there is considerable evidence.[16] Kammerer reports that the investigative services had to be reformed after many complaints were voiced by public and press. These complaints centered around the investigators' "bias against liberal affiliations" and their indiscriminate application of the "guilt by association standard established by the Dies Committee." Kammerer records Leonard D. White as saying in a personal interview that "the orientation of these investigators as a group was distinctly conservative." In a letter written to Kammerer, Mr. Floyd M. Reeves stated:

> The major interest of almost all of them seemed to be that of finding out whether or not the person being investigated might be sympathetic toward Communism, toward our ally, Russia, or toward the Spanish Loyalists. The questions asked relating to matters such as membership in national or local associations, books and literature read, and associations with other persons, seemed to imply that one who had read books about Russia, visited Russia, was a friend of someone who had visited Russia, or had been sympathetic with the Spanish Loyalists was a dangerous person to employ in a government agency. I cannot recall ever having been asked a question that implied that the person under investigation might be or might have been sympathetic toward Germany or Japan.

Testimony even more enlightening issued from the Civil Service Commission itself. In response to criticism, the commission issued instructions in August of 1942 detailing types of questions that were not to be asked by investigators. These instructions revealed more clearly than could mountains of critical personal testimony just what criteria of loyalty were being applied by the investigators. This list of prohibited questions should be sampled.

> Under no circumstances should any question be asked . . . involving union membership, union associations, or union activities. . . .
> Do not ask any question whatever involving the applicant's sympathy with Loyalists in Spain.
> Under no circumstances ask any question or make any statement . . . relating . . . to the color, race, creed, or religion of an applicant or witness.
> Do not ask any question regarding the type of reading matter read by the applicant. This includes especially the *Daily Worker* and all radical and liberal publications.
> Do not ask any questions as to so-called mixed parties, that is to say, whether the applicant associates with Negroes or has had Negroes in his home.
> Do not ask any general questions regarding the political philosophy of the applicant, such as whether he believes in capitalism or what his opinion is regarding certain events of a current or historical nature. . . .
> Exercise intelligence. Keep in mind what you are looking for. Remember that you are investigating the loyalty of the applicant to the United States. You are not investigating whether his views are unorthodox or do not conform with those of the majority of the people.

As one scans this panel, and recalls the personal statements of White and Reeves, he perceives implicit in them a rather curious concept of loyalty. White concludes that the investigators were "distinctly conservative." Reeves adds that they had a keen eye for anyone who was interested in, or knew about, or knew people who knew about, Russia and things Russian. The list of questions which the commission had to forbid its investigators covers such matters as attitudes toward unionism and capitalism, attitudes toward Negroes and Spanish Loyalists, liberal and radical publications, and whether one's views were generally orthodox. Could it be possible that the investigators were confusing nonconformity with communism and disloyalty? There is certainly more than a hint of that in the record. It appears that the operative concept of loyalty equated loyalty with orthodoxy. The loyal citizen is one who shares the views of the conservative majority on matters of interracial relations, economic and social policy, and reading tastes. Apparently, if one deviated from such views there was enough doubt about his loyalty to the United States to require full investigation.

What came of it all? What was the product of all this zeal directed against disloyalty and subversion? This. The Civil Service Commission reported that its Investigation Division closed out 273,429 cases between July, 1940, and December 31, 1944. Of these, 1,180 persons were found ineligible solely on loyalty grounds. During this period of war and defense more than 7,500,000 persons were recruited into federal employment. Therefore, only .0157 per cent of federal employees were barred for disloyalty reasons; that is, out of about every 6,356 employees you could expect to find one who was *suspected* of disloyalty.[17]

These figures permit either of two conclusions: (1) there were very few disloyal employees, or (2) the methods used to discover disloyalty were hopelessly inefficient. The figures themselves do not indicate which is the better conclusion. We know, for example, that none of the proven cases of sabotage and espionage which have come to light since 1940 were discovered in the course of routine work under the loyalty program. It may be, therefore, that the methods employed simply were inadequate to the job of finding the disloyal. On the other hand, given the "shotgun" approach of the program, its vague and comprehensive criteria, and the fact that all "doubtful" cases were decided in favor of the government, it is hard to conclude otherwise than that the federal services were staffed overwhelmingly by persons of steadfast and unquestionable loyalty. On this note of doubt the first phase of the loyalty program ended.

The second phase began soon after the close of the war. Whittaker Chambers and Elizabeth Bentley had published their accounts of underground activities in Washington and elsewhere. In the offices of the magazine *Amerasia* were found hundreds of classified documents from the files of military and security agencies. In June, 1946, the Canadian government disclosed its report on military and atomic espionage.[18]

The Canadian report was disturbing. It showed the nefarious operations of a circle of men, mostly Canadian citizens, engaged in the systematic betrayal of their country. It traced the steps by which persons were led, almost unwittingly, from innocent beginnings into an entrapping web of crime. Soviet espionage agents would select as targets persons in critical positions who had some personal defect which could be exploited and who were vulnerable to Communist ideology. These potential victim-spies would be led into study groups where Communist ideology would be presented and the "students" would be analyzed closely for their promise as future undercover agents. The discussions would shade imperceptibly from mere exposure to Communist ideas to criticism of Western democracy, and then to indoctrination in the Communist alternative. At the same time, the target individuals gradually were being absorbed into the social life of their new-found companions. Previous ties were discouraged and intense efforts made to get the converts deeply involved in a new organizational life. Then appeals would be directed to the idealism of the converts in order to effect a transfer of loyalty from country to humanity, from nation to international brotherhood. The ultimate receptacles of this new loyalty were, of course, the Soviet Union and the Communist party. After the victim had made this shift he would be sounded out and, if possible, induced to deliver state secrets, always on the plea that this was the way he could most effectively serve his new loyalty. The last act in this grim drama of spider and fly came when the victim was seduced into accepting "gifts" for services rendered. His corruption was now complete: he was trapped. Here was political seduction worked by masters in the arts of temptation. Igor Gouzenko indicated that the same game was being played in the United States.

These revelations, coming when America was in a troubled time of change from open war to uneasy peace, had an instantaneous impact. From all sides arose the clamor for stronger loyalty-security measures. Russia, with whom we had entered into a "strange alliance" during the war, fell under dark suspicion. What is equally important, it became ever clearer that the real criteria of loyalty are subjective, and that the only way to separate the loyal from the disloyal is to probe their thoughts and attitudes, ideas and beliefs. It was in this atmosphere of emergency that the President, on November 25, 1946, promulgated Executive Order 9806, creating the President's Temporary Commission on Employee Loyalty.[19] The commission reported in March of 1947,[20] and its recommendations became the basis for Executive Order 9835, of March 21, 1947, establishing a comprehensive loyalty program for the executive branch.[21] This program, with few amendments, remained in effect until the advent to power of the Eisenhower Administration.

Executive Order 9835 opens with an announcement of its bases and goals. Each employee, it begins, "is endowed with a measure of trusteeship over the democratic processes which are the heart and sinew of the United States." Therefore, "It is of vital importance that persons employed in the Federal service be of complete and unswerving loyalty to the United States." In order to achieve this goal and at the same time protect loyal employees against "unfounded accusations of disloyalty," the program was created.

The order required a loyalty investigation of every applicant for employment and of every person already employed in the executive branch. It made each department or agency head responsible for eliminating disloyal workers from his jurisdiction. Those charged with disloyalty could have a hearing before a loyalty board, and decisions of the boards could be appealed to the Loyalty Review Board of the Civil Service Commission. The Loyalty Review Board returned only advisory opinions in appellate cases. The order directed the Attorney General to furnish the board with a list of subversive organizations. The Federal Bureau of Investigation was the primary investigative agency under the program and, very importantly, was permitted to conceal the identity of confidential informants provided it "furnishes sufficient information about such informants on the basis of which the requesting department or agency can make an adequate evaluation of the information furnished by them and provided it advises the requesting department or agency in writing that it is essential to the protection of the informants or to the investigations of other cases that the identity of the informants not be revealed." [22] The order prescribed that the standard for refusal of employment or for expulsion from employment was that "on all the evidence, reasonable grounds exist for belief that the person involved is disloyal to the Government of the United States." * The factors relevant in determining loyalty or disloyalty were:

1. Sabotage, espionage, or attempt or preparations therefore, or knowingly associating with spies or saboteurs;
2. Treason or sedition or advocacy thereof;
3. Advocacy of revolution or force or violence to alter the constitutional form of government of the United States;

---

* Executive Order 9835, Part V, 1. This standard was altered subsequently to read: "The standard for the refusal of employment or the removal from employment in an executive department or agency on grounds relating to loyalty shall be that, on all the evidence, there is a reasonable doubt as to the loyalty of the person involved to the Government of the United States." Executive Order No. 10241, 16 Fed. Reg. 3690 (April 28, 1951).

4. Intentional, unauthorized disclosure to any person, under circumstances which may indicate disloyalty to the United States,
of documents or information of a confidential or non-public
character . . . ;
5. Performing or attempting to perform his duties, or otherwise
acting so as to serve the interests of another government in
preference to the interests of the United States;
6. Membership in, affiliation with or sympathetic association
with any foreign or domestic organization, association, movement, group or combination of persons, designated by the Attorney General as totalitarian, fascist, communist, or subversive, or as having adopted a policy of advocating or approving
the commission of acts of force or violence to deny other persons their rights under the Constitution of the United States,
or as seeking to alter the form of government of the United
States by unconstitutional means.

The investigative procedure under the program, as it developed,
had a number of steps. First the name of the applicant or employee
was checked against the files of all appropriate federal government
bodies (such as the FBI and congressional investigating committees),
local law-enforcement files, schools, employers, and so forth.[23] If
this initial check revealed any "derogatory information" a full field
investigation followed. If a loyalty board considered the FBI report
damning, it gave the accused an opportunity to appear with counsel
and present evidence in his own behalf, or through witnesses, or
by affidavit. He was given a statement of the suspicions surrounding
him and of the charges against him "in sufficient detail, so that
he will be enabled to prepare his defense." [24] He could appeal his
case to the agency head and then on to the Loyalty Review Board.
Appeal from administrative to regular judicial tribunals was not
provided.

But events move rapidly in this area. "Truman's Loyalty Program,"
as the procedures utilized under Executive Order 9835 came to be
called, fell on hard days. Hardly had it been launched when the
attack struck. Some thought it inordinately harsh, sweeping, and in-
considerate of private rights and public good. Others thought it
insufficiently stern for the job it was designed to do. Some thought
it should be revised in major or minor part, others that it should
be abandoned. Few spoke to defend it. Moreover, candidate Eisenhower promised that, should he be elected to the Presidency, the
entire security program would be brought under review with a view
to improvement. So it was; and the result was Executive Order 10450,

of April 27, 1953, revoking the prior order and instituting a new program.[25]

The new order established a combined loyalty-security program, whereas during the Truman regime these two were kept distinct. Under the Truman system, security was handled as a separate operation. Until 1950, most departmental security programs functioned without specific statutory basis, and with widely varying standards and procedures. On August 26, 1950, the Congress passed Public Law 733, prescribing security procedures for State, Justice, Commerce, Defense, and other departments—eleven altogether—and empowering the President to extend it to such other agencies as he thought "necessary in the best interests of national security." [26] Under this statute, heads of agencies or departments might summarily suspend employees in the interests of national security. The law also entitled the employee to a written statement of charges, a hearing, and review by the agency head or his agent. Order 10450 extended this law to all agencies and departments in the federal service.

The new order, like its predecessor, has a dual objective: (*a*) to assure that all employees "shall be reliable, trustworthy, of good conduct and character, and of complete and unswerving loyalty to the United States," and (*b*) to assure that they shall be adjudged by "mutually consistent and no less than minimum standards and procedures . . . ," as required by the American tradition that all persons should receive "fair, impartial, and equitable" treatment by the government. The factors relevant in determining whether employees are good loyalty-security risks are stated in detail, although they are not to be considered exhaustive. They include all those listed in Order 9835, plus a number of others. Among the most important of these additional criteria are:

1. Any behavior, activities, or associations which tend to show that the individual is not reliable or trustworthy.
2. Any deliberate misrepresentations, falsifications, or omissions of material facts.
3. Any criminal, infamous, dishonest, immoral, or notoriously disgraceful conduct, habitual use of intoxicants to excess, drug addiction, or sexual perversion.
4. An adjudication of insanity, or treatment for serious mental or neurological disorder without satisfactory evidence of cure.
5. Any facts which furnish reason to believe that the individual may be subjected to coercion, influence, or pressure which may cause him to act contrary to the best interests of the national security.

In addition, the criteria include sympathetic association with subversive persons or representatives of any foreign nation whose interests may be inimical to the interests of the United States, and willful disregard of security regulations. Finally, the provision of the new order with regard to membership in subversive organizations is broader than that of the old order. It does not limit such groups to those appearing on the Attorney General's list, nor does it provide that membership must be treated as one item of evidence only, nor that such factors as time and duration of membership, and knowledge of the organization's aims, must be taken into account.

Under the new order, each agency head is responsible for security and loyalty within his jurisdiction; the Loyalty Review Board no longer exists. All persons in the federal service must undergo at least a minimum examination, including a check with the FBI and other "national agencies," with former employers, persons cited as references, and local law officers. Those who hold "sensitive" positions, defined as those whose occupants could have "a material adverse effect on the national security," undergo a far more rigorous investigation. The order provides that each agency head shall define the sensitive positions within his jurisdiction. The State Department, with more zeal than prudence, has designated all its positions sensitive. The order further provides that any person previously cleared after a full field investigation under Order 9835 shall have his case reëxamined. If the person was cleared under a standard less stringent than that of "clearly consistent with the interests of the national security," the case must be readjudicated.

Such are the outlines of the present program.* It is notorious

---

* Some estimate of the scope of the program is afforded by the following data: As of March, 1952, 4,000,000 employees had to be checked. Charges had been issued in 9,077 cases and hearings held in 2,961. Three hundred and seventy-eight persons had been dismissed or denied employment. (Figures from Eleanor Bontecou, *The Federal Loyalty-Security Program* [Ithaca: Cornell University Press, 1953], p. 145.) A better picture of the number of suspected disloyals emerges from these figures: On May 5, 1950, the FBI stated that 11,813 of 2,500,000 cases merited full field investigation. Of the 11,813, the Civil Service Commission announced that as of March 31, 1950, 202 had been severed on loyalty grounds. The Loyalty Review Board reversed findings of suspected disloyalty in 143 cases. While their investigations were pending, 1,406 left the service, and 1,028 left prior to adjudication of their cases by review boards. From Morris L. Ernst, "Some Affirmative Suggestions for a Loyalty Program," *American Scholar*, XIX (Autumn, 1950), 452–453. Under the intensified program of the present Administration, these totals have increased. The Civil Service Commission announced that during the year from May 28, 1953, to June 30,

that this program, like its predecessor, has come under heavy critical fire. In this area cool and impartial thinking is rare. Therefore, the analyst must move cautiously among the hazards of conflicting claims and assertions. And, in trying to estimate the virtue and workability of the program, he must be keenly aware of the role his own attitudes are playing. It must be remembered, however, that what follows is no attempt to present a comprehensive study of the entire program. The questions of major concern are: What appear to be the concepts of loyalty operative in the program? How do they influence action?

POTENTIAL LOYALTY AND DISLOYALTY

Executive Order 9835 lists six categories of evidence relevant to a determination of disloyalty.* The first four categories are clear and precise. They deal with overt acts, all of which long have been illegal under numerous statutes. They add nothing to the traditional American concept of disloyalty as meaning overt acts inimical to the security and well-being of the government. Moreover, none of those discharged under the program were charged with having committed any of these acts. On this point, Mr. L. A. Nikolorić, attorney with the law firm of Arnold, Fortas, and Porter, which has handled more loyalty cases than any other firm, writes:

> Not an employee fired has been charged with the commission of a wrongful act. During a recent public discussion with me, Mr. Seth Richardson, Chairman of the Loyalty Review Board, stated that the loyalty program has not discovered a single instance of espionage or any other overt action contrary to the best interests of the United States.[27]

Eleanor Bontecou reports that of eighty-five cases selected at random, "not one was found which involved charges of treason, sedition, espionage, sabotage, or advocacy of the overthrow of the Government

---

1954, 6,926 federal employees had been dismissed as security risks or had resigned while adverse information was in their files. Of this total, 2,611 were dismissed, and 4,315 resigned. In 1,743 cases of the total dismissed and resigned, adverse information referred to subversive activities or associations. The causes were not listed in 3,657 cases. Of the rest, 618 were characterized as sexual perverts, and 2,272 had records of misdemeanors or felonies. It is not known how many of the 4,315 who resigned did so because they knew their files contained adverse information. (Reported by Anthony Leviero, New York *Times*, Oct. 12, 1954, p. 1.)

* It should be noted that neither order provides a positive definition of loyalty. They work from the opposite end and deal with the indicia of disloyalty.

by force or violence, and no such cases were reported by the agency officials interviewed." [28]

It is clear, then, that categories five and six are the crucial ones for determining loyalty and disloyalty. In these categories inhere the basic concepts of the whole program. For all practical purposes, category five also can be excluded. It is so nebulous that even the loyalty boards hesitate to utilize it. Nearly all cases arise under the last category.[29]

Here a vital distinction must be made, namely, the distinction between actual and potential disloyalty. The first four categories are tests for actual disloyalty, the latter two for potential disloyalty. They look to the future. Their purpose is to investigate an individual's past and present attitudes and associations and, on this basis, assess his tendencies toward future disloyalty. Not only is this distinction implicit in the categories themselves, but it reappears time after time in the charges, hearings, and adjudications in cases before the loyalty boards. One employee, for example, was suspected of holding views of freedom of speech deemed dangerously "liberal" by the board. The case merits quotation *in extenso* for it very neatly points up the distinction between actual and potential disloyalty—as the hearing boards see it. It should be noted that the charges contained in the interrogatory had nothing to do with free speech. Indeed, when counsel for the accused tried to steer discussion back to the charges, the chairman rather testily responded that "you're dealing with a phase of the case that doesn't concern me at all. . . . What causes us concern is your *basic philosophy,* which seems to go so far as to defend the right of advocacy even to overthrow the government of the United States, unless the conditions at the time are such as that that would probably incite a dangerous upheaval." Extracts from the record follow.

> Chairman: What do you mean now by saying that you believe in the right of any individual to advocate the overthrow of our government by force?
>
> Witness: I believe that an individual must have the right to express any opinions, whether they're cockeyed or reasonable, whether they're agreed to by his fellows or not. . . . I think I would honestly have to stick by the statement that people have no right to plan or plot, or to organize action. Thinking is one thing, speaking is one thing; action is quite a different thing. . .

This disturbed the board. As the hearing approached its end, the issue was made sharper. When asked the standard question as to whether he felt his hearing had been fair and adequate, the witness responded:

> Witness: I do feel that I've had as adequate a hearing as it's possible to have. I do not feel that I have explained to you adequately my position. I have the feeling that you have very strong doubts as to whether at some time I would irrationally espouse some cause——
>
> Chairman: No. Now let me explain. I'm not concerned about that. I don't believe that you would advocate communism personally, I'm not at all sure that you believe in communism.
>
> Witness: Well, I don't believe in communism.
>
> Chairman: That's not the point. Let's get this clear. The point that I'm disturbed about is that while you would *neither advocate* communism nor *do anything consciously to implement it*, nevertheless you would go the limit in defending the right of other people . . . to advocate communism, . . . and the only limitation that you placed on that right . . . was that you would limit it, or forbid it, if the conditions at the time happened to be such that a political upheaval of some kind might result.[30]

It is apparent from this colloquy that the witness was trying to restate in homely terms Justice Holmes' doctrine of the clear and present danger. But this unorthodoxy, in the opinion of the board, rendered him something less than loyal and reliable. He bore the taint of possible disloyalty. There was no question that he had committed any illegal or disloyal acts, nor even that he had indulged in any illicit or suspicious advocacy. There was only the suspicion that any man who held such opinions as he did concerning the meaning of free speech might possibly, sometime, in the future, on some occasion, perform a disloyal act or engage in disloyal utterance. He might even defend others who mouthed disloyal doctrines so long as they did not try to put them into effect by illegal means. This man was declared disloyal by the board; the Loyalty Review Board sustained.

Seth Richardson has contested this argument. Yet, and in the same article which contains the denial, he slips into language which indicates that the test of potential disloyalty is the one actually used. He explains, first of all, that the primary purpose of the loyalty program is "to insure that no employees with substantial disloyalty elements in their records remain in the Government Executive service."[31] Therefore, he proceeds, the "fact to be determined is, of course, *present disloyalty*."[32] This fact is to be discerned by delving into remote events insofar as they are pertinent as indicators of present attitudes. But then the ground of discussion shifts. The first hesitant shift appears when Richardson explains that the loyalty boards' chief problem has not been to determine the meaning of loyalty, but to uncover the facts of an individual's record. He puts it this way: "The difficulty arises when we attempt to ascertain whether a particular employee has been, *or is likely to be,* seduced away from his belief in constitutional processes." [33] Now, it may be difficult for one untrained in the subtleties of loyalty-probing to appreciate this distinction between the meaning of loyalty and the facts which are indicators of its presence or absence: If you do not know what you are looking for, how do you know when you have found it? But that is not the important point. The point is that the argument has shifted to apply to a future state of affairs. If any doubt remains, Richardson dispels it in his concluding passages. Countering the argument that loyalty investigations should take cognizance only of overt acts of disloyalty, he writes:

> The employee who does not join, affiliate, or associate himself with subversive organizations and companions is less susceptible to subversive influence than the employee who does so but who, cautiously, refrains from committing overt acts of subversion. Such an employee may be a potential danger to the Government, corrupted beneath the surface by the company he has kept. I believe that the Government is justified in endeavoring to remove from employment those extra-susceptible persons in order to reduce the chance of subversive infiltration. The time to lock the Government door is *before* the loyalty horse is stolen, not afterwards. [34]

This brief passage contains some ideas and implications that give considerable cause for concern about the loyalty program. Take the first sentence. Richardson declares that one who has no intercourse with "subversives" is less susceptible to their influences than one who has such intercourse. Webster defines "susceptible" as "such in constitution or temperament as to be unresistant; exposed or liable through weakness." Either Richardson has confused the word "susceptible" for "exposed," or else he really means that association with "subversives" proves a susceptibility to their blandishments. If the latter meaning is intended, his assertion is not only questionable as an empirical matter, but highly dangerous as a premise for judging cases of loyalty. It assumes that mere exposure—degree unspecified —to subversive influences is tantamount to, or at least shows a dangerous proclivity to, reception of subversive ideas. This kind of reasoning lies at the base of the abuses of the guilt-by-association concept. Furthermore, what is said here does not even mention the broad and shadowy meanings currently attached to the word "subversive" in official and public thinking. It is notorious that that word has been stretched into bizarre shapes.

The extract's facile assumption that the only "reliable," the only "safe," Americans are those who never have been exposed—let alone susceptible—to persons or ideas that might "corrupt" them shows a shocking ignorance of the meaning of free speech and free association in the democratic society. Even more, it reveals a total lack of faith in the ability of men to choose wisely among political alternatives. It seems to say that Americans are not to be trusted with new and "foreign" ideas. It hopes to protect political virtue by removing all temptations. Such thinking is very far removed from the philosophy upon which this Republic was founded. Have Americans shown the immaturity and imprudence that might justify the mistrust revealed in this passage?

But we must refrain from pursuing all the themes in the passage, lest the one of immediate importance escape. The task of the loyalty program, Richardson makes clear, is to nip the bud of potential disloyalty before it can ripen into actual disloyalty. Moreover, although Richardson was still reluctant to admit the point, it is now openly avowed doctrine. The present security chief of the Department of State explicitly states that the job of his office is "to project a future judgment as to the security potential of the individual." [35]

An instructive comparison can be made here with the so-called bad-tendency standard sometimes applied in freedom of speech cases. The government does not propose to sit idly by until one who bears the seeds of evil can deposit them in soil where they may mature into actions constituting a clear and present danger of bringing about evils which it has a right to prevent. The loyalty program is designed to apprehend potential disloyalty. It attempts to do this by investigating past and present associations and attitudes, and, on this basis, judging the future likelihood of a person's committing disloyal or treasonous deeds. The basic concept of loyalty and disloyalty operative in the federal program is that of potential rather than actual loyalty and disloyalty. From this concept much of the rest of the program takes its impetus.

LOYALTY AND DISLOYALTY BY ASSOCIATION

The idea of potential loyalty and disloyalty is empty of content. What loyalty and disloyalty are it does not say. It asserts only that the future likelihood of their appearance in an individual can be determined. For the content of loyalty, that is, for the indicators by which future loyalty can be estimated, it is necessary to look to two other ideas. The first, and the subject of this section, is the idea of loyalty and disloyalty by association. The second, and the subject of the next section, is the concept of loyalty as conformity.

Category six of indicative factors in Executive Order 9835 begins with these words: "Membership in, affiliation with, or sympathetic association with. . . ." On first impression, the chief terms appear to be precise and to permit of testing by objective data. But are they? It will be suggested here that, as a measure of loyalty, this criterion of association is not wholly satisfactory.

First of all, the Loyalty Review Board never defined "sympathetic association." [36] Of the remaining two, take the one that appears to be the more precise, membership.[37] It can mean at least technical or legal membership; but it can also mean, in a broader psychological sense, membership implying involvement in, or identification with, or sympathy for, a given organization. In the first sense, it is clear. This is the kind of membership a court, for example, would be interested in if it were inquiring into one's obligations as an alleged member of a business corporation. The court would simply read the bylaws and membership rolls of the corporation, and then ask whether this person now before it, on the evidence, falls within their scope. Here there is little ambiguity.

However, this is not the meaning the loyalty probers give to the term. They want to know whether one subscribes to, is involved in, or sympathizes with the programs and goals of specified organizations. And here we enter the realm of the subjective. Membership in a political organization may mean quite different things to different persons. One may subscribe wholeheartedly to its complete program; another may have no other commitment to the organization than that of personal material interest. Another's membership may satisfy a need for group-belongingness and he may have little or no interest in policy and program. Membership is a matter not simply of degree—though that is part of it—but may include varieties of thought and conduct essentially different in kind. Carey McWilliams supplies a list of the meanings of "membership" he has extracted from loyalty hearings and un-American activities investigations. That list should show the hopeless vagueness and ambiguity of the term as a tool for discovering potential disloyalty. It should show, as McWilliams concludes, that ". . . membership is like a spectrum; that it has many gradations of meaning; and that the real test goes to the intensity of feeling, which is purely subjective." [38] He finds at least the following meanings:

1. Admitted membership
2. Concealed membership
3. Strategic nonmembership
4. Membership by interest
5. Subject to the discipline of
6. Membership by assumption
7. Membership by reputation
8. Lapsed membership
9. Fellow traveler
10. Former member [39]

As additional illustration of the inappropriateness of this sixth category for its appointed task, take the phrase "designated by the Attorney General as totalitarian, fascist, communist, or subversive. . . ." The practice of listing organizations and using the lists as bases for punitive action against individual members dates from the Deportation and Exclusion laws of 1917, 1918, and 1920, which forbade any alien who belonged to a group advocating overthrow of the government by force from entering or remaining in the country. Attorney General A. Mitchell Palmer read them as a license to conduct relentless warfare against radical groups. Radicalism, in his view, was synonymous with alien agitation and he undertook to implement his views through proscribing organizations, and through waging the notorious "red raids." [40] The Attorney General immediately listed twelve organizations and declared that membership in any of them constituted automatic grounds for exclusion or deportation. Personal beliefs and actions were irrelevant; the sole question was membership.

> The grounds for deportation in these cases will be based solely upon membership in the Communist Party of America and the Communist Labor Party, and for that reason it will not be necessary for you to go into the particular activities of the persons apprehended.[41]

Mr. Palmer's crusading ardor was blunted by the cautious interpretation given the statutes by Secretary of Labor Wilson and his assistant, Louis F. Post. The Department of Labor was charged with the duty of conducting hearings in deportation cases. Wilson and Post held that guilt must be personal and that, for the purposes of the law, "membership" must be strictly defined as meaning conscious knowledge of the nature of the organization and voluntary participation in its illegal activities. The Secretary further ruled that no organization could be listed as subversive unless its purposes were made known in ways discoverable by the membership. Furthermore, he distinguished between legitimate and illegitimate radical activities and purposes on the ground that only those that included the intention to use force and violence were invalid. Mere teaching and advocacy of radical doctrines did not make a group subversive.[42]

Not until the middle 1930's did the government again become active in the field of proscribing organizations. With the threat of Nazi propaganda and agitation hanging darkly over the country, Congress went to work with a will. The first Special Committee on Un-American Activities, under Representative McCormack, defined its scope narrowly and adopted a threefold test to determine whether an activity or organization was un-American: (1) whether it was under foreign control, (2) whether it promoted racial and religious bigotry, and (3) whether it wished to establish the Führer Principle in its internal affairs. Under these criteria, eight organizations were listed. Following this, the Dies Committee entered the field with a zeal far outstripping that of its predecessors. Ogden reports that the committee adopted a restricted definition of "un-American" but failed to adhere to it in practice. *

During this same period, executive agencies were required to draw up lists under a number of statutes. The Foreign Agents Registration Act of 1938, amended in 1939, required all groups conducting propaganda on behalf of a foreign principal to register.[43] The 1939 Hatch Act required the listing of organizations having as their purpose the overthrow of constitutional government. The Voorhis Anti-Propaganda Act of 1940 required groups subject to foreign control or intending to control or overthrow the government by force to register.[44] The Department of Justice had to interpret and enforce these statutes and

---

* The committee defined un-American groups as those ". . . directed, controlled, or subsidized by foreign governments or agencies which seek to change the policies and form of government of the United States in accordance with the wishes of such foreign governments." Raymond Ogden, *The Dies Committee* (Washington, D.C.: Catholic University of America Press, 1945), p. 177. It should be noted that, although Ogden calls this a restricted definition, he does so in relation to other statements by the Dies Committee. Actually, to call un-American any group that seeks to change the policies of our government to correspond with those of another government is to go very far indeed. If such a criterion were followed literally, it would mean that to urge upon our government any policies favored by any other government would be un-American. The Dies definition, sadly enough, is representative of the shoddy thinking so prevalent in this field.

that, of course, meant that it must engage in the practice of proscribing organizations. Under the Voorhis and McCormack acts the department had to deal with difficult problems of propaganda analysis. Recognizing the complexity of the task, the department retained social scientists who, under the direction of Harold D. Lasswell, began the job. They made elaborate studies preparatory to final decision as to the character of an organization. Decisions could be appealed to the courts. Frequently, however, the department did not make the lists public. The complete listing of forty-seven organizations under the Hatch Act was not published until 1947.[45]

Since March of 1947, when the new loyalty program began, the listings have been of extremely broad scope and have been prepared almost entirely in secrecy. The Attorney General has built his lists on ideological bases often unrelated to national security or to the enforcement of particular statutes. The first list of eighty-two organizations was made public on March 20, 1948.[46] Since that time, new groups have been added until, in November of 1950, the list included 197 organizations.[47]

How does the Attorney General arrive at his conclusions? Only he knows that. It is known only that before the Supreme Court ruled otherwise, he did not have to consult members of the listed organizations.[48] Nor did he have to grant representatives of the organizations an opportunity to appear in their behalf. By processes unknown, he makes his judgments and drafts his lists. In more precise terms, the listing is a strictly ex parte proceeding.

> Neither the criteria adopted nor the information upon which the departmental judgment is based has ever been made public. The listing is purely a matter of executive fiat and for that reason not subject to analysis.[49]

Many of the organizations have been long defunct. Few advocate the use of force or violence as a political method.

The hearing boards may not question the Attorney General's decisions. Although the Loyalty Review Board incorporated in its rules the President's admonition that membership is but one piece of evidence, it adopted additional rules which all but deny this. The boards, for example, may not inquire into the actual activities and professed objectives of the groups. Nor may they explore, prior to the filing of charges, a person's motivations and activities in the groups. The result is that membership is taken as a presumption of disloyalty and as a prima-facie case upon which charges may issue.

The one charged is then put to the burden of overthrowing the presumption. In this situation, as Tocqueville warned, persons are reluctant to engage in organizational activity. Furthermore, it is ingenuous to think otherwise when the list is changed from time to time. An employee may join an organization today which is blacklisted tomorrow.

Executive Order 10450 extends this concept in two ways. First of all, it includes associations with individuals. The relevant portion of the order follows.

> Establishing or continuing a sympathetic association with a saboteur, spy, traitor, seditionist, anarchist, or revolutionist, or with an espionage or other secret agent or representative of a foreign nation, or any representative of a foreign nation whose interests may be inimical to the interests of the United States, or with any person who advocates the use of force or violence to overthrow the government of the United States or the alteration of the form of government of the United States by unconstitutional means.[50]

Secondly, the order does not contain the limitation that only organizations appearing on the Attorney General's list are to be considered. It extends to *any* organization that is totalitarian, Fascist, Communist, or subversive, or that has a policy of approving violence to deny other persons their rights, or that seeks to alter the government by unconstitutional means. Now, apparently, each loyalty-security official may construct his own list of proscribed persons and groups.

From this discussion it emerges that the concept of loyalty operative in the loyalty program has as its second dimension (the first was its future referent) the notion of disloyalty by association. Loyalty is no longer a matter to be determined on a strictly personal basis. If one is a member of a proscribed group, or associates with "subversive" persons, his loyalty automatically is in doubt. No account is taken, in the first instance, of personal motivations, attitudes, and activities. Apparently on the adage that "birds of a feather flock together," one's loyalty is judged by the company he keeps. He can be loyal or disloyal according as he associates with persons of one or the other kind. The Attorney General and loyalty boards distinguish one kind from the other. But that is not entirely accurate. A really curious part of this whole business is that there is no articulate doctrine of "innocence by association" as a counterpart to the guilt-by-association doctrine. One may belong to any number of "loyal" organizations but what weighs most heavily is membership in the "disloyal" ones. Do only *black* birds flock together?

It is obvious that this dimension of the loyalty concept makes severe inroads into the traditional notion of pluralist loyalty and the voluntary bestowal of loyalty on private associations. Eleanor Bontecou, who has made the most careful study of this entire question, should be permitted to summarize the point.

> There can be no doubt of the impact of the list on the right and practice of freedom of association. As far as Government employees are concerned, the effect of a list which reaches into the past as well as the future and is issued piecemeal is an effective barrier to organizational activity. . . . The blight of the practice . . . extends far beyond the ranks of Government employees. No one can be sure that at some future date the Communists may not attempt to capture the organization to which he belongs. This is particularly true if the organization is dedicated to any project of social reform or has some special mass appeal. . . . The only safe course is to refrain from joining—a course of action which leaves the field of social reform free for the Communists.[51]

The practice of determining potential loyalty and disloyalty on the basis of group membership has given rise to one of the most vehement public discussions of the day. In the words "guilt by association," we have what one writer called "three words in search of a meaning." [52] Fortunately, Professors Sidney Hook and Henry Steele Commager, eminent scholars and skillful writers both, have recently addressed themselves to the subject.[53] The two authors state the issues fairly and ably. Their essays are especially valuable since each holds a different opinion on the utility and morality of the principle. An exposition of their arguments should contribute to the clarity which both agree is badly needed.

Hook holds that the doctrine can be a useful instrument for determining loyalty, if properly understood and applied. He undertakes to examine individually the two principal terms. There are, Hook begins, two kinds of guilt: criminal and moral. Criminal guilt is that "which makes a man subject to penal sanctions." The law recognizes criminal guilt by association only in a certain kind of conspiracy where the association is of a certain form. Moral guilt is that "which is not legally punishable but which may incur, in addition to a judgment of blame and disapproval, certain social sanctions from the community." Of course "criminal guilt usually carries with it the stigma of moral guilt." In current controversy the guilt-by-association concept is applied most often to cases of moral guilt, and it is "common sense and common practice" to recognize that one's associations are relevant to a judgment of fitness for positions of public confidence. Surely, a man known as a crony of criminals is unfit for a judicial post, even though nobody alleges his criminal guilt.

The real question, however, is "the degree and justification of the sanctions the community adopts toward those who are presumably guilty." This question, in turn, hinges on the meaning of "association," and cannot be resolved until the kind of relationship existing between the subject and his colleagues is known. "Association" is ambiguous; it covers relationships ranging from "active co-operation through membership in an organization, to chance meetings and other innocuous contacts, to continuous encounters for purposes of debate and refutation." It is clear, however, that a member of the Communist party, which has conspiratorial purposes, and a structure such that none can remain in it without coöperating in those purposes, by the *act* of joining is personally and morally guilty. No one today stumbles blindly into the party. And if he remains in it, that is "*prima facie* evidence that he is a hardened conspirator and that he accepts its orders and directives."

Membership in front or subversive organizations is another matter altogether. Often the actual purposes of such organizations are disguised. Here extreme care must be exercised in determining the significance of association. The judgments must be made by men with expert knowledge of front groups and of Communist ideology and tactics. In judging the significance of membership in subversive organizations, the following considerations are among the more important: (1) the number of such organizations one belongs to, (2) the degree and character of his activity in the organizations, (3) the time and place of the activity, and (4) the "extent of the open co-operation between the front organization and the Communist Party."

Commager opens his discussion as a good historian should. The doctrine of guilt by association, he states, is as old as the Pharisees and as new as the Loyalty Order of March, 1947. For, though the Pharisees murmured against Jesus for associating with publicans and sinners, it remained for our generation to adopt the concept as policy, law, and sin. This cloud now darkens the land, and under its shadow the witch-hunters pursue their sinister designs. But the doctrine is pernicious—logically, legally, practically, historically, and morally. Commager argues each point in turn.

Guilt by association is unsound in logic because it assumes that "a good cause becomes bad if supported by bad men." But the validity of a cause or a principle is independent of its sponsorship: is the

Declaration of Independence tarnished because the Communists endorse it?

Guilt by association is wrong legally because guilt is personal and attaches only to illegal acts, not to dangerous thoughts or suspicious associations. Criminal law, of course, knows the concept of collective guilt in a conspiracy, but conspiracy concerns only illegal acts. Moreover, the Supreme Court has repudiated the doctrine of guilt by association and the corollary concept that any one man can decide which organizations are legal and which illegal.[54] Finally, under our system guilt is not retroactive; but to punish a man in 1952 for joining in 1937 an organization which was declared subversive in 1950 clearly violates the spirit if not the letter of the constitutional prohibition against ex post facto laws.

Third, the doctrine is defective on practical grounds. It is impossible to import clarity and definiteness into a definition of subversive organizations. Consequently, those who try to apply the definition take refuge in a "woolly vagueness," and each lister comes up with a different listing. Moreover, it is neither possible nor desirable for us to engage in a check of membership, past and present, of all organizations we belong to or are asked to join. Not only would the practice be socially disruptive, but it also overlooks the gap between membership and responsibility so characteristic of organizations in our society. In application, the doctrine of guilt by association is actually "more one of chain reaction than of association." That is, it holds that one's specific beliefs and affiliations entail all sorts of other beliefs, whether or not the person in question actually holds them. Formerly it was held that the abolitionist was also ". . . an anti-hanging man, woman's rights man, an infidel, . . . a socialist, a red republican, a fanatical teetotaler, a believer in mesmerism and Rochester rappings." Finally, the principle of collective contamination has been applied selectively. No one questions associations such as the American Legion, the Daughters of the American Revolution, or the Democratic party, although each has been guilty of un-American intolerance or of trying to violate the First and Fourteenth Amendments.

The doctrine of guilt by association is wrong historically. The voluntary association is the most characteristic of American social institutions, and it underlies nearly all others. We are "a nation of joiners," and we have learned to accomplish our ends through such means rather than through reliance on government. This has taught Americans how to run their own affairs, and has kept government much smaller and closer to the people than it would otherwise be. Private organizations also have played a leading part in tying together peoples of various states, sections, classes, and interests. If we strike at the principle of voluntary association our people will become fearful of joining and our democracy "will dry up at the roots."

Finally, the doctrine is wrong morally because it assumes a "far greater power in evil than in virtue." It is based on the "rotten-apple theory of society—the theory that one wicked man corrupts all virtuous men, and that one mistaken idea subverts all sound ideas." It is based upon fear and lack of faith in freedom. Why tremble if we find one or two ex-Communists on a faculty? Why not take comfort from the thousands of loyal teachers and students? Why fear for a community that has a few of the works of Marx on its library shelves, rather than take reassurance from the thousands of books written by "the great host of the free"? Also, the doctrine caters to spiritual pride and vanity for it assumes that some men know surely the good and the true, and have no difficulty distinguishing them from the bad and the false. "It is time," Commager concludes, "that we see this doctrine of guilt by association for what it is; not a useful device for detecting subversion, but a device for subverting our constitutional principles and practices, for destroying our constitutional guarantees, and for corrupting our faith in ourselves and in our fellow men."

Hook and Commager argue the issues and present alternative points of view about as effectively as the job can be done. Elaboration would be superfluous. If one agrees with Professor Commager the loyalty program would have to be discarded, for it rests squarely upon the concept of testing loyalty by delving into associations. If one agrees with Professor Hook, he would be satisfied with reforms in the present program, provided they were broad enough and incorporated the ideas he suggests. Both writers agree that the modern notion of loyalty or disloyalty by association works basic revisions in our traditional views.

LOYALTY AS CONFORMITY

Hidden under layers of opaque language, and sometimes kept deliberately in shadow by men afraid or ashamed to recognize it, lies another aspect of the modern concept of loyalty. Although not easy to strip from its husk, this principle lies at the center of the program and forms an essential part of the modern concept of loyalty itself. With it many facets of the program otherwise obscure may be understood.

It is hard to find a brief phrase to describe the concept without undue distortion. Yet such a phrase would be a most convenient asset in expounding the idea. So, admitting the limitations of labels, but recognizing also their usefulness, we can open by calling this principle "loyalty as orthodoxy-conformity." A canvass of the relevant materials discloses that loyalty, as the federal boards understand it, tends to imply adherence to some rather definite articles of belief; conversely, dissent carries at least a suspicion of disloyalty. This is what is suggested by "orthodoxy." The word "conformity" was adopted to suggest that this tendency runs beyond the realm of belief into some spheres of action. The principle of loyalty as orthodoxy-conformity means that the modern concept of loyalty tends to equate loyalty with adherence to specified articles of belief and behavior.

Often the best clues as to exactly what these articles are come by indirect routes, as when, for example, the Civil Service Commission had to instruct its investigators to cease asking certain questions. Another source of insight is the concept of "derogatory information." Since a full-scale field investigation and hearing are undertaken only when a preliminary report contains derogatory information, it is crucial to know what kind of information is considered to cast unfavorable light upon one's loyalty. This information comes in the first place from the reports of the Federal Bureau of Investigation. Unfortunately for the researcher, FBI investigative documents are among the most confidential of government papers. Although never available for public inspection, now and then some event occurs— as when a Judith Coplon steals a handful of them and a judge forces disclosure of their contents—to lift for a moment the cloak of secrecy. Transcripts of loyalty board proceedings provide many clues to the thinking of board members, and sometimes offer insights into the FBI investigative reports. Beyond this, little is known. However, this tantalizing glimpse shows that some very strange things get into the reports.[55]

For example: In the Coplon trial disclosed records revealed that the FBI had seen fit to include in its reports the statement of an unidentified informant that she had seen her neighbors "moving about the house in a nude state." Bontecou relates that the subject in one loyalty hearing confronted this astonishing challenge: "Information has been received that you were opposed to the institution of marriage, which is one of the tenets of the Communist party." In another hearing a board member asked an employee if, as the record charged, he opposed segregation of blood donated by colored and and white people to the Red Cross. Another was challenged: "There is a suspicion in the record that you are in sympathy with the underprivileged. Is that true?" During the struggle over Senate confirmation of Mr. Charles E. Bohlen in March of 1953, it appeared that one of the derogatory reports, on the basis of which Mr. Scott McLeod thought it dangerous to clear Mr. Bohlen, came from an unidentified informant who said he possessed a sixth sense which enabled him to look at a man and tell whether there was any immoral element in his make-up. This clairvoyant had pierced Mr. Bohlen's camouflage and discovered behind it a tendency toward immorality which made him unfit for an ambassadorial position in the Soviet Union. Another confidential informant, according to Bontecou, had visited a suspect's house. While there he was entertained by a recorded opera entitled *The Cradle Will Rock.* This work, he reported, "followed along the lines of a downtrodden laboring man and the evils of the capitalist system." The miserable employee was asked to explain this incident. In recent years many federal agencies have employed the polygraph in the battle against so-called security risks and suspected disloyals. Some of the uses to which the instrument has been put are appalling, and some of the incidents which have arisen are disgusting. Investigators have shown a prurient interest in the sexual morality of employees which runs not simply beyond the bounds of legitimate official interest, but beyond the limits of decency as well. This snooping and prying into privacy, in the name of loyalty and security, offers many illustrations of the meaning of loyalty as conformity and orthodoxy. But to cite those cases is an ugly task, and it is better that this shameful chapter in our government be understood only in general, than that we excite ourselves with the squalid details.[56] Other cases show an intense interest in one's reading habits and in those of his friends. Still others are concerned with one's connections with "radical" (not even subversive) movements and ideas, and with his attitudes toward capitalism.[57]

It is unfortunate that Executive Order 10450 extends a certain official approval to this kind of approach to problems of loyalty and security by listing a number of personal characteristics which must be taken into account when determining whether the employment of a person is "clearly consistent with the interests of the national security." Now the officials are to look for behavior which tends to show that the individual is "not reliable or trustworthy," and they are to inspect his record for deliberate falsifications, for "criminal, infamous, dishonest, immoral, or notoriously disgraceful conduct." They are to see whether he is addicted to drugs or intoxicants. They are to determine whether he has a sexual perversion, or has suffered "serious mental or neurological disorder without satisfactory evidence of cure." Such categories, of course, invite unrestrained subjectivity of judgment. Moreover, although they are relevant in determining an applicant's general *suitability* for employment, it is questionable whether they belong in a document dealing with loyalty and security. For under the loyalty-security program, very few procedures are afforded the individual by which he may present his side of the case. Moreover, since loyalty and security are practically synonymous in the public mind, a person discharged as a "security risk" may be identified as disloyal and have his good name besmirched for reasons that have nothing at all to do with loyalty.

What these examples and criteria add up to is that the loyalty boards mistrust persons who may not share the values of the larger community on certain issues. The person who has had associations with atypical persons or groups, or who shows an interest in exotic subjects, or who is simply firm about forming his own opinions, is far more likely to find himself in trouble than the citizen of average tastes and habits who takes his views from the mass media, who never is engaged with strange associations or ideas, and who passively shares community values. This fear of the deviant sometimes goes to ridiculous lengths: one man was actually asked why he was dissatisfied with the Book-of-the-Month-Club and preferred the Book Find Club, when, after all, most people found the former quite satisfactory. His simple reply that the Book Find selections pleased him more pleased the board not at all. Boards also have shown an inordinate interest in folk whose tastes run to foreign films and to rather unpopular or obscure newspapers and periodicals. The boards are vigilantly on watch for those who show an "unusual attachment" to foreign systems. Sometimes, rather than being ridiculous, fear of nonconformity is dangerous. Agencies such as the CIA, the NSA, or the State Department need men of education and originality who possess sophisticated knowledge of foreign ideas and isms. Yet they want people who have not been exposed to radical or foreign ideas and suspect those who have. The two wishes are incompatible. This kind of exaggerated emphasis on conformity can have dire consequences for the national interest: at a time when we most need men of broad knowledge and imagination we most suspect and harass them. Witness the statement by Norman Armour, Robert Woods

Bliss, Joseph C. Grew, William Phillips, and G. Howland Shaw that fear of nonconformity in the State Department is so great as to threaten the national interest:

> The conclusion has become inescapable, for instance, that a Foreign Service officer who reports on persons and events to the very best of his ability and who makes recommendations which at the time he conscientiously believes to be in the interest of the United States may subsequently find his loyalty and integrity challenged and may even be forced out of the service and discredited forever as a private citizen after many years of distinguished service. A premium therefore has been put upon recommendations which are ambiguously stated or so cautiously set forth as to be deceiving.
>
> When any such tendency begins its insidious work it is not long before accuracy and initiative have been sacrificed to acceptability and conformity. The ultimate result is a threat to national security.[58]

We might turn to one final example of the emergent tendency to equate loyalty with conformity. The case of Dr. J. Robert Oppenheimer is especially valuable, not only because it involved issues and persons of prime importance, but also because the essential documents are available for inspection. Both the Personnel Security Board of the Atomic Energy Commission and the commission itself published their findings and decisions. The publications are the clearest statements we have of the kind of thinking present within two of the highest loyalty-security boards in the entire program.[59]

Twenty-three of the twenty-four charges against Dr. Oppenheimer concerned his connections with organizations and individuals; the last concerned his role in the hydrogen bomb program. Nearly all the affiliations cited took place before 1942, and some as early as 1937. Thus, in 1940 he was a sponsor of the Friends of the Chinese People, characterized in 1944 as a Communist-front organization by the House Un-American Activities Committee. In 1937 he joined the American Committee for Intellectual Freedom and was active in it for a very short time. The House committee also cited this group in 1942. For about a year during 1938–1939, he belonged to the Western Council of the Consumers Union. In 1944 the House committee called it a Communist front. He had known one Jean Tatlock and saw her between 1936 and 1939 with some frequency. From 1939 to 1943 he saw her rarely. He knew she was a Communist, and said he had no reason to believe she was not one still in 1943. Before her marriage to him, Oppenheimer's wife had been a Communist from 1934 to 1936. His brother had been a Communist during the 1937–1941 period, as had his brother's wife. Oppenheimer associated with a number of Communists rather often before 1942. During 1941–1942, he subscribed to the *Daily People's World*. He frequently contributed to political causes (especially to the Spanish Republicans) from the winter of 1937 to the early winter of 1941. Many of these contributions were made through Communist channels. Oppenheimer attended a few Communist meetings between 1937 and early 1941, and probably attended a meeting where Communists were present on January 1, 1946.

On a very few occasions after 1943 Dr. Oppenheimer had met, sometimes accidentally, sometimes intentionally, personal acquaintances who had been, or perhaps still were, Communists. And, in 1943, he had been approached by Haakon Chevalier, a Communist, with a guarded proposal to obtain information about his work for Soviet scientists. Oppenheimer replied that this was "terribly wrong." For some months he failed to report this incident to security officials, and then did so in a false version. Not until he was told by General Groves that he would be ordered to reveal all circumstances did he give a full account to security officers. Oppenheimer's evasiveness in this matter was apparently inspired by a wish to protect a friend. In December of 1945, Mr. and Mrs. Oppenheimer saw Chevalier briefly in Paris.

Here is a picture of a man who for a few years was actively involved in a number of reform and pressure groups, some of which counted Communists among their members. Oppenheimer described his interest as "very brief and very intense." He characterized himself as a fellow traveler from late 1936 or early 1937 until shortly after 1939, when his interest began to taper off. After 1942 he no longer considered himself one. He defined a fellow traveler as "someone who accepted part of the public program of the Communist Party, who was willing to work with and associate with Communists, but who was not a member of the Party."

The last item of the charges concerned the physicist's role in the H-bomb program. During World War II he apparently had "no misgivings about a program looking to thermonuclear development, and, indeed, during the latter part of the war, he recorded his support of prompt and vigorous action in this connection." In the autumn of 1949, and subsequently, he opposed the program on moral, political, and technical grounds. After January 31, 1950, when it was determined to proceed with the H-bomb, he "did not oppose the project in a positive or open manner, nor did he decline to cooperate in the project." But his previous views were well known, and his influence within the scientific community great. Since he did not make it known that he had abandoned those views, "his attitude undoubtedly had an adverse effect on recruitment of scientists and the progress of the scientific effort in this field. In other words, . . . if Dr. Oppenheimer had enthusiastically supported the thermonuclear program . . . , the H-bomb project would have been pursued with considerably more vigor, thus increasing the possibility of earlier success in this field." Although the board was unable to make a categorical finding that this opposition had slowed down H-bomb development, it did conclude that "the opposition to the H-bomb by many persons connected with the atomic energy program, of which Dr. Oppenheimer was the 'most experienced, most powerful, and most effective member' did delay the initiation of concerted effort which led to the development of a thermonuclear weapon.

On the basis of these facts and findings, first the Personnel Security Board of the Atomic Energy Commission, then the general manager of the commission, and then the commission itself, declined to renew Oppenheimer's security clearance. By a vote of two to one in the Personnel Security Board, and by four to one in the AEC, he was officially declared a security risk. The Personnel Security Board found no evidence of disloyalty, but it did conclude that Oppenheimer was not blameless "in the matter of conduct, character, and association." The board thought, first of all, that Oppenheimer had not shown sufficient regard for the security system. Indeed, he had "repeatedly exercised an arrogance of his own judgment with respect to the loyalty and reliability of other citizens to an extent which has frustrated and at times impeded the workings of the system." Since individuals must understand and support the security system, must subordinate their personal judgment to the professional experience of security officers, and must be wholeheartedly committed to the preservation of the system, the board had to take a serious view of the kind of "continuing judgment" Oppenheimer exercised in regard to the system. His associations and conduct showed lack of respect for the security system.

The board also found a "susceptibility to influence which could have serious implications for the security interests of the country." This statement is not easily reconciled with the board's declaration that Oppenheimer "seems to have had a high degree of discretion reflecting an unusual ability to keep to himself vital secrets," but this did not deter the board from its course.

Finally, the board thought Dr. Oppenheimer "may have departed his role as scientific adviser" on the H-bomb question, and that, while he was entitled to hold any opinions he wished, he "did not show the enthusiastic support for the program which might have been expected of the chief atomic adviser to the Government. . . ." This conduct was "sufficiently disturbing as to raise a doubt as to whether his future participation, if characterized by the same attitudes in a Government program relating to the national defense, would be clearly consistent with the best interests of security." The board also "regretfully concluded" that the witness had been "less than candid" in several parts of his testimony.

Dr. Ward W. Evans disagreed with his two colleagues. Dr. Evans thought there was nothing wrong with Oppenheimer's character, that he had shown himself "extremely honest," that he had proven himself totally reliable in matters of secrecy, that his judgment and discretion were far better now than they had been in 1947 when the board had cleared him on substantially the same materials as were now before it, that he was being put in double jeopardy, and that he had in no way hindered development of the H-bomb.

By a vote of four to one, the Atomic Energy Commission upheld the Personnel Security Board. The commission found "fundamental defects" in Oppenheimer's character: he had fallen "far short" of acceptable standards of reliability, trustworthiness, and self-discipline. He had committed "falsehoods, evasions and misrepresentations" at least six times before various official agencies. He had shown a "persistent and willful disregard for the obligations of security." And, finally, his associations with known Communists and fellow travelers extended "far beyond the tolerable limits of prudence and self-restraint" required of one in his high position. Moreover, these associations "lasted too long to be justified as merely the intermittent and accidental revival of earlier friendships."

Commissioner Thomas E. Murray concurred in the decision but for very different reasons. His argument was simple: at the present time, wholehearted support and unquestioning acceptance of the security system is the acid test of loyalty. Loyalty must be judged by the "standard of their [government employees'] obedience to security regulations." But Oppenheimer had shown "frequent and deliberate disregard of those security regulations which restrict a man's associations." Therefore, he was disloyal.

Commissioner Henry DeWolf Smyth dissented from the opinions of his colleagues. The only question before the commission, he thought, was "whether there is a possibility that Dr. Oppenheimer will intentionally or unintentionally reveal secret information to persons who should not have it." And, since "there is no indication in the entire record that Dr. Oppenheimer has ever divulged any secret information," Smyth could find no reason for denying him security clearance. Commissioner Smyth also made the point that the evidence before the commission was not newly discovered, but had been known for years and had been previously evaluated. The incidents and associations which the majority thought proof of fundamental defects in Oppenheimer's character he thought "thin" and "singularly unimpressive" when seen in the context of the rich and active fifteen years of life from which they had been drawn. Dr. Oppenheimer had shown no disregard for the security system. That system, first of all, was "nothing to worship." Nor did it give the government the right "to dictate every detail of a man's life." The security system was but a means to the end of protecting secrecy. "If a man protects the secrets he has in his hands and his head, he has shown essential regard for the security system." To argue that one who does not bow to the security system in every detail is thereby a security risk, "extends the concept of 'security risk' beyond its legitimate justification and constitutes a dangerous precedent." In conclusion, he thought the few incidents dredged up by the investigators, none of which Smyth found unexplainable and only one of which he found reprehensible, could not permit the judgment that Oppenheimer was a security risk unless one started from the assumption that he was disloyal.[60]

But this résumé fails to communicate the temper of the decisions. What is most striking about the documents is their harsh and dogmatic air. Here were boards judging a man who, so they thought, had manifested inexcusable eccentricities in his behavior. He refused to surrender his right of private judgment about his own friends and relatives, about the workings of the security system, and about the desirability and feasibility of the hydrogen bomb. The Personnel Security Board did once bend to what might more generously than accurately be called charity. Discussing the principle "once a Communist, always a Communist, once a fellow-traveler, always a fellow-traveler," the board asked whether a man might not "rehabilitate" himself so as to remove the suspicion of security risk. It answered that a man should not be denied the right to have made a mistake "if its recurrence is so remote a possibility as to permit a comfortable prediction as to the sanity and correctness of future conduct." In discussing Dr. Oppenheimer's advice concerning the H-bomb, the board feared that he had allowed emotional considerations to color his view, and, it sternly announced, "emotional involvement in the current crisis, like all other things, must yield to the security of the nation." Yet, while demanding advice unstained by sentiment, the board went on to announce this proposition:

> In evaluating advice from a specialist which departs from the area of his specialty, Government officials charged with the military posture of our country must . . . be certain that underlying any advice is a genuine conviction that this country cannot in the interest of security have less than the strongest possible offensive capabilities in a time of national danger.

In other words, a specialist must have the *correct* bias. He must be convinced that nothing short of the strongest *offensive* might can be the objective of national military policy. That this aggressive hint was not merely the result of imprecise language was demonstrated when the board, a bit later, recorded its concern that Oppenheimer may have exercised influence "in matters in which his convictions were not necessarily a reflection of technical judgment, and also not necessarily related to the protection of the strongest offensive military interests of the country." One wonders how widespread this kind of thinking is in our high councils of state, and whether it has become so firm that dissent is heresy.

Similar expressions critical of those who exercise their own values appear in many other places. The board, for example, thought it "arrogant" of Oppenheimer to believe it possible to know Communists and still not betray your country. An astonishing passage appears where the board takes notice of the quick and strong support given to Oppenheimer by many other scientists. This encouraged the board to feel that there was still much vitality in the country.

> However, the Board feels constrained to express its concern that in this solidarity there have been attitudes so uncompromising in support of science in general, and Dr. Oppenheimer in particular, that some witnesses have, in our judgment, allowed their convictions to supersede what might reasonably have been their recollections.

The board also sharply reminded Oppenheimer that whereas "loyalty to one's friends is one of the noblest of qualities, being loyal to one's friends above reasonable obligations to the country and the security system, however, is not clearly consistent with the interests of security." Even if one grants that Dr. Oppenheimer did show a superior loyalty to friends, and the present writer finds scant evidence to support that, it is doubtful whether the doctrine that the government may decide what loyalties are legitimate is itself "clearly consistent" either with our democratic traditions or, indeed, with the national interest. Forced conformity, as Justice Black emphasized, leads to the unanimity of the graveyard. It appears, however, that during his service in the loyalty program Mr. Seth Richardson also accepted the view that the government may determine legitimate behavior for its employees. He puts the argument this way:

> In the first place, the [Loyalty Review] Board is of the opinion that, legally, the government is entitled to discharge any employee for reasons which seem sufficient to the government and without extending to such employees any hearing whatsoever. We believe that the rights of the government in that respect are at least equal to those possessed by private employers.[61]

This doctrine of "reasons sufficient to the government" not only proves too much, but is obnoxious to the philosophy of limited government and individual rights under the law. It proves too much because it simply is not true that the government may fire employees for any reason at all. It is one of the triumphs of civil service reform that millions of federal employees cannot be fired at whim, but only for cause and by proper procedure. Moreover, no private employer has the right to defame character as an incident to hiring and firing. Should a private employer state publicly that he fired a man because of suspected disloyalty he could be made to justify those allegations before a court of law in a trial for slander and defamation of character. But the government does not permit those it labels disloyal or security risks to plead their causes before a court. The doctrine is obnoxious to the philosophy of limited government and individual rights under the law because it assumes the government may judge the whole of a man's life by whatever standards it chooses to adopt. This is the essence of what is meant here when it is said that the concept of loyalty implicit in the federal program tends to equate loyalty with conformity and orthodoxy. Moreover, the doctrine places the government in a special position vis-à-vis the law. A recent author puts the point this way:

> The loyalty program also distorts the concept of equal justice before the law. It assumes that a democratic government may exact from its employees special standards of conduct wholly offensive to constitutional guarantees of freedom and justice as applied to ordinary citizens.[62]

And, in assuming this authority, the government appears to have lost sight of that "fixed star" which Justice Jackson thought must always guide its policy.

If there is any fixed star in our constitutional constellation, it is that no official, high or petty, can prescribe what shall be orthodox in politics, nationalism, religion, or other matters of opinion or force citizens to confess by word or act their faith therein.[63]

A TENTATIVE APPRAISAL OF THE NEW LOYALTY

Although it is no primary purpose of this chapter to offer a critique of the loyalty program, the program does raise a number of questions which should be asked, even if not fully answered. The questions of prime importance are: (1) Are the purposes of the program ones that the government may validly and usefully pursue? (2) Are the standards and techniques employed useful? (3) Considered in terms of its stated purposes and its consequences on society, is the program wise policy?

1) Executive Order 9835 states the purposes of the program to be: (*a*) to assure that "persons employed in the federal service be of complete and unswerving loyalty to the United States," and (*b*) to protect loyal employees against "unfounded accusations of disloyalty." Order 10450 reaffirms these principles. Now, surely, these are laudable objectives. No government staffed by persons bent on its destruction could long endure. No government of a society that prides itself on its regard for individual rights would want to injure individuals innocent of treasonous intent. Nor can it be argued that the government lacks authority to pursue these purposes. The government may require whatever conditions it wishes as qualifications for public employment, so long as the conditions specified do not violate the Constitution. Therefore, it may prescribe loyalty as among these qualifications.

2) But it does not necessarily follow that the standards and practices employed are either useful or legitimate. Is it not a supreme paradox that a program designed to assure loyal workers has never defined the meaning of loyalty? Disloyalty, we must presume, is the opposite of loyalty. But how can you distinguish the disloyal from the loyal until you have defined at least one of the terms? To be sure, one can educe from the program a working concept of loyalty, a concept including the three dimensions already described. Of these three, the first (potential loyalty and disloyalty) is empty. It asserts that you can judge propensities toward future disloyalty, but it does not say what loyalty is. That—the content of loyalty—must come from the other two standards.

Of these two, Executive Order 9835 stated only one (the matter of association) as relevant to a judgment of loyalty or disloyalty. Under the order, the Attorney General discriminated between proscribed and legitimate organizations. What criteria he used we do not know. We do know that many of the organizations listed could not be described by the few criteria specified in the order. Order 10450 even removed the limitation that the only proscribed organizations are those listed by the Attorney General. "Membership in," "affiliation with," and "sympathetic association with" remain vague and largely amorphous notions. Therefore, we still lack a fundamental standard of loyalty.

The remaining dimension of the concept operative in the federal program (loyalty as conformity) *could* stand as a definition of loyalty: the loyal man is the man whose thoughts and actions conform to dominant opinion. The defects of this as a definition of loyalty are twofold: (1) the federal boards do not admit they use it, and (2) neither executive order specifies conformity as a criterion of loyalty. Therefore, in strictest logic, whenever the boards apply this standard they go beyond their delegated powers. All this, of course, is quite apart from the question of whether it is wise to equate loyalty with conformity.

Moreover, even if the federal program had a clear and explicit definition of loyalty, there are additional grounds for questioning the utility of these standards for measuring it. Take the idea of potential loyalty and disloyalty. It is difficult at best to reason from a man's opinions to his actions. Man is an inconstant creature; there is no simple one-to-one correlation between his thoughts and his behavior. And, even if the connection could be established, the government has neither the proper kind of evidence and standards nor the skilled personnel needed for this work. To estimate the likelihood of future disloyalty on the basis of even the best evidence would require men who combined the subtlety of the Jesuit casuist with the canny insight of the Viennese psychoanalyst. The techniques available to the administrative and judicial processes are simply too cumbersome and plodding, too undiscriminating for the task. It is true that administrative agencies often must deal with cases too demanding of individual disposition to permit of treatment under regular law and through regular judicial channels. That, in fact, is one of the chief arguments in support of administrative adjudication. But here that argument misses the point. The loyalty testing process uses concepts and techniques which are not too fine, but are too broad and blunt to cut through the fine layers of thought and sentiment which must be bared if a predilection toward future disloyalty is to be found. Although only the notion of potential loyalty has been analyzed here, similar arguments and conclusions hold true for the ideas of loyalty and disloyalty by association and loyalty as conformity: as standards, they are too vague to be useful.

Certain empirical evidence points the same way. On June 30, 1953, the Loyalty Review Board published figures summarizing its work to that time. It reported that it had considered 26,236 cases. Of these, 2,748 had been dropped because the persons involved resigned from the service or withdrew their requests for review. In 3,634 cases, adjudication was never finished for similar reasons. Also, 1,015 cases had been referred to the Department of the Army, and 1,779 were still pending. Of the remaining 17,060, the board dismissed or denied employment to 557, whereas 16,503 were adjudged loyal. This means that about 2 per cent ended with action adverse to the applicant. These figures do not prove that there was little disloyalty in the service. They do suggest that the program suffered from grave defects in standards and procedures.

Everyone can cite instances of erroneous arrest; grand juries often return true bills against persons subsequently shown innocent; there are some appalling instances of individuals proved innocent after trial, conviction, and sentence. But despite occasional and regrettable mistakes, our police and courts have a satisfactory record of administering justice. Can the same be said of the loyalty program? If 98 per cent of the people arrested by the police were subsequently cleared, if 98 per cent of grand jury indictments were found to be without substance, if 98 per cent of court trials were found on review to have been faulty—then we would certainly conclude that somewhere there was deep error. When people are put in jeopardy of any kind, under any program and before any deciding agency, and 98 per cent are cleared, then something is profoundly wrong. Yet, this is the actual record of the Loyalty Review Board.

Since one of the stated objectives of the loyalty program is to protect the innocent from unfounded accusations of disloyalty, it is necessary to estimate the practices employed in the program from this point of view. Here, however, only the major themes will be presented, for the subject of loyalty board procedures, although important, is a whole field in itself, and basically of a technical rather than a philosophic character.

Over the slow decades and centuries, Anglo-American law has arduously established a number of elements which must be present in a trial situation if the accused is to receive justice, and if approximate truth is to emerge from the trial. These essentials are summarized under the heading "due process." Now, it is true that an employee whose loyalty is challenged is not charged with a crime. Still, as the Supreme Court pointed out in the Lovett case, to discharge a man for disloyalty is to work severe punishment on him. Given the current climate of opinion, one whose loyalty is merely questioned already moves under a heavy handicap, as numerous victims of various investigations will testify. Therefore, it is reasonable to conclude with the President's Committee on Civil Rights that "The federal government must maintain a loyalty program which adequately protects the civil rights of its employees." The Committee specified that in the loyalty program ". . . provision should be made for such traditional procedural safeguards as the right to a bill of particular accusations, the right to subpoena witnesses and documents where genuine security considerations permit, the right to be represented by counsel, the right to a stenographic report of proceedings, the right to a written decision, and the right of appeal." [64]

Many of these defenses were provided the accused by Order 9835. In this category fall the right to a bill of particular charges, the right to counsel, the right to present evidence through witnesses or by affidavit, and the right of administrative appeal. However, the right to a bill of particular charges is limited by the requirement that the charges need only be as specific and complete as the employing department decides is permitted by security considerations. The order did not specify that accused persons may subpoena witnesses and documents, nor that the accused be given a stenographic report of proceedings and a written decision. It should be mentioned also that the accused may not confront his accusers if to do so would jeopardize protection of the informants or investigation of other cases. Finally, Order 10450 omits any mention of any specific procedural rights, although in practice those provided under Order 9835 are still usually granted to the employee.

Without written decisions it is impossible to develop a jurisprudence of loyalty which board members can use in preparing charges and deciding cases, and which accused and their counsel can use in preparing the defense. Without a stenographic report of proceedings, which in fact usually is not given, the accused is at great disadvantage in preparing his defense. Moreover, charges often are so general that the accused does not really know what he is being charged with, nor how to reply. Different charges than appeared on the formal bill of charges are sometimes aired in the hearings. Not permitting one to confront and cross-examine witness against him, nor even to know the sources of information against him, is perhaps the severest disability of all. There is no perfectly just solution to this problem of the "confidential informant." The important thing about the solution adopted in the loyalty program is that it places full power to decide whether a source should be revealed in the hands of a police investigative agency, usually the FBI. Order 9835 expressed a pious hope that "Investigative agencies shall not use this discretion to decline to reveal sources of information where such action is not essential," but provided no way to enforce the hope, nor to guard against abuses of discretion.

These handicaps under which the accused labors injure more than his personal cause. They also weaken the loyalty-security effort as such, because they make it excessively difficult for the hearing agencies to reach a considered decision on the best possible evidence. Secretary of State John Foster Dulles, in what he termed a "little educational statement" about the work of the FBI, emphasized that the investigators prepare only one side of the case.

> The investigators' job is to find information that is adverse, if there is any, because their business is to try to detect anything which is suspicious. Then, when the field reports are concluded, the FBI makes summaries and these summaries deal primarily with the derogatory material because what we are looking for is [*sic*] danger signals.[65]

Hence, the hearing agencies often hear but one side of the case, for the accused lacks opportunity to develop his own defense. Moreover, the hearing agencies, under the doctrine of the secrecy of the "confidential informant," often cannot even tell whether the side of the case they do hear is fairly and competently made. How, then, can a hearing board, even when motivated by the best intentions, discriminate wisely?

Add to these specific defects the further fact that the standards by which loyalty is determined are not clearly defined, and it becomes evident that the procedures of the program are defective. It is doubtful whether they are very useful in achieving either of the program's two major purposes. Nor, for two reasons, would it be profitable to propose an alternative list of procedures designed specifically for the loyalty program: (1) given the lax standards by which loyalty is measured, no set of procedural safeguards can protect the government against disloyalty and the individual against unfounded accusation (the root evil here is in the standards; procedures are secondary), and (2) because it has not been proven that abridgments of our traditional system of procedural due process need be made for loyalty cases. It is enough to say that:

> Our system of democratic justice has proved again and again
> its ability to protect us in peace and in war. To make a conspicu-
> ous departure from it against government workers would surely
> weaken the safeguards of the right of all citizens to speak freely
> and to organize in furtherance of their opinions. Here, as else-
> where, the federal government must set an example for the rest
> of the country by being uncommonly scrupulous in its respect
> for the civil rights of all its citizens.[66]

3) Is the program wise public policy? The present writer thinks not.
Stating only conclusions of previous facts and arguments, the program
is unwise in that it cannot be proven to have cleansed the government
of disloyal elements. No case of espionage, sabotage, delivery of secrets
to foreign powers, nor any of the other overt acts listed in the categories of evidence constituting disloyalty has been brought to light
under the program. It is true that men of suspect loyalty have been
separated for failure to meet the tests of potential loyalty, purity of
association, and conformity. But these standards are defective. It will
be argued in the next chapter that the entire ideological cast of the
program is unwise from the point of view of protection for the government. The real problem of protection is not one of loyalty judged on
vague ideological grounds, but one of security. That is fundamentally
a technical problem, best handled by intelligent police and counter-
espionage techniques, not by random inquiries into opinions and associations.

It may be objected that Order 10450 did make a shift to an emphasis
on security, technically considered. Although the order undoubtedly
contemplated it, such a shift has not in fact occurred. The following
summary of the State Department's loyalty-security procedures clearly
suggests that the "security" investigators are interested in something
other than security.

> You will observe that this system is in no way analogous to our
> court system since we are not trying to prove anyone is guilty of
> violating a law. That is the business of the Justice Department.
> If our investigation discloses the possibility that anyone is vio-
> lating a law or that an individual poses a possible threat to the
> Nation's security, we must turn the matter over to the Justice
> Department because the FBI is charged with the responsibility
> for investigating violations of the laws . . . and for the primary
> responsibility of protecting the internal security of the United
> States.[67]

The program can be indicted too as unwise policy in that it has not
protected the rights of employees. In addition, it has injured the public service. Evidence already presented shows that the loyalty program

has reduced morale, lowered the sense of initiative and freedom, driven worthy men from the service, dissuaded others from applying, restricted the associative activities of employees, and engendered fear and suspicion. Additional brief evidence on these points will be offered in the final chapter.

A few words should be said about the broader social impact of the program. First of all, no government whose employees are so handicapped can properly serve society. But, secondly, the program has had destructive impact on some traditional American legal and moral standards.

To say that the government has authority to prescribe conditions of employment is not to say that that authority includes carte blanche prerogative to inquire into one's innermost thoughts and sentiments. It must stop where action stops. Anglo-American law long has known the principle of inferring motive or intent from deeds, and assessing punishment on that basis. But it has not known, since at least the eighteenth century, the principle of punishment merely for entertaining thoughts that some deciding agency believes might lead to illegal action. Nor can these practices be defended by the doctrine of unlawful conspiracy. Disloyalty is defined in the federal program as the absence of loyalty; but loyalty is left undefined. In conspiracy cases the act conspired at *is* specified and defined. The government violates traditional standards of law and justice when it concerns itself with the potential disloyalty of persons as determined by their past and present attitudes and associations, and by their conformity to generally held views.

The government violates more than the law. It assaults standards of decency and privacy basic to American mores. A determination of possible future disloyalty necessarily involves search into areas of life which Americans jealousy guard as private and outside legitimate official concern. It must inquire into past and present associations, into intimate personal relationships, into opinion and sentiment, motive and sincerity—in a word, into the most secret and sacred realms of life. When this happens we have the contemptible spectacle of a great and dignified government prying, with the perverted energy and mean spirit of any common gossip, into the private affairs of citizens. Whoever doubts that this in fact has been done need but consult the records of the loyalty boards, the dossiers of the FBI (so far as they are known), the testimony of attorneys defending loyalty cases, and the numerous statements of individuals who have been caught in the sticky web of alleged disloyalty.

Indeed, a long and dreary footnote could be appended here, a footnote which would show investigations into attitudes regarding governmental policies (especially foreign policies and the loyalty program itself), into the intelligence level and personal habits of oneself and of his friends and associates, into one's attitudes about Negroes and the underprivileged, into one's reading tastes, his ancestry, his economic and social status, his private hopes and fears. If government is granted this authority, even as applied to its own employees, a chief distinction between loyalty in the limited state and loyalty in the totalitarian state is erased for a large segment of the population. But that perhaps is not the worst of it. No reasonable American expects tyranny and totalitarianism to issue from the loyalty program. At the same time, no man of dignity can tolerate the official meddling that is an integral part of the investigations. "We could," wrote Macaulay, "make shift to live under a debauchee or a tyrant; but to be ruled by a busybody is more than human nature can bear." [68]

There is much over-simplification in the argument that, after all, these practices fall only on those who work for the federal government. That is not true. Government investigative agencies have collected data on many, many persons other than government employees. Moreover, if one considers the great number directly employed in the civilian and military agencies of the federal government, plus those indirectly involved in government programs (e.g., scholars engaged in subsidized work, recipients of federal scholarships), as well as employees' friends and acquaintances who may be interrogated by the loyalty investigators, he begins to get some measure of the throng directly affected by the loyalty program. Also, many state and local jurisdictions, and some private employers, utilize practices similar to those of the federal government in their own loyalty programs. It is now commonplace for contracts between the Department of Defense and private corporations to include a clause permitting security officials of the department to designate individuals, and categories of individuals, as loyalty-security risks, and specifying that the corporation will discharge such employees upon request. [69] Even if one were to admit authority in the government to investigate the loyalty of its employees by the practices now used, does it follow that that authority can be extended to others not its employees?

PART THREE

6

American Loyalty and American Democracy

"THE SIN OF THE ACADEMIC," WROTE PROFESSOR MICHAEL Oakeshott at the conclusion of a brilliant short essay on political education, "is that he takes so long in coming to the point. Nevertheless, there is some virtue in his dilatoriness; what he has to offer may, in the end, be no great matter, but at least it is not unripe fruit, and to pluck it is the work of a moment." [1] Anyone who has followed the present effort this far doubtless will agree that the development has been tortuous and slow, the argument long in coming to the point. Still, there is promise in Oakeshott's judgment. It may be true that what is yet to come is of little import, but at least it will come with directness and

---

[1] For numbered notes to chap. 6, see pp. 207–208.

speed. The work of summary should indeed be but the work of a moment.

In these final pages, three matters will receive special attention: (1) a comparison of old and new conceptions of loyalty, (2) a redefinition of the problem of disloyalty, and (3) analysis of the relations between the new loyalty and emergent concepts of mass democracy. So, then, to the first.

THE OLD AND THE NEW LOYALTIES COMPARED

So patent are the contrasts between the traditional and the modern conceptions of loyalty that it is hardly necessary to mark them. The emergent concept includes the elements of potential loyalty and disloyalty, loyalty and disloyalty by association, and loyalty as conformity. All alter one or another component of the traditional concept.

The first, potential loyalty and disloyalty, revises the conception of disloyalty as meaning overt acts hostile to the safety and well-being of the political community. We have accepted a new doctrine of disloyalty which encompasses thought as well as action and applies to future as well as to present time. This "cold war treason," as Barth calls it, does not demand the strict proofs and procedural guarantees required by the older notion. Congressional committees have branded men disloyal without having afforded them the opportunity of a fair hearing. Loyalty boards often do not permit the accused to confront his accusers. Charges against him may be so vague that defense is virtually hopeless. During the hearing he may be challenged by accusations entirely different from those in the formal statement. Those who come before the boards or committees, with their loyalty in question, struggle under a heavy weight of prejudice and unfair procedure. Apparently under the adage that "where there is smoke there is fire," the judges are impatient with confining procedures. The following passage illuminates this frame of mind.

> It is also true that in many instances the crimes of treason and espionage are so difficult to punish by conviction because of technical devices and the necessity of so tightly defining these crimes, that if near treason and "virtual espionage" and "cold-war treason or espionage" are to be guarded against, it is imperative that not only must the power of public opinion be marshaled against these disloyal and self-serving practices but legislation must be enacted which will provide appropriate punishment for these specific derelictions.[2]

The concept of loyalty and disloyalty by association adds whole new dimensions to the picture. It is directed at the very source of the traditional doctrine, namely, its individualism—an individualism holding that each must determine his own loyalties and be judged solely on his own actions. The modern doctrine holds that an individual's loyalty may be measured by the associations he holds; if they are disloyal, so is he. Moreover, the new doctrine repudiates that whole complex of ideas stemming from what was called earlier the "pluralist conception of loyalty." In setting aside some groups as subversive, a cloud is put on joining as such. The former theory held that diversity of private loyalties was not incompatible with loyalty to the whole community. In fact, it held that loyalty to the political community is the final product of loyalties to lesser associations and ideals. In assuming the right to distinguish legitimate from illegitimate associations, the government has cut the groundwork from the old ideal which held that each citizen may make such determinations for himself.

Third, the concept of loyalty as conformity alters the entire spirit of the early conception of loyalty. Most importantly, it attacks those portions of the traditional ideal which stemmed from faith in the dignity and integrity of private life. This belief safeguarded provinces of life in which the categories of loyalty and disloyalty did not apply, and into which the state might not trespass. Should this development run unchecked, it must ineluctably eventuate in the absorption of the saving *tertium quid,* nonloyalty, by the loyalty-disloyalty dichotomy. The new concept corrodes the principle that no official can decree the relative priority of different loyalties—the principle that political loyalty cannot compel all other loyalties, that loyalties are different in kind but equal in validity. The idea of loyalty as conformity also debases the former doctrine that loyalty must be voluntarily given and is owed only to a just government. Consider how far we have traveled from these once accepted notions when a member of the Atomic Energy Commission can announce that the acid test of loyalty is unquestioning obedience to the security system, with all that that system implies.

In summary, it is accurate to say that the new official concept of loyalty leaves intact no single important part of the former (relatively) formal theory of loyalty. Moreover, and this is the second point, the new loyalty takes one strand of the two opposing traditions of popular loyalty which have been present throughout our history and elevates it to a superior position. Perhaps a quotation from a previous page might fix the point. Of course, the new loyalty favors what is called in the following passage the "latter strand" of loyalty.

> This brief sketch of the popular meanings of loyalty and Americanism has indicated two opposing traditions. The first, which is essentially rational, pluralistic, dedicated to certain principles, and extranational, has been complemented in the course of time by an idea of Americanism wholly unlike it in tone and content. This latter strand is irrational, nationalistic, and conformist. The first views America as an uncompleted process; the latter views it as a finished and organic being. In the current "great debate" over loyalty these two opposed conceptions define the central positions of the contending forces.*

There is in this new loyalty something terrible, and yet pathetic. Our whole interpretation of loyalty has become a negative and frightened one; we define loyalty by reference to something called "un-Americanism." And by that we mean nonconformity. Gone is the grand confidence of the time when we believed that men would be loyal to America simply because the American promise would inspire loyalty in all who were given a chance to share it. Now we rely on ritual professions of loyalty, we suspect diversity and unorthodoxy, we build a massive administrative system to assure us that our schools, factories, and governments are not riddled by subversives.

This new loyalty is also pathetic. Can we really believe that it is loyalty we are after? Is it loyalty we shall achieve? Has loyalty not sunk to the level of what Veblen would call an "honorific" word? It is possible to compel conformity and obedience, surely, but is it possible to compel loyalty? When a state can attract loyalty and evoke a sense of duty from its members—that is its supreme achievement. Admittedly, part of its power to do so rests on the fact that the state embodies for its citizens those qualities that distinguish them from others outside their group. But the state attracts loyalty also because most men feel a need for a devotion to something larger than their own self-seeking and narrow group allegiances. If the state is to receive this loyalty, it must earn it. Loyalty, like love, to which it is closely related, cannot be forced; it must be nourished by the beauty and power of its objects. Can we really believe that the use of oaths, police systems, and stool pigeons by the government will make us more loyal?

---

* Chap. 3, pp. 88–89.

> Behind the dozens of sedition bills in Congress last session, behind teachers' oaths and compulsory flag salutes, is a desire to make our citizens loyal to their government. Loyalty is a beautiful idea, but you cannot create it by compulsion and force. A government is at bottom the officials who carry it on: legislators and prosecutors, school superintendents and police. If it is composed of legislators who pass shortsighted sedition laws by overwhelming majorities, of narrow-minded school superintendents who oust thoughtful teachers of American history and eight-year-old children whose rooted religious convictions prevent them from sharing in a brief ceremony—a government of snoopers and spies and secret police—how can you expect love and loyalty? You make men love their government and their country by giving them the kind of government and the kind of country that inspire respect and love; a country that is free and unafraid, that lets the discontented talk in order to learn the causes for their discontent and end those causes, that refuses to impel men to spy on their neighbors, that protects its citizens vigorously from harmful acts while it leaves the remedies for objectionable ideas to counter-argument and time.[3]

And with this a fresh view of an old problem unfolds. Chafee makes it clear that much of the compulsive agitation against disloyalty may be sadly misdirected. That suggestion is the base from which the following discussion begins. It is the thesis of the following pages that much of the current concern with disloyalty is misdirected because it starts from a radical misunderstanding of the real problem of disloyalty in modern America.

THE PROBLEM OF DISLOYALTY REAPPRAISED

The problem of what to do about the disloyal in our ranks has troubled Americans for some time. Nor is concern with it on the wane. Each week press and periodical register new expressions of opinion on the subject. Nor can it be said that the problem is near solution; indeed the more it is considered, the more remote a solution seems to become. Public discussion, though not wanting in intensity and volume, has contributed little toward clarification and resolution of the issues involved. That has been so for a number of reasons: the inherent complexity of the issues, the capacity of the subject to excite violent and doctrinaire attitudes, and the fact that some men have exploited the situation for selfish ends.

But these factors account only in part for the muddled state of public thinking. From the beginning the whole debate has been out of focus. The issues dealt with have been superficial and peripheral

rather than basic and central. Public discussion has revolved around
what might be called "active disloyalty." An inordinate amount of
energy has been spent, for example, on the question of what to do
about the Communists. That there are problems here no one will
deny. What is denied is that such problems are the really basic ones.
In addition, when the problem of disloyalty is framed in such terms
it usually marks a challenge to battle rather than an invitation to
dispassionate inquiry. There is a problem of disloyalty in America,
but only its smallest part consists in the menace posed by Communists,
Fascists, and other subversives.

Furthermore, most of these problems can be handled by intelligent
legislation and alert police work. The significant threat posed by
the active disloyalists is their ability to work espionage and sabotage.
That ability can be reduced not by inflammatory speech, not by
legislation whose chief purpose is the symbolic one of expressing
hatred, or the active one of stifling opinion, not by heated debate over
the role of hostile minorities within the polity, but by wise laws
designed to deter potential spies and saboteurs by the clarity and
scope of their provisions and the firmness of their sanctions, coupled
with aggressive police activity designed to block the potential criminals
from working their schemes, and, if that fails, to make swift and
certain their capture and punishment.

To punish a man solely because he professes doctrines which, you
think, predispose him to dangerous actions is illiberal and ineffective
policy. If proof were needed to support this obvious but often
forgotten truth, it could be mustered in massive quantity from the
whole melancholy history of suppression. The problem would be not
to find evidence, but to select judiciously a few persuasive cases from
the legion recorded. But why toil to rehearse what already has been
done so thoroughly by so many learned writers? The argument of
Macaulay is decisive. After citing numerous cases to show that there
is no constant relation between a man's beliefs and his action,
Macaulay concludes: "Man, in short, is so inconsistent a creature
that it is impossible to reason from his belief to his conduct, or
from one part of his belief to another." [4]

The problem with the active disloyalist, then, is not to suppress
his doctrine, but to regulate his actions. Probably, given the present
condition of affairs, portions of the federal legislation directed
against the Communists are necessary. Certainly some of the provisions
of the Subversive Activities Control Act of 1950 (known as the
McCarran Act) [5] must be included within this category. Thus, its

provisions strengthening existing laws against sabotage and espionage are wise and necessary. So too its effort to deal with the contingent danger of fifth-column activities in time of emergency by permitting the detention of suspected potential spies and saboteurs. And its provisions for the registration of "communist-action" and "communist-front" organizations also must be deemed stringent but salutary prophylactic measures. But when the act moves into the realm of suppression of doctrine, as in its provision for labeling the source of Communist propaganda, it deals directly with doctrine and not with action. The provision of the Alien Registration Act of 1940 (known as the Smith Act),[6] which makes it a crime to advocate or teach the overthrow of the government by force or violence, or to join or help organize any group that so advocates, shares in the same character. Although that law was declared valid by the highest court in the land, one may still, with Justices Black and Douglas, doubt its wisdom and doubt also whether it was shown that the convicted persons actually had taught methods of espionage and sabotage.[7]

But these issues, exciting and important as they are, do not deal with the real meaning of disloyalty in America. The real problem of disloyalty in the United States today is posed not by the weak and miserable band of the actively disloyal, but by the legions without loyalty. This is the real, the crucial problem. Yet this vital phase of the problem of disloyalty has been neglected or misunderstood. For too long we in America have overlooked the facts of mass society and their pitiless implications for the theory and practice of liberal democracy. As a nation we have failed to cultivate the conditions that support rich and meaningful loyalties. Loyalty has never held a position of dignity among our national ideals. When we have cultivated loyalty, too often it has been urged as an intolerant and narrow attachment to our own nation and government in time of stress. Many of the symbols employed to express national loyalty exemplify this narrow view. They are the symbols of economic and military power and of superiority over other nations. When spiritual values are invoked they are usually pressed into service as rallying cries and asserted as doctrinaire slogans. Most dangerous of all, our favored method of teaching loyalty now is by indulging in passionate denunciation of the wicked foreign forces arrayed against American virtue. That method is deceptively easy and attractive in the short view, but any appeal to hatred and to bigotry stirs up emotions which bode ill for the long run.

For a great many Americans loyalty means the prosecution of

parochial designs. Group contends against group, section against section, with each in the contest not for what it can contribute to the general good but for what it can extract for its own good. The ethic of competition turns men's eyes toward personal material success rather than toward harmonious and creative devotion to the common weal. Moreover, one of the darker refinements of American politics is that each special group tends to identify its particular desires with Americanism, thereby suggesting that opposing interests may be deficient in the finer qualities of patriotism and altruism. Thus, when we do instruct men in the ways of loyalty that loyalty too easily and too often is equated with aggressive selfishness.

National loyalties are too narrowly partisan and gathered around symbols of power and superiority. Parochial loyalties too often are exclusionist and aggressive. In addition to these two aspects of the character of present-day loyalty in America, there is a third of imponderable importance: many of today's citizens have never had, or have lost, personal experience of genuine loyalty. This is the problem of the men without loyalty, men not actively disloyal, but simply unattached and devoid of abiding loyalties. Moreover, the a-loyal man is an authentic creature of mass society. The loyal ties of the past have lost their vitality for many persons and are watered down into slogans and advanced as an orthodoxy to which one is compelled to subscribe. Social conditions have conspired to make it increasingly difficult for vital loyalties to flourish. Family loyalties pale. Most craft and guild loyalties have succumbed to the huge corporation and union, both of which mean for the masses only the powers that control their destinies but do not evoke their sympathies. Small communities have surrendered to the impersonal and lonely life of megalopolis. Religious loyalties play a role of declining significance. Despite all that is said and written about the "joining" characteristics of the American, the fact is that most Americans are without profound organizational loyalties.*

As a result of these transformations there emerges a growing

---

* Political scientists accept almost as a "given" the belief that voluntary group life in America is extraordinarily rich and diverse. So it is; but there is considerable evidence that this is not the whole story. See the study by Barnard Barber entitled "Participation and Mass Apathy in Associations," in Alvin W. Gouldner, ed., *Studies in Leadership: Leadership and Democratic Action* (New York: Harper, 1950), pp. 477–504. The following data are from Barber's article. His numerous documentary footnotes have been omitted. Investigation of participation in voluntary associations reveals: "(1) There is an almost countless number of associations in this country; (2) There is a large number of people who have

multitude whose members have either selfish loyalties or none at all. And the sloganization of values without the life experience that gives them content can only engender a cynical contempt for all loyalty. It is lamentable that men must see loyalty as either synonymous with the assertion of selfish interests against others, or as standing in the way of personal gain. It is a darker tragedy that modern social conditions have produced large numbers of men with no real and living experience of loyalty whatever. Lacking loyalties, the self is blemished and life a thing without direction. Without the masses of men experiencing shared loyalties the bonds of community are threatened. Such men, and the social conditions that have produced them, constitute a threat of awful aspect for the future of liberal democracy. In their longing to mend their injured spirits, men without loyalties may turn to the demagogue who offers them security and purpose if they will but deliver over their liberty. They are the "lean and hungry" men who form the shock battalions of the onslaught

---

no memberships in any associations at all; (3) There exists, in any given association, an active minority and an inactive majority among the members." First, Barber surveys some of the well-known facts showing the great extent of voluntary associations. On the second point, he says that the evidence reveals "the little-known fact that many have not even a single such affiliation." This uniformity holds true for all types of areas. Thus, in a sample of 5,500 residents of metropolitan Chicago, "approximately 30 per cent of the men and 40 per cent of the women had no memberships at all in associations." And, in New York City, unaffiliated persons constitute a large majority. In a sample reported by Komarovsky, "60 per cent of the working class and 53 per cent of the white-collar men did not belong to a single association, with the possible exception of a church." A similar situation was observed in suburban New York City. A little less than 50 per cent of the residents of a typical medium-sized city in Ohio's Erie County belonged to no associations. In Yankee City, with 17,000 population, only 41 per cent belonged to even one association. For the rural areas nonparticipation has been documented even more heavily. It appears that a minority engage in multiple memberships, a majority in very few or none. Barber then supplies some estimate of the amount of apathy present even among association memberships. He reports a universal pattern of mass apathy and minority control. For illustration, he cites James P. Warbasse's statement that even ". . . in the most powerful and deeply rooted People's Organizations in this country the degree of popular participation reached a point varying between five and seven per cent!" David B. Truman, *The Governmental Process: Political Interests and Public Opinion* (New York: Knopf, 1951), p. 521, after canvassing the evidence, concludes that participation in voluntary associations is tending toward concentration in particular classes or strata. The evidence indicates: "(1) that the frequency of membership in formal organizations of the association type increases from the lower to the upper reaches of the class structure, and (2) that the members of many, if not most, such groups are drawn from the same or closely similar status levels." See also the references cited in Truman, *op. cit.*, p. 522 n. 28.

against liberty. They are the men who in some other countries became the willing victims of fascist totalitarianism.

But if the a-loyal (the "alienated" of a previous chapter) pose the real problem of disloyalty, a host of new questions appears. It was suggested, cryptically perhaps, that "the a-loyal man is an authentic creature of mass society." If that is so, it raises questions of a fundamental order about the nature and significance of political loyalty in modern American democracy. Particularly, it poses the question of how far conditions and ideas have pushed us toward a conception of democracy very different in theory and substance from the liberal democratic order we usually think of as being ours, and what impact this movement has had on the concept of loyalty.

It is far too early to offer definitive answers. But quite as important as solutions is recognition of the problems. In these concluding pages, then, an effort will be made to sketch the outlines of the problem of the relations between loyalty and mass democracy.

LOYALTY AND MASS DEMOCRACY

In a certain sense, a free society is a contradiction in terms. Society means order, constraint, conformity. Freedom means initiative, independence, diversity. The chief problem of government is to effect a working balance between the opposing tendencies of freedom and society. Dewey frames the dilemma this way:

> Some cultural conditions develop the psychological constituents that lead toward differentiation; others stimulate those which lead in the direction of the solidarity of the beehive or anthill. The human problem is that of securing the development of each constituent so that it serves to release and mature the other.[8]

This "human problem," as Dewey names it, is difficult; most attempts to solve it have failed. The American resolution, as outlined in the sections of this study on the (relatively) formal theory of loyalty, was itself complicated and precarious. Most importantly, it depended upon a given set of conditions; those conditions have changed beyond hope of restitution.

Community was to be built in the New World from two ingredients, namely, shared experience and commitment to the ideal of individual freedom. Community was to grow not because all men believed in the same political ideology, the same theology, or belonged to the same race. The creators of the Republic repudiated the idea that community must be based upon established creed and enforced conformity. They hoped to fashion community by permitting men to share the same experiences and to live together in freedom. Their doctrine of loyalty, in a word, did not mean loyalty to established dogmas and institutions, but loyalty to freedom—to the right of each man to be free in thought and, as far as possible, action. It was their firm belief that, given the inevitable variety of human nature and of indigenous conditions, loyalty to the principle that every citizen may believe and do as he chooses would endure long beyond loyalty to any particular creed or dogma.

The component parts of this general theory of loyalty already have been spelled out. The ideas of limited and just government, privacy, right of voluntary association, accepted diversity of religious and political thought—these and the others—sum up to the over-all doctrine that the American theory of loyalty meant loyalty to the principle of freedom. This was a grand and noble conception. It was perhaps the finest flower of the Age of Enlightenment. It exudes optimism, faith in man, and belief in progress. It was a resolution of the age-old problem of liberty versus authority that has yet to be improved upon.

But if it was the Enlightenment's finest flower it was also the most fragile. By no means did it resolve for once and all the inherent contradiction between the two opposing forces. That is achieved only when all members of the community believe and feel alike. But such systems are static: the archetype is the communistic order of the anthill. It was a resolution that could last only if a balance could be kept between the opposing emotional needs of freedom and conformity. As one of those needs shifts in weight relative to the other, then the resolution itself must suffer.

We have tried to show that there has been a movement away from freedom and toward conformity. "There has been," writes a contemporary poet-moralist, "a massive, almost glacial, shift away from the passion for individual freedom and toward a desire for security of association, of belonging, of conformity." [9] As a result of this "glacial" shift in popular feeling, loyalty is put before freedom. And loyalty does not mean loyalty to the principle of freedom; it means loyalty to the beliefs—economic, political, and social—of the majority. It means conformity to the dominant creed. When this is understood much of the apparent confusion of the contemporary scene falls into pattern. We are in search of community. Community is most easily secured when all men think and feel alike. So we look on silently while our schools are converted into agencies of indoctrination, while liberal politicians and thinkers are accused of disloyalty, while individual freedoms are attacked in the name of loyalty, while the voices of tolerance and liberality become faint. We have become convinced that we must believe in *something* in common; otherwise, the Communists, with their faith, will overwhelm us. How can we confront such a challenge without a faith of our own? How can a faith in nothing more than freedom stand up to such a challenge? We have transferred our faith in freedom over to a faith in community, conformity, discipline. Modern social conditions no longer support our traditional ideas of freedom and diversity; conditions are urging toward faith in community and conformity. In the last analysis, it comes down to this:

> Faith in freedom rests necessarily upon faith in man. The American belief in man was the condition precedent to the existence of the American Republic. A *loss* of faith in freedom results . . . from a *loss* of faith in man. . . . We no longer wholly trust the power of the institutions of freedom to defend themselves by the methods of freedom because we no longer wholly believe in the capacity of men to live as men in a world such as our technicians and scientists have revealed to us.[10]

MacLeish is not in public favor today but his words probe to the essence of the present concern with loyalty. No longer are we entirely sure man is able to control the social and physical forces he has released. Lacking this faith, it is easy to argue that individual freedom is not an ultimate value, that what is more necessary than freedom is conformity or security. MacLeish, of course, writes only as an observer. Yet it is interesting to remark that Mr. Seth Richardson, chairman of the Loyalty Review Board in its formative years, did very clearly lack the faith in freedom that MacLeish writes of. His view of human nature was that men cannot be trusted to distinguish good from bad; they must, therefore, be protected against malign influences. Mr. Richardson argues that it would be difficult, if not impossible, to find a formula to distinguish between sensitive and nonsensitive agencies. He continues:

> Moreover, the presence in even a non-sensitive Government organization of a disaffected non-sensitive employee, might, through contact and association, lead to the infection of loyal, and possibly sensitive employees. One bad apple may ultimately infect the whole barrel! [11]

This "bad apple" theory of man and society is transparent; its core is lack of faith in man and freedom. Mr. Richardson believes that one "disaffected" employee may "infect" co-workers with his own ideological germs. Therefore, others must be protected by removing the diseased agent to a safe distance. Mr. Richardson's view of the individual's inability to inspect ideas for himself and arrive at his own reasonable conclusions is a far cry from any theory of human nature that could support an argument for freedom. It is a theory that would have revolted the Jefferson who, in his first inaugural address, spoke that "Error of opinion may be tolerated where reason is left free to combat it."

Loss of faith in freedom and the individual, and thus in individual freedom, has its counterpart in a growing emphasis on man in the mass, on conformity, uniformity.* That has been suggested often in these pages and now it too may be adjusted to its proper historical context. The nineteenth century was a century of great isms and collective movements. In that era, so rich and varied, may be found the forerunners of most present-day intellectual and social tendencies. But while Science, Socialism, Progress, Materialism, and other Great Systems appeared to be sweeping the field of all opposition, a few voices spoke out in protest. Kierkegaard in Denmark, Nietzsche in Germany, and Dostoevsky in Russia foretold that the balance sheet was not complete, that the new movements would spawn counter-movements whose effects would be devastating. Nietzsche spoke of the crisis of values, Dostoevsky foretold the birth of fanaticism and the denial of liberty, and Kierkegaard wrote that individuality was being crushed by the new Systems. Kierkegaard's words, long unheeded, ring today with the tone of authentic prophecy:

---

* For a suggestive essay on the powerful stress toward group primacy and the urge to conform, see William H. Whyte, Jr., "The Social Engineers," *Fortune*, XLV (Jan., 1952), 88–89, 108. Whyte concentrates on expressions of these tendencies in the writings of educators, social scientists, and public relations men. He calls the type that asserts such doctrines "social engineers," and points out that to qualify as a social engineer one needs but two premises: "The first is the primacy of the group. Its harmony is the important goal, and the individual has meaning chiefly as he contributes to that goal. . . . The second premise flows naturally from the first. To achieve this 'integration' one must turn to 'scientific' techniques. By measurement and codification you enable people to find out how everyone else is thinking and unthinking and to adjust accordingly. In a word, groupthink." (Pp. 88–89.) See also "Groupthink," *Fortune*, XLV (March, 1952), 114–117, 142, 146.

The more the collective idea comes to dominate even the ordinary consciousness, the more forbidding seems the transition to becoming a particular existing human being instead of losing oneself in the race, and saying "we, our age, the nineteenth century." That it is a little thing merely to be a particular existing human being is not to be denied; but for this very reason it requires considerable resignation not to make light of it. For what does a mere individual count for? Our age knows only too well how little it is, but here also lies the specific immorality of the age. Each age has its own characteristic depravity. Ours is perhaps not pleasure or indulgence or sensuality, but rather a dissolute pantheistic contempt for the individual man. In the midst of all our exultation over the achievements of the age . . . , there sounds a note of poorly conceived contempt for the individual man; in the midst of the self-importance of the contemporary generation there is revealed a sense of despair over being human. Everything must attach itself so as to be a part of some movement; men are determined to lose themselves in the totality of things, in world-history, fascinated and deceived by a magic witchery; no one wants to be an individual human being.[12]

But the real prophet of mass democracy spoke well before the nineteenth century. What now can be discerned clearly is what Rousseau, that *enfant terrible* of the Age of Reason, saw only "through a glass, darkly"; that is, the emergence of mass democracy based upon a concept of the general will.

To turn from the pages of Helvetius or Holbach, Turgot or Diderot, Voltaire or Condorcet, to the pages of Rousseau, is to depart the clear day of reason for the obscure night of sentiment. As compared to the characteristic thinkers of the Enlightenment, Rousseau is *sui generis*. Where they emphasized reason, he emphasized feeling. Where they gloried in natural law, progress, and science, he apotheosized the homely virtues of family, tillage, and the simple life—in a word, primitivism. Where they stressed cosmopolitanism, he reveled in parochialism. Where they announced the dawn of a new individualism, he trumpeted the claims of the community. Rousseau is, par excellence, the philosopher of community; that means he is the philosopher of loyalty.

Rousseau's model was the city-state. Although he used such phrases as the "natural man," the "noble savage," or the "state of nature," he was really concerned with them only so far as they were the clichés of political speculation of his time, and so far as it was necessary to use them in order to deny them. Rousseau stood on its head the rationalist and utilitarian view of society as an association of fully developed rational men, each possessed of natural rights, and co-operating with others mainly for his own ends. He saw society as having value in and of itself, rather than as simply an instrument for protecting individuals' values. Indeed, before Rousseau was done, the individual had no moral attributes outside society. Man is a social creation; his rights are social rights. The reader is warned of this on the very first page of the *Social Contract:* "The social order is a sacred right which is the basis of all other rights." [13] Community, Rousseau insisted, rests not upon reason and self-interest but upon emotional ties among persons. And the distinctive fact about a community is that it has being and will, interests and goods of its own apart from those of its members. Rosseau's shorthand expression of this is the general will (*volonté générale*).

So far the doctrine is reasonably clear. But soon, conquered by his passion for paradox, and displaying his usual contempt for logic, Rousseau entangles himself in some very sticky ideas. Starting from the premise that rights and privileges are the gift of society, and must be justified in terms of their contribution to social good, he goes on to "prove" what, logically, he need not have dealt with at all, namely, that society can never deny freedom. He puts the problem this way:

> The problem is to find a form of association which will defend and protect with the whole common force the person and goods of each associate, and in which each, while uniting himself with all, may still obey himself alone, and remain as free as before.[14]

Rousseau solves his problem by positing a form of social contract in which each gives all his rights to the whole community:

> Each of us puts his person and all his power in common under the supreme direction of the general will, and in our corporate capacity, we receive each member as an indivisible part of the whole.[15]

Clearly, then, "the Sovereign, being formed wholly of the individuals who compose it, neither has nor can have any interest contrary to theirs. . . . The Sovereign, merely by virtue of what it is, is always what it should be." [16] An individual, however, may have a particular will contrary to his general will as a citizen. But, since the general will is always right,* when one opposes his particular will to the general will he displays either selfishness or ignorance. Therefore:

---

* Professor Sabine points out that this proposition is a truism: The social good is the standard of right. The general will is synonymous with the social good. Therefore, "What is not right is merely not the general good." George H. Sabine, *A History of Political Theory* (New York: Henry Holt, 1937), p. 591.

> Whoever refuses to obey the general will shall be compelled to
> do so by the whole body. This means nothing less than that he
> will be forced to be free; for this is the condition which, by giv-
> ing each citizen to his country, secures him against all personal
> dependence.[17]

Rousseau completes his audacious paradox and rounds out the doctrine
of the infallibility of the general will and the fallibility of particular
wills by writing:

> The citizen gives his consent to all the laws, including those
> which are passed in spite of his opposition, and even those which
> punish him when he dares to break any of them. The constant
> will of all the members of the State is the general will; by virtue
> of it they are citizens and free. When in the popular assembly a
> law is proposed, what the people is asked is not exactly whether
> it approves or rejects the proposal, but whether it is in conformity
> with the general will, which is their will. . . . When therefore
> the opinion that is contrary to my own prevails, this proves neither
> more nor less than that I was mistaken, and that what I thought
> to be the general will was not so. If my particular opinion had
> carried the day I should have achieved the opposite of what was
> my will; and it is in that case that I should not have been free.[18]

Then there appears what must surely be the most sardonic footnote
in all political writing, when Rousseau tells us that "At Genoa, the
word 'Liberty' may be read over the front of the prisons and on the
chains of the galley-slaves."

This concept of the general will comes closer to the spirt of modern
democracy than does its rival conception of individualist democracy.
The individualist doctrine of democracy held that the individual
conscience was the ultimate source and judge of right and wrong.
Along with this ran a belief in the natural and inalienable rights of
individuals: the purpose of government was but to protect rights
which already existed. Hence government must be limited to performing the terms of the political compact. Majority rule was accepted
as a practical expedient, but minorities were always protected. Majority rule meant not that the majority was necessarily right, but
that it was right to obey the majority so long as certain characteristics
were present in the political process: there must be the right to
criticize, free access to information, and unrestricted right to organize
politically. Individualist democracy also insisted the individual possessed certain rights even against the whole society. This theory of
democracy was militantly antistatist and anticonformist.

Then observe Rousseau's revisions of democratic theory. The

general will, whose repository was the sovereign, is right and just. The individual who opposes it displays either selfishness or ignorance; in either case he has shown himself a defective member of the community. Rousseau sometimes even speaks in language which suggests that dissent is treason. If these ideas are combined with the Utilitarian destruction of natural rights, and their replacement of natural rights with the greatest good of the greatest number as the supreme directive of political conduct, then the ideological foundations of mass democracy are complete. If to these ideological foundations are added the environmental conditions of mass population, mass production, mass media of communication, and the massive state, then the social bases of mass democracy are also in place. That poses the chief political problem of our day: how far have we gone toward a conception of democracy that postulates a general will? It becomes increasingly clear that we have traveled farther than we would care to recognize. Such ideas as those contained in the phrase "un-American activities," such practices as test oaths for loyalty, such factors in the social atmosphere as the felt need to "clear oneself," i.e., to proclaim one's patriotism and Americanism, before discussing certain sensitive subjects—all these suggest the operation of a theory of the general will which is really a theory of orthodoxy. And, like all orthodoxies, those who differ are heretics and can be suppressed without qualm. In moving from the individualistic democracy of yesterday to the mass democracy of today we have moved far from the idea that truth emerges from controversy, that each individual may assert his inalienable rights against all opposition, and that minorities must not be silenced. We have moved toward a theory that postulates certain dogmatic articles as expressive of the "true" will of the nation. And under these conditions, as E. H. Carr has pointed out, "Loyalty has come to mean the submission of the individual to the general will of the party or group." [19]

But Oakeshott's promise already is threatened. It is time to stop, not because the final word has been said, but because it is time to stop. On loyalty the final word will never be written. Out of his "forced coöperation" man has created a virtue, and he has called this virtue loyalty. But it is a troublesome virtue at best. For loyalty, on the one hand, means obedient service to the object of loyal attachment; it means discipline and devotion. On the other hand, loyalty also affords men some of the richest experiences of freedom. The sentiment of loyalty, coupling as it does freedom and devotion, combines elements that can war with one another. Invaluable is loyalty

Notes

CHAPTER 1

[1] Ralph Barton Perry, *Realms of Value: A Critique of Human Civilization* (Cambridge: Harvard University Press, 1954), p. 1.

[2] William Aylott Orton, *The Liberal Tradition: A Study of the Social and Spiritual Conditions of Freedom* (New Haven: Yale University Press, 1945), p. 19.

[3] Thomas Hill Green, *Lectures on the Principles of Political Obligation,* introduction by A. D. Lindsay (London: Longmans, Green, 1950), p. 29.

[4] Josiah Royce, *The Philosophy of Loyalty* (New York: Macmillan, 1908), pp. 16–17.

[5] Herbert Aaron Bloch, *The Concept of Our Changing Loyalties* (New York: Columbia University Press, 1934), p. 36.

[6] Some social psychologists even assert that the study of attitudes is the core of their science. A recent text devotes large sections to the principles governing the formation and operation of beliefs and attitudes. David Krech and Richard S. Crutchfield, *Theory and Problems of Social Psychology* (New York: McGraw-Hill, 1948). Another remarks that "during the past two decades the problem of attitudes has become central in social psychology." Muzafer Sherif and Hadley Cantril, *The Psychology of Ego-Involvements* (New York: John Wiley and Sons, 1947), p. 9.

[7] The following works have been used extensively throughout the subsequent discussion: (1) Krech and Crutchfield, *op. cit.,* pp. 158–165; (2) Sherif and Cantril, *op. cit.,* pp. 17–27; (3) E. Nelson, "Attitudes: Their Nature and Development," I, *Journal of General Psychology,* XXI (Oct., 1939), 367–399; (4) A. Strauss, "The Concept of Attitude in Social Psychology," *Journal of Psychology,* XIX (April, 1945), 329–339.

[8] Sidney Hook, *Heresy, Yes—Conspiracy, No* (New York: John Day, 1953), p. 74.

[9] John Dewey, *The Public and Its Problems* (New York: Henry Holt, 1927), p. 151.

[10] P. F. Lazarsfeld, B. Berelson, and H. Gaudet, *The People's Choice:*

How the Voter Makes Up His Mind in a Presidential Campaign (New York: Duell, Sloan and Pearce, 1944).

¹¹ T. M. Newcomb and G. Svehla, "Intra-Family Relationships in Attitude," *Sociometry,* I (July–Oct., 1937), 180–205.

¹² E. L. Horowitz, "The Development of Attitude Toward the Negro," *Archives of Psychology,* no. 194 (Jan., 1936).

¹³ Orton, *op. cit.,* p. 190.

¹⁴ Krech and Crutchfield, *op. cit.,* pp. 87–88.

¹⁵ Sherif and Cantril, *op. cit.,* p. 4.

¹⁶ Gustav Icheiser has done some excellent work on this problem of the selectivity of perception and its social consequences. See *Misunderstandings in Human Relations* (Chicago: University of Chicago Press, 1949); "Misunderstandings in International Relations," *American Sociological Review,* XVI (June, 1951), 311–316.

¹⁷ Among many excellent studies on modification of attitudes, a few might be cited to illustrate their tenacity and resistance to change: (1) A. M. Rose, *Studies in Reduction of Prejudice* (Chicago: American Council on Race Relations, 1947); (2) F. T. Smith, *An Experiment in Modifying Attitudes Toward the Negro* (New York: Columbia University Press, 1943); (3) Harold H. Kelley and Edmund H. Volkart, "The Resistance to Change of Group-Anchored Attitudes," *American Sociological Review,* XVII (Aug., 1952), 453–465.

¹⁸ Tönnies' principal work was *Gemeinschaft und Gesellschaft,* 1887; it was translated by Charles P. Loomis under the title *Fundamental Concepts of Sociology: Gemeinschaft and Gesellschaft* (New York: American Book Co., 1940). A brief exposition of his ideas may be found in Rudolf Heberle's chapter entitled "The Sociological System of Ferdinand Tönnies: Community and Society," in Harry Elmer Barnes, ed., *An Introduction to the History of Sociology* (Chicago: University of Chicago Press, 1948), pp. 227–248. The following presentation is drawn from Heberle.

¹⁹ The distinction is similar to that employed by the political analyst in the concepts of mechanistic and organic political associations. See esp. T. D. Weldon, *States and Morals: A Study in Political Conflicts* (New York: McGraw-Hill, 1947).

²⁰ Hans Gerth and C. Wright Mills, *Character and Social Structure* (New York: Harcourt, Brace, 1953), p. 174.

²¹ The point was suggested by J. T. MacCurdy, *The Structure of Morale* (Cambridge: Cambridge University Press, 1943), pp. 77–81.

²² Plato, *The Dialogues of Plato,* trans. by Jowett (Amer. ed.; New York: Random House, 1937), I, 434–435.

²³ Ranyard West, *Conscience and Society: A Study of the Psychological Prerequisites of Law and Order* (2d ed.; London: Methuen, 1950), p. 215.

²⁴ Rebecca West, *The Meaning of Treason* (2d ed.; London: Reprint Society Ltd., 1952), pp. 3, 248.

CHAPTER 2

¹ David Easton, *The Political System: An Inquiry into the State of Political Science* (New York: Knopf, 1953), pp. 125 ff.

[2] Alan Barth, *The Loyalty of Free Men*, foreword by Zechariah Chafee, Jr. (New York: Viking, 1951), p. 6.

[3] Walter Bagehot, *The English Constitution*, introduction by Lord Balfour (World Classics ed.; London: Oxford University Press, 1928), p. xxiv.

[4] Josiah Royce, *The Philosophy of Loyalty* (New York: Macmillan, 1908), pp. 22, 43, 171, 225.

[5] Lord Acton, *Essays on Freedom and Power*, selected and with introduction by Gertrude Himmelfarb (Glencoe: Free Press, 1948), pp. 32–33.

[6] *The Federalist*, No. 47.

[7] Salvador de Madariaga, *Anarchy or Hierarchy* (New York: Macmillan, 1937), p. 29.

[8] Dostoevsky, *The Brothers Karamazov*, trans. by Constance Garnett (New York: Random House, n.d.), pp. 267–268.

[9] R. M. MacIver, *The Web of Government* (New York: Macmillan, 1947), p. 411.

[10] *Ibid.*, pp. 429–430.

[11] Hegel, *The Philosophy of Hegel*, ed. and with introduction by Carl J. Friedrich (Modern Library ed.; New York: Random House, 1953), p. 166.

[12] Jacques Maritain, *The Range of Reason* (New York: Charles Scribner's Sons, 1952), p. 167.

[13] Henry V. Dicks, "Personality Traits and National Socialist Ideology," *Human Relations*, III, no. 2 (1950), 137, 140.

[14] Credit for suggesting these quotations goes to Howard B. White, "Patriotism and the Citizen Soldier," *Social Research*, XVIII (Dec., 1951), 493, 487.

[15] *West Virginia State Board of Education* v. *Barnette*, 319 U.S. 624, 632–633 (1943).

[16] Gabriel Marcel, *Homo Viator: Prolégomènes à une Métaphysique de l'Espérance* (Aubier: Editions Montaigne, 1944), pp. 123–124. Present writer's translation.

[17] Henry Steele Commager, "Who Is Loyal to America?" *Harper's Magazine*, CVC (Sept., 1947), 195, 196. The essay has been reprinted in Commager's spirited little volume, *Freedom, Loyalty, Dissent* (New York: Oxford University Press, 1954).

[18] Sidney Hook, *Education for Modern Man* (New York: Dial Press, 1946), p. 172.

[19] The following discussion draws heavily from White, *op. cit.*, pp. 486–501.

[20] The Nuremberg Judgment, Cmd. 6964 (1946). Reprinted in part in L. C. Green, *International Law through the Cases* (New York: Frederick A. Praeger, 1951), pp. 697–713. Quotation from Green, p. 706.

[21] Green, *op. cit.*, p. 706.

[22] Quoted in Georg Schwarzenberger, *A Manual of International Law* (3d ed.; London: Stevens and Sons, 1952), p. 285.

[23] These points were recognized by G. D. H. Cole in two essays separated by years during which his thinking underwent a decisive shift. The discussion here owes much to Cole. See his "Conflicting Social Obligations," *Proceedings of the Aristotelian Society*, n.s., XV (1915), 140–160, and "Loyalties," *Proceedings of the Aristotelian Society*, n.s., XXVI (1926), 151–171.

[24] David Riesman, "Marginality, Conformity, and Insight," *Phylon,* XIV (Sept., 1953), 244, 258, makes a cognate point. He emphasizes that the position of the "marginal man"—one not quite in the group, not quite out of it—often enhances self-knowledge and development. It is a position affording the broader vision which total conformity rarely gives, and which is so necessary to creative activity.

[25] The germ of the idea comes from Philip Selznick, "Foundations of the Theory of Organization," *American Sociological Review,* XIII (Feb., 1948), 26. Selznick writes: "From the standpoint of organization as a formal system, persons are viewed functionally, in respect to their *roles,* as participants in assigned segments of the cooperative system. But in fact individuals have a propensity to resist depersonalization, to spill over the boundaries of their segmentary roles, to participate as *wholes.*"

[26] Jan Valtin, *Out of the Night* (New York: Alliance Book Corporation, 1941), p. 659.

[27] R. M. MacIver, *The Elements of Social Science* (9th ed., rev.; London: Methuen, 1949), p. 166.

[28] 310 U.S. 586 (1940); 319 U.S. 624 (1943).

[29] 310 U.S. at 596 (1940).

[30] For an incisive analysis of these and other shortcomings in congressional forms, see James MacGregor Burns, *Congress on Trial: The Legislative Process and the Administrative State* (New York: Harper, 1949).

[31] David Spitz, "Democracy and the Problem of Civil Disobedience," *American Political Science Review,* XLVIII (June, 1954), 397–404.

[32] *Ibid.,* p. 397.

[33] *Ibid.,* p. 402.

CHAPTER 3

[1] Merle Curti, *The Roots of American Loyalty* (New York: Columbia University Press, 1946).

[2] Ralph Waldo Emerson, "Politics," *Essays: Second Series.*

[3] *Syllabus in Civics and Patriotism,* University of the State of New York, Bulletin no. 704 (Feb. 15, 1920), pp. 7, 9. For an earlier period, a compilation by Selim H. Peabody is a valuable source. See Selim H. Peabody, *American Patriotism: Speeches, Letters, and Other Papers Which Illustrate the Foundation, the Development, the Preservation of the United States of America* (New York: American Book Exchange, 1880).

[4] Thus, antipathy to foreign ideologies has roots which began long before Depew delivered his sentiments on the subject. "The ranks of anarchy and riots number no Americans. The leaders boldly proclaim that they come here not to enjoy the blessings of our liberty and to sustain our institutions but to destroy our government, cut our throats, and divide our property." Curti assures us that this sentiment, announced in 1892, was "widely held." John D. Champlin, ed., *Orations, Addresses, and Speeches of Chauncey Depew* (New York: Austin and Lipscomb, 1910), III, 264–273; Curti, *The Growth of American Thought* (2d ed.; New York: Harper, 1951), p. 494.

[5] C. H. McIlwain, ed., *The Political Works of James I* (Cambridge: Harvard University Press, 1918), p. 333.

6 William Sherlock, *The Case of the Allegiance Due to Sovereign Powers* (London, 1691), pp. 4, 9.

7 25 Edw. III, stat. 5, c. 2.

8 Nathaniel Weyl, *Treason: The Story of Disloyalty and Betrayal in American History* (Washington, D.C.: Public Affairs Press, 1950), p. 18. It is worthy of note, also, that the statute of 1351 was itself enacted in order to put a bridle on the judges: "The reason for such an enactment was the wide interpretation given to treason by the judges; and accordingly the Statute further provided that if future questions should arise, whether anything not in the Statute specified should be adjudged treason, such question should be referred to Parliament. . . . [But this] did not in practice prevent the Judges from holding that certain acts outside the Statute were 'constructive treasons'. . . ." Wilfred George Carlton Hall, *Political Crime: A Critical Essay on the Law and Its Administration in Cases of a Certain Type* (London: George Allen and Unwin, Ltd., 1923), p. 16.

9 John Locke, *Second Treatise . . .* , ed. Charles L. Sherman under title *Treatise of Civil Government and a Letter Concerning Toleration* (New York: D. Appleton-Century, 1937), secs. 13, 119, 131, 232.

10 The first case was *Minersville School District* v. *Gobitis,* 310 U.S. 586 (1940). The second was *West Virginia State Board of Education* v. *Barnette,* 319 U.S. 324 (1942).

11 Samuel D. Warren and Louis D. Brandeis, "The Right to Privacy," *Harvard Law Review,* IV (Dec., 1890), 196. For a discussion bringing Warren and Brandeis' survey of forces encroaching upon privacy up to date, see Harold D. Lasswell, "The Threat to Privacy," in R. M. MacIver, ed., *Conflict of Loyalties,* Religion and Civilization Series, The Institute for Religious and Social Studies (New York: distributed by Harper, 1952), pp. 121–141.

12 *Pavesich* v. *New England Life Insurance Company,* 122 Ga. 190 (1906).

13 *Prudential Insurance Company of America* v. *Cheek,* 259 U.S. 530, 543 (1921).

14 *Wolf* v. *Colorado,* 338 U.S. 25, 27 (1949).

15 *Olmstead* v. *United States,* 277 U.S. 438, 478 (1928).

16 Quoted in Ralph Barton Perry, *Puritanism and Democracy* (New York: Vanguard Press, 1944), p. 69.

17 *Ibid.,* pp. 74–75.

18 Richard D. Mosier, *The American Temper: Patterns of Our Intellectual Heritage* (Berkeley and Los Angeles: University of California Press, 1952), p. 27.

19 Inability to curb religious enthusiasts and harness their energies to institutional ends, has always been one of the first sources of weakness and faction in the Protestant churches. Macaulay has written a keen analysis comparing Catholic and Protestant policy and success in this matter. See his essay on Ranke's "History of the Popes" in *Critical and Historical Essays* (1840).

20 Vernon Louis Parrington, *Main Currents in American Thought: An Interpretation of American Literature from the Beginnings to 1920* (New York: Harcourt, Brace, 1927–1930), I, 65.

21 Nathaniel Ward, *The Simple Cobbler of Aggawam* (1647), as quoted by Alpheus T. Mason in *Free Government in the Making* (New York: Oxford University Press, 1949), p. 59.

[22] Roger Williams, *The Bloudy Tenent of Persecution for Cause of Conscience Discussed* . . . (1644), as quoted in Mason, *op. cit.*, p. 63.

[23] Roger Williams, . . . *Conference between Truth and Peace* (1644), as quoted in Mason, *op. cit.*, pp. 66–67.

[24] For an elaboration of these points, see Perry Miller, "The Location of American Religious Freedom," in Miller *et al.*, *Religion and Freedom of Thought* (Garden City: Doubleday, 1954), pp. 9–24.

[25] For a general introduction to utopian thought and practice, see Lewis Mumford, *The Story of Utopias* (New York: Boni and Liveright, 1922). Some forty-five experiments to set up isolated communities after the doctrines of Owen and Fourier were conducted in late eighteenth- and early nineteenth-century America. For their histories, see C. Nordhoff, *The Communistic Societies of the United States* (New York: Harper, 1875).

[26] The relevant sections are Tocqueville, *Democracy in America,* trans. by Henry Reeve, ed. by Henry Steele Commager (Galaxy ed.; New York and London: Oxford University Press, 1946) pp. 109–116, 319–333. See also A. M. Schlesinger, Jr., "Biography of a Nation of Joiners," in *Paths to the Present* (New York: Macmillan, 1949), pp. 23–50; and Currin V. Shields, "The American Tradition of Empirical Collectivism," *American Political Science Review*, XLVI (March, 1952), 104–121. Much of the massive body of writing on pressure politics and public opinion in American politics centers around this same approach. For two outstanding recent examples see Alfred de Grazia, *Public and Republic* (New York: Knopf, 1951), and David B. Truman, *The Governmental Process* (New York: Knopf, 1951).

[27] Tocqueville, *op. cit.*, p. 331.

[28] *Ibid.*, pp. 114–115.

[29] *Ibid.*, p. 329.

[30] Plato, *The Republic,* Jowett Translation, secs. 558, 563.

[31] *Joint Anti-Fascist Refugee Committee* v. *McGrath*, 341 U.S. 123 (1950).

[32] See *United States* v. *Classic*, 313 U.S. 299 (1941); and *Smith* v. *Allwright*, 321 U.S. 649 (1944). The doctrine that economic corporations "affected with a public interest" are subject to public regulation has, of course, long been accepted in American jurisprudence. See *Munn* v. *Illinois*, 94 U.S. 113 (1876). The decision in *American Communications Association* v. *Douds*, 339 U.S. 382 (1950), upholding the provisions of the Labor-Management Relations Act requiring unions wishing to avail themselves of the opportunities of the act to have their officials execute non-Communist affidavits, could be the first step in regulating private associations by defining conditions of access to publicly afforded advantages.

[33] *Beauharnais* v. *Illinois*, 343 U.S. 250 (1952).

[34] For an example of this line of argument, see Shields, *op. cit.*, pp. 104–121.

[35] Alexander H. Pekelis, *Law and Social Action*, selected essays, ed. by Milton R. Konvitz (Ithaca: Cornell University Press, 1950), esp. pp. 66–71.

[36] Ralph Henry Gabriel, *The Course of American Democratic Thought* (New York: Ronald Press, 1940), p. 19. Gabriel's book throughout is rich with source quotations and capable discussion of the complex ramifications of individualism in American life. See also Curti, *The Growth of American Thought.*

[37] Wilbur J. Cash, *The Mind of the South* (Doubleday Anchor ed.; Garden City: Doubleday, 1954), pp. 45, 44, 55, 46.

[38] Curti, *The Roots of American Loyalty,* pp. vii–viii.

[39] Earle L. Hunter, *A Sociological Analysis of Certain Types of Patriotism* (New York: Columbia University Press, 1932), p. 21.

[40] Percy Holmes Boynton, *Changing Ideals of American Patriotism,* Public Policy Pamphlet no. 21 (Chicago: University of Chicago Press, 1936), p. 2.

[41] Philip Freneau, *Literary Importations* (1786).

[42] Tocqueville, *op. cit.,* p. 226.

[43] Charles M. Wiltse, "From Compact to National State in American Political Thought," in Milton R. Konvitz and Arthur E. Murphy, eds., *Essays in Political Theory Presented to George H. Sabine* (Ithaca: Cornell University Press, 1948), pp. 153–179.

[44] Gabriel, *op. cit.,* p. 396. The discussion here draws heavily on Gabriel's evocative treatment of the same points, pp. 396–418.

[45] Henry R. Estabrook, *Proceedings of the Annual Meeting of the Missouri Bar Association* (1913), p. 278, as quoted in Gabriel, *op. cit.,* p. 402.

[46] W. I. Thomas and Florian Znaniecki, *The Polish Peasant in Europe and America* (New York: Knopf, 1927).

[47] Quoted in Howard K. Beale, *Are American Teachers Free?* (New York: Scribner's, 1936), p. 702.

[48] Quoted in Mosier, *op. cit.,* p. 135.

[49] Beale, *op. cit.,* pp. 19–20.

[50] Clinton Rossiter, "The American Mission," *American Scholar,* XX (Winter, 1950–1951), 19–29.

[51] Frank Thistlethwaite, "What Is Un-American?" *Cambridge Journal,* V (Jan., 1952), 215.

[52] Reported in Curti, *The Growth of American Thought,* pp. 397–398.

[53] *Texas* v. *White,* 7 Wall 700 (1869).

[54] Curti would place the triumph of the nationalism here under discussion at a somewhat earlier date. See his chapter on "The Nature of the New Nationalism," in *The Growth of American Thought,* pp. 481–507.

[55] For one example, see D. W. Brogan, *The American Character* (New York: Knopf, 1944), pp. 96 ff., 135 ff.

[56] Thistlethwaite, *op. cit.,* pp. 220–221.

[57] In Zechariah Chafee's Foreword to Alan Barth, *The Loyalty of Free Men* (New York: Viking, 1951), p. x.

CHAPTER 4

[1] This formulation, though less formal in style and abbreviated in content, does not differ significantly from that expounded by Gerth and Mills. They list the components of social structure as: (1) roles, (2) institutions, (3) the institutional order, and (4) spheres of activity common to all orders (i.e., education, status, conduct, symbols, and technology). See Hans Gerth and C. Wright Mills, *Character and Social Structure* (New York: Harcourt, Brace, 1952), pp. 21–32.

[2] "Institutions are those patterns which define the essentials of the legitimately expected behavior of persons in so far as they perform *structurally important roles* in the social system." Talcott Parsons, *Essays in Sociological Theory Pure and Applied* (Glencoe: Free Press, 1949), p. 311. See also *ibid.,* p. 14 n. 5.

[3] Edmond Taylor, *Richer by Asia* (New York: Houghton Mifflin, 1947).

[4] Parsons, *op. cit.*, p. 13.

[5] James B. Conant, *Modern Science and Modern Man* (Anchor ed.; Garden City: Doubleday, 1953), p. 12.

[6] "The affect [*sic*] of a change in the realistic situation while an institutional definition remains unchanged is to create a strain. The line of least resistance in reaction to this strain will usually be an attempt more aggressively than before to reassert the old definition of the situation and to shape the realistic situation in conformity with it." Parsons, *op. cit.*, p. 314.

[7] In Robert Redfield, *The Primitive World and Its Transformations* (Ithaca: Cornell University Press, 1953), p. 69.

[8] See Clement Eaton, *Freedom of Thought in the Old South* (Durham: Duke University Press, 1940).

[9] Hugh Nibley, "The Unsolved Loyalty Problem: Our Western Heritage," *Western Political Quarterly*, VI (Dec., 1953), 631–658.

[10] See for one example, W. H. R. Rivers, ed., *Essays on the Depopulation of Melanesia* (Cambridge, England: The University Press, 1922).

[11] This concept of the accursed group comes from Yves R. Simon, *Community of the Free* (New York: Henry Holt, 1947), pp. 63–72.

[12] Pitirim Sorokin, *The Crisis of Our Age* (New York: E. P. Dutton, 1941), p. 187.

[13] A comparative analysis of the older large-family system and the newer small-family way of life may be found in James H. S. Bossard and Winogene Pratt Sanger, "The Large Family System," *American Sociological Review*, XVII (Feb., 1952), 3–10.

[14] Carle C. Zimmerman, "The Social Conscience and the Family," *American Journal of Sociology*, XLII (Nov., 1946), 263.

[15] The term "culture" is used in the sense of ". . . a body of common understandings enabling the group to act effectively toward the realization of recognized values. . . ." Margaret Park Redfield, "The American Family: Consensus and Freedom," *American Journal of Sociology*, XLII (Nov., 1946), 181.

[16] This list of conditions congenial to the rise of culture is adapted from M. P. Redfield, *op. cit.*, *passim*.

[17] Zimmerman, *op. cit.*, p. 263.

[18] M. P. Redfield, *op. cit.*, p. 183.

[19] Montesquieu, *Esprit des Lois*, Bk. IV, chap. 5.

[20] Herbert W. Schneider, "The Old Theory and the New Practice of Religious Loyalty," *American Quarterly*, V (Winter, 1953), 295–296.

[21] For a trenchant statement of this thesis, Marx and Engels' *Manifesto* of 1848 is unexcelled. R. H. Tawney's *The Acquisitive Society*, first published in 1921, has given the idea its classic formulation in the modern period. Karen Horney, in her widely cited *Neurotic Personality of Our Time* (New York: Norton, 1937), approaches the same problem from a modified psychoanalytic point of view.

[22] Rebecca West, *The Meaning of Treason* (2d ed.; London: Reprint Society Ltd., 1952), p. 177.

[23] John Dewey, *Individualism Old and New* (New York: Minton, Balch, 1930), pp. 52–53.

[24] Two citations from the enormous literature must suffice. The urban

youthful gang has been much studied by sociologists, but F. M. Thrasher's *The Gang* (Chicago: University of Chicago Press, 1927) remains a basic work. Thrasher shows that gangs are formed to provide members with a status and identity not given them by society at large. These gangs encourage and regulate activities that satisfy basic human needs and relieve deprivations where families and communities have failed to do so. "Gangs represent the spontaneous effort of boys to create a society for themselves where none adequate to their needs exists. . . . [The gang] offers a substitute for what society fails to give; and it provides a relief from suppression and distasteful behavior." (Pp. 37–38.) A more recent book fortifies Thrasher's conclusions. See W. F. Whyte, *Street Corner Society* (Chicago: University of Chicago Press, 1943).

[25] An invaluable study of the middle classes is furnished by C. Wright Mills, *White Collar: The American Middle Classes* (New York: Oxford University Press, 1951).

[26] Leo Lowenthal and Norber Guterman, *Prophets of Deceit: A Study of the American Agitator* (New York: Harper, 1949)

[27] *Ibid.*, p. 14.

[28] *Ibid.*, p. 15.

[29] Erich Fromm, *Escape from Freedom* (New York: Farrar and Rinehart, 1941).

[30] David Riesman, *The Lonely Crowd* (New Haven: Yale University Press, 1950).

[31] Sebastian de Grazia, *The Political Community* (Chicago: University of Chicago Press, 1948).

[32] Grazia's assertion of the internal conflicts in the ideology of modern Western civilization is made more definite and applied specifically to the American scene by Lynd, who says that one of the characteristic aspects of American life is an attempt to orient life under ambivalent or conflicting "rules of the game." He has drawn up a panel of these conflicting directives operative in American society. Robert S. Lynd, *Knowledge for What?* (Princeton: Princeton University Press, 1939), pp. 60–61.

[33] John H. Hallowell, *Main Currents in Modern Political Thought* (New York: Henry Holt, 1950), pp. 618, 651.

[34] Bertrand Russell, "A Free Man's Worship," in *Mysticism and Logic* (London: George Allen and Unwin, 1917), pp. 56–57.

[35] José Ortega y Gasset, *The Revolt of the Masses* (New York: W. W Norton, 1932), p. 80.

[36] Melville Herskovitz, *Man and His Works* (New York: Knopf, 1948), pp. 61–78.

[37] *Ibid.*, p. 63.

[38] *Ibid.*, pp. 76–77.

[39] Robert Redfield, *op. cit.*, p. 147.

[40] Francis Downing, "Graham Greene and the Case for 'Disloyalty,'" *Commonweal*, XLV (March 14, 1952), 565.

[41] Henry Steele Commager, *The American Mind: An Interpretation of American Thought and Character since the 1880's* (New Haven: Yale University Press, 1950), p. 425.

[42] Dewey, *op. cit.*, pp. 9, 82.

[43] The poll is reported in Theodore M. Newcomb, *Social Psychology*

(New York: Dryden Press, 1950), p. 177. Newcomb cites the case as a "horrible example" of shortcomings in question-phrasing on opinion polls. In our view, it is an excellent example of the watering down of ideals.

[44] President's Committee on Civil Rights, *To Secure These Rights* (Washington, D.C., 1947), pp. 139–140.

[45] American Civil Liberties Union, *Our Uncertain Civil Liberties: U.S. Liberties, 1947–48* (New York: American Civil Liberties Union, 1948), pp. 8–9.

[46] W. H. Auden, "Letter to Lord Byron," 1937.

[47] Michael Oakeshott, "Rationalism in Politics," *Cambridge Journal,* I (Nov., 1947), 86. Oakeshott, with obvious glee, cites as the most sublime of these projects—"so sublime that even a Rationalist . . . might think it eccentric" —Owen's proposal for "a world convention to emancipate the human race from ignorance, poverty, division, sin and misery."

[48] Josiah Royce, *The Philosophy of Loyalty* (New York: Macmillan, 1908), p. 164.

[49] *Ibid.,* p. 229.

[50] *Ibid.,* p. 242.

[51] It is unfortunately true, as one student reports, that "the isolation of man . . . is not a central problem of contemporary sociological thought." Two recent books offer at least an introduction to the subject. See Paul Halmos, *Solitude and Privacy: A Study of Social Isolation, Its Causes and Therapy* (London: Routledge and Kegan Paul, 1952), and Margaret Mary Wood, *Paths of Loneliness: The Individual Isolated in Modern Society* (New York: Columbia University Press, 1953). The quotation above is from Halmos, p. xv. R. M. MacIver, *The Ramparts We Guard* (New York: Macmillan, 1950), pp. 85–87, offers a suggestive classification of types of anomic (alienated) personalities.

[52] The best analysis of political apathy known to the present writer is David Riesman and Nathan Glazer, "Criteria for Political Apathy," in Alvin W. Gouldner, ed., *Studies in Leadership: Leadership and Democratic Action* (New York: Harper Brothers, 1950), pp. 505–560.

[53] See, for example, C. E. Merriam and H. F. Gosnell, *Non-Voting* (Chicago: University of Chicago Press, 1924); J. K. Pollock, *Voting Behavior: A Case Study* (Ann Arbor: University of Michigan Press, 1939); and P. F. Lazarsfeld and Associates, *The People's Choice* (New York: Duell, Sloan and Pearce, 1944).

[54] Lazarsfeld, *op. cit.,* pp. 45–46.

[55] Morris Janowitz and Dwaine Marvick, "Authoritarianism and Political Behavior," *Public Opinion Quarterly,* XVII (Summer, 1953), 185–202, have made a pioneering study in this area. Their article is one of the many minor studies which have their roots in T. W. Adorno *et al., The Authoritarian Personality* (New York: Harper Brothers, 1950). Janowitz and Marvick explore the hypothesis that ". . . high authoritarians tend to participate less and have less political self-confidence than low authoritarians in politics as presently organized." (Pp. 186–187.) They conclude, *inter alia,* that: "(a) Personality tendencies measured by authoritarian scale served to explain political behavior at least as well as those other factors traditionally included in political and voting behavior studies (age, education, class) . . . ; (c) The incidence of authoritarianism not only was significantly related to political isolationism and to feelings of political effectiveness, but also to non-voting. Authoritarianism was helpful in explaining candidate preferences." (P. 201.)

⁵⁶ Rousseau, *The Social Contract and Discourses,* trans. and with introduction by G. D. H. Cole (Everyman's ed.; London: J. M. Dent, 1913), Bk. III, chap. 15, p. 78.

⁵⁷ There is other, more "empirical," support for the point. Groups of American combat soldiers in World War II were asked this question: "When the going was tough how much were you helped by thoughts of hatred for the enemy?" About *one-third* replied such thoughts "helped a lot." But in response to the query "When the going was tough how much did it help you to think that you couldn't let the other men down?" roughly *two-thirds* answered "It helped a lot." S. A. Stouffer *et al., The American Soldier: Combat and Its Aftermath* (Princeton: Princeton University Press, 1949), p. 174.

⁵⁸ An excellent short account of the causes and forms of "scapegoating" is provided by a pamphlet published under the direction of the Central YMCA College, *The ABC's of Scapegoating,* foreword by Gordon W. Allport (Chicago: Central YMCA College, n.d.).

⁵⁹ See Nathaniel Weyl, *The Battle against Disloyalty* (New York: Thomas Y. Crowell, 1951).

⁶⁰ David C. Williams, "The Cold War in America," *Political Quarterly,* XXI (July–Sept., 1950), 282.

⁶¹ For an example, see Philip Selznick, *The Organizational Weapon: A Study of Bolshevik Strategy and Tactics,* The Rand Corporation Series (New York: McGraw-Hill, 1952).

⁶² In Theodore H. White, *Fire in the Ashes: Europe in Mid-Century* (New York: William Sloane Associates, 1953), p. 125.

⁶³ Alistair Cooke, *A Generation on Trial: U.S.A. v. Alger Hiss* (New York: Knopf, 1950), esp. pp. 3–43.

⁶⁴ Julien Benda, *La Trahison des Clercs,* trans. by Richard Aldington as *The Treason of the Intellectuals* (New York: William Morrow, 1928), pp. 44, 51.

⁶⁵ Williams, *op. cit.,* p. 282.

⁶⁶ Eric Hoffer, *The True Believer: Thoughts on the Nature of Mass Movements* (New York: Harper, 1951), p. 103.

CHAPTER 5

¹ 53 Stat. 1148.

² *Hatch Act Enforcement Order,* Civil Service Circular no. 222 (June 20, 1940). See also William G. Torpey, *Public Personnel Management* (New York: D. Van Nostrand, 1953), pp. 283–284.

³ *Civil Service War Regulations,* sec. 18.2c(7), (Sept. 26, 1942).

⁴ *Testimony of Arthur Flemming, Independent Offices Appropriation Bill for 1945,* Hearings, Subcommittee of the House Committee on Appropriations, U.S. 78th Cong., 2d sess. (1944), p. 1083.

⁵ 54 Stat. 611.

⁶ 54 Stat. 713; 56 Stat. 1053.

⁷ 64 Stat. 476.

⁸ In reporting on the bill to fortify the Secretary of the Navy with summary dismissal powers, Chairman Vinson of the House Naval Affairs Committee stated: "In times like these it is of the utmost importance to the Navy and to the Nation that every single civilian employee be a loyal patriotic worker and that the Navy Department be permitted to remove without question any employee who

there is reason to believe renders more loyalty to possible enemies of this country than to the United States. . . . It [the bill] is a direct way of getting rid of subversive influences that might be in the Department." 85 *Cong. Rec.* p. 7023. Quoted in Eleanor Bontecou, *The Federal Loyalty-Security Program* (Ithaca: Cornell University Press, 1953), p. 13.

⁹ *Ibid.*, p. 17.

¹⁰ *Ibid.*, pp. 17–18.

¹¹ For an account of the committee's work see *ibid.*, pp. 18–21.

¹² A good brief account of the wartime period appears in Gladys M. Kammerer, *Impact of War on Federal Personnel Administration, 1939–1945* (Lexington: University of Kentucky Press, 1951), pp. 117–136. See also Robert E. Cushman, "The Purge of Federal Employees Accused of Disloyalty," *Public Administration Review*, III (Autumn, 1943), 297–316; and Thomas I. Emerson and David M. Helfeld, "Loyalty Among Government Employees," *Yale Law Journal*, LVIII (Dec., 1948), 1–143.

¹³ *Fitness for Continuance in Federal Employment of Goodwin B. Watson, and William E. Dodd, Jr., and Robert Morss Lovett . . .* , Hearings before the Special Subcommittee of the House Committee on Appropriations, U.S. 78th Cong., 1st sess. (April 9, 12, 13, 15, 1943).

¹⁴ The standard work on the Dies Committee is August Raymond Ogden, *The Dies Committee: A Study of the Special House Committee for the Investigation of Un-American Activities, 1938–1944* (Washington, D.C.: Catholic University of America Press, 1945). See also William Gellerman, *Martin Dies* (New York: John Day, 1944). A perusal of either volume will show that the Dies Committee had very flexible notions of "fellow traveling."

¹⁵ The affair is reported by Frederick L. Schuman, " 'Bill of Attainder' in the Seventy-Eighth Congress," *American Political Science Review*, XXXVII (Oct., 1943), 819–820. See also *United States v. Lovett*, 328 U.S. 303 (1945).

¹⁶ Much of the following comes from Kammerer, *op. cit.*, esp. pp. 120–127. Kammerer's work, based as it is on reports of the Civil Service Commission, on congressional hearings, and on personal interviews with officials either in or fully acquainted with the program, appears to be reliable.

¹⁷ The basic figures come from *ibid.*, pp. 120, 133. The calculations are the present writer's. Kammerer calculates that .014 per cent were barred for loyalty reasons. But if her basic figures are correct, then her calculation is incorrect.

¹⁸ *Report of the Royal Commission Appointed . . . to Investigate the Facts Relating to . . . the Communication by Public Officials and Other Persons in Positions of Trust of Secret and Confidential Information to Agents of a Foreign Power*, June 27, 1946 (Ottawa: E. Cloutier, 1946).

¹⁹ 11 Fed. Reg. 13863.

²⁰ *Report of the President's Temporary Commission on Employee Loyalty*, Civil Service Commission (Washington, 1947).

²¹ 12 Fed. Reg. 1935.

²² Executive Order 9835, Part IV, 2.

²³ Although the order lists a number of "pertinent sources of information" to be referred to in this initial step, the listing is not meant to be exhaustive. The list of specific sources is followed by a blanket provision reading that "any other appropriate source" may be used. Executive Order 9835, Part I, 3(j).

²⁴ Executive Order 9835, Part II, 1b.

²⁵ 18 Fed. Reg. 2489.

[26] 64 Stat. 476.

[27] L. A. Nikolorić, "The Government Loyalty Program," *American Scholar*, XIX (Summer, 1950), 292.

[28] Bontecou, *op. cit.*, p. 105.

[29] In testimony before a Senate committee, Seth Richardson stated that "all of these cases that we have had had to do with this question of association, affiliation, membership with organizations which have been certified by the Attorney General to be subversive." *State Department Employee Loyalty Investigation*, Hearings, Subcommittee of the Senate Committee on Foreign Relations, U.S. 81st Cong., 1st sess. (1950), Part I, p. 409.

[30] As reported in Alan Barth, *The Loyalty of Free Men* (New York: Viking, 1951), pp. 119–122. Italics are present author's.

[31] Seth W. Richardson, "The Federal Employee Loyalty Program," *Columbia Law Review*, LI (May, 1951), 546.

[32] *Ibid.*

[33] *Ibid.*, p. 556; present writer's italics.

[34] *Ibid.*, p. 557.

[35] Scott McLeod, "Security in the Department of State," *Department of State Bulletin*, XXX (March 29, 1954), 471.

[36] Marver H. Bernstein, "The Loyalty of Federal Employees," *Western Political Quarterly*, II (June, 1949), 260.

[37] The analysis here follows that of Carey McWilliams, *Witch Hunt: The Revival of Heresy* (Boston: Little, Brown, 1950), pp. 282–289.

[38] *Ibid.*, p. 289.

[39] *Ibid.*, pp. 284–287.

[40] See Zechariah Chafee, Jr., *Free Speech in the United States* (Cambridge: Harvard University Press, 1941), pp. 196–241.

[41] *Attorney General A. Mitchell Palmer on Charges Made against the Department of Justice by Louis F. Post and Others*, Hearings, House Committee on Rules, U.S. 66th Cong., 2d sess. (1920), Part 1, p. 151. Quoted in Bontecou, *op. cit.*, p. 160.

[42] For a good account of this early period, see John Lord O'Brian, "Loyalty Tests and Guilt by Association," *Harvard Law Review*, LXI (April, 1948), 592–611.

[43] 53 Stat. 1244.

[44] 54 Stat. 1201.

[45] Bontecou, *op. cit.*, p. 167.

[46] 13 Fed. Reg. 1473.

[47] Bontecou, *op. cit.*, p. 171.

[48] *Joint Anti-Fascist Refugee Committee* v. *McGrath*, 341 U.S. 123 (1950).

[49] Bontecou, *op. cit.*, p. 170.

[50] Executive Order 10450, sec. 8,(a),(3).

[51] Bontecou, *op. cit.*, p. 204.

[52] John Lord O'Brian, "Guilt by Association—Three Words in Search of a Meaning," *University of Chicago Law Review*, XVII (Autumn, 1949), 148–162.

[53] Sidney Hook, *Heresy, Yes—Conspiracy, No* (New York: John Day, 1953), pp. 84–94; Henry Steele Commager, *Freedom, Loyalty, Dissent* (New York: Oxford University Press, 1954), pp. 93–135.

⁵⁴ To support this thesis, Commager cites a number of cases. Some are listed here in order to make it clear that the citations Commager uses are a mixture of obiter dicta and minority opinions. In *Dennis* v. *United States,* 341 U.S. 494, 572 (1950), Jackson wrote: "What really is under review here is a conviction of conspiracy, after a trial for conspiracy, on an indictment charging conspiracy, brought under a statute outlawing conspiracy." In *De Jonge* v. *Oregon,* 299 U.S. 353, 365 (1936), Chief Justice Hughes said: "The holding of meetings for peaceable political action cannot be proscribed. Those who assist in the conduct of such meetings cannot be branded as criminals on that score. The question . . . is not as to the auspices under which the meeting is held but as to its purpose. . . . If the persons assembling have committed crimes elsewhere, if they have formed or are engaged in a conspiracy against the public peace and order, they may be prosecuted for their conspiracy or other violation of valid laws." In *Schneiderman* v. *United States,* 320 U.S. 118, 136 (1942), Murphy stated: ". . . under our traditions, beliefs are personal and not a matter of mere association, and . . . men in adhering to a political party or other organization notoriously do not subscribe unqualifiedly to all of its platforms or asserted principles." He notes further (p. 147) that: "The Government frankly concedes that 'it is normally true . . . that it is unsound to impute to an organization the views expressed in the writings of all its members, or to impute such writings to each member. . . .' " In *Bridges* v. *Wixon,* 326 U.S. 135, 163 (1944), Murphy notes: "The doctrine of personal guilt is one of the most fundamental principles of our jurisprudence."

⁵⁵ Max Lowenthal, *The Federal Bureau of Investigation* (New York: William Sloane Associates, 1950), although obviously biased, rests on documented and available sources and is replete with excerpted material from bureau reports and statements. Eleanor Bontecou, in her thorough study (*The Federal Loyalty-Security Program*), supplies additional insights into the loyalty work of the bureau. See also Alan Barth, "How Good Is an F.B.I. Report?" *Harper's Magazine,* CCVIII (March, 1954), 25–32.

⁵⁶ If some of this language seems extravagant, and not "objective," see the articles by Dwight Macdonald, "The Lie-Detector Era," *Reporter,* X (June 8, 1954), 10–19; X (June 22, 1954), 23–30.

⁵⁷ Illustrations of many of these points can be found in an article containing actual statements of charges against one person before a loyalty board. See Adam Yarmolinsky, "How a Lawyer Conducts a Security Case," *Reporter,* X (March 2, 1954), 18–23.

⁵⁸ New York *Times,* Jan. 17, 1954. Nothing has been said here of the impact of the loyalty-security program on employee morale and efficiency because it, however important, is essentially another subject. That the impact has been considerable, and unfavorable, is beyond dispute. Marie Jahoda and Stuart Cook, psychologists, made an extensive study of the matter. They reported widespread attitudes of suspicion and reluctance to express opinions. Many employees felt that persons had often been singled out unfairly as targets of attack. Those who had belonged to "voluntary organizations with definite social purposes" were most frequently subjected to unfounded attacks. "Security Measures and Freedom of Thought: An Exploratory Study of the Impact of Loyalty and Security Programs," *Yale Law Journal,* LXI (March, 1952), 295–334. Dr. Vannevar Bush testified to Congress that the program had demoralized the scientific community, almost destroyed mutual respect between the military services and the scientific community, and greatly hindered weapons research programs. Dr. John von Newmann stated

that the program was the greatest single threat to free scientific research, that as now applied the program tended to confuse technical opinion with political intention, and that it could lead to thought control. (As reported in the New York *Times,* Oct. 19, 1954, pp. 1, 12.) Professor Hans J. Morgenthau argues that the program has weakened morale and caused such a drastic decline in quality of personnel in the Department of State that the department is "hardly competent to serve any government. . . ." He maintains also that the department "is probably not more immune to subversion and treason than it was before." "A State of Insecurity," *New Republic,* CXXXII (April 18, 1955), 8–14.

[59] For the full transcript of the Oppenheimer hearings before the Personnel Security Board see *In the Matter of J. Robert Oppenheimer,* U.S. Atomic Energy Commission, . . . Hearings before Personnel Security Board, April 12, 1954 through May 6, 1954 (Washington: U.S. Govt. Printing Office, 1954). The report of the Personnel Security Board may be found in *Findings and Recommendations in the Case of Dr. J. Robert Oppenheimer,* U.S. Personnel Security Board, May 27, 1954 ([Washington], 1954). The official text of the decisions of the Atomic Energy Commission is conveniently reprinted in *U.S. News and World Report* (July 9, 1954), 71–81.

[60] For an inquiry into the political interests involved in the case and a scathing review of the board's judgment on the evidence, see Joseph and Stewart Alsop, "We Accuse!" *Harper's Magazine,* CCIX (Oct., 1954), 25–46.

[61] United States Civil Service Commission, *Statement by Seth W. Richardson, Chairman of Loyalty Review Board, December 23, 1947.* Mimeographed release. Quoted in Bernstein, *op. cit.,* p. 262.

[62] Nikolorić, *op. cit.,* pp. 285–286.

[63] *West Virginia State Board of Education* v. *Barnette,* 319 U.S. 624, 642 (1943).

[64] President's Committee on Civil Rights, *To Secure These Rights* (Washington, D.C., 1947), p. 51.

[65] Press release dated March 20, 1953, in *Department of State Bulletin,* XXVIII (April 6, 1953), 518–519.

[66] PCCR, *To Secure These Rights,* p. 51. A specific discussion of procedural defects in the program, and ways to reform them, may be found in Maurice J. Goldbloom, *American Security and Freedom* (New York: American Jewish Committee, 1954). Something of value here also may be learned from the English experience. See H. H. Wilson and Harvey Glickman, *The Problem of Internal Security in Great Britain, 1948–1953,* Doubleday Short Studies in Political Science (Garden City: Doubleday, 1954).

[67] McLeod, *op. cit.,* p. 471.

[68] Thomas Babington Macaulay, *Critical and Historical Essays* (Everyman's ed.; London, 1907), p. 145.

[69] For a discussion of this problem in private industry, see Adolf A. Berle, Jr., *The 20th Century Capitalist Revolution* (New York: Harcourt, Brace, 1954), pp. 83–115.

CHAPTER 6

[1] Michael Oakeshott, *Political Education* (Cambridge: Bowes and Bowes, 1951), p. 23.

[2] *Interim Report . . . on Hearings Regarding Communist Espionage*

in the United States Government, House Committee on Un-American Activities, U.S. Cong. (Washington, Aug. 28, 1948), p. 3, as quoted in Alan Barth, *The Loyalty of Free Men* (New York: Viking, 1951), p. 74.

[3] Zechariah Chafee, Jr., *Free Speech in the United States* (Cambridge: Harvard University Press, 1941), pp. 564–565.

[4] Thomas Babington Macaulay, "Hallam," in *Critical and Historical Essays* (Everyman's ed.; London, 1907), p. 8.

[5] 64 Stat. 987.

[6] 54 Stat. 670.

[7] For a description and analysis of existing law dealing with loyalty and security, see the two studies prepared for the Special Subcommittee on Security Affairs of the Senate Committee on Foreign Relations: (1) *Adequacy of United States Laws with Respect to Offenses against National Security,* U.S. 83d Cong., 1st sess. (April 17, 1953); (2) *Federal Case Law Concerning the Security of the United States,* U.S. 83d Cong., 2d sess. (Sept., 1954).

[8] John Dewey, *Freedom and Culture* (New York: G. P. Putnam's Sons, 1939), p. 22.

[9] Archibald MacLeish, "Loyalty and Freedom," *American Scholar,* XXII (Autumn, 1953), 395.

[10] *Ibid.,* 397–398.

[11] Seth W. Richardson, "The Federal Employee Loyalty Program," *Columbia Law Review,* LI (May, 1951), 553.

[12] Soren Kierkegaard, *Concluding Unscientific Postscript,* trans. by David F. Swenson and Walter Lowrie (Princeton: Princeton University Press, 1941), p. 317.

[13] Rousseau, *Social Contract* (1762), Bk. I, chap. 1. English translation by G. D. H. Cole, *The Social Contract and Discourses* (Everyman's ed.; London: J. M. Dent, 1913), p. 3.

[14] *Ibid.,* chap. 6, p. 12.

[15] *Ibid.,* p. 13.

[16] *Ibid.,* chap. 7, pp. 14–15.

[17] *Ibid.,* p. 15.

[18] *Ibid.,* Bk. IV, chap. 2, p. 88.

[19] Edward Hallett Carr, *The New Society* (London: Macmillan, 1951), p. 65.

Index

Accursed group, 96–97

Acton, Lord: definition of liberty, 22

Age of Anxiety, 94

Age of Reason, 97, 115; idea of liberty, 184–185

Alien and Sedition Acts, 61

Alienation: and current stress on loyalty, 115–122; Josiah Royce on, 118, 119; evidence for and extent of, 119–120; and urge toward conformity, 120–122; of intellectuals, 127–128. *See also* A-loyal man; *Anomie;* Apathy

Alien Registration Act of 1940, 181

Allegiance: etymology, 58n. *See also* Obligation

A-loyal man: and mass society, 181, 182–183, 184

Amerasia, 137

American Civil Liberties Union, 114

American Committee for Intellectual Freedom: as Communist front, 160

American heritage: importance of loyalty in, 54–55

Americanism: dual tradition of, 84–86

Americanization of immigrants, 87, 98–99

American loyalty: separation of political and religious loyalties, 67–69; slow growth of, 77–79; isolationist aspect of, 79; and sectionalism, 80; symbols of, 80–82; dual tradition of, 84 ff.

Anglo-American loyalty, 78

Anomie, 108–109, 113, 115n

Antiforeignism, 82–83, 86, 87

Anti-intellectualism, 126–128

Apathy, political, 182n; danger to liberal democracy, 183–184

Aristotle, 8, 23, 38

Association: as source of loyalty, 8; Tocqueville on diversity of, 69–70; as test of loyalty, 152 ff., 177; defined by Sidney Hook, 154; prevalence of, in America, 182n. *See also* Group living; Group membership; Voluntary association

Atomic Energy Commission: action of, in Oppenheimer case, 160–166, 177

Attitude: loyalty as, 5–7; formation of, 9; determinants of, 11; resistance to change of, 12–13; and selective perception, 13

Attorney General's Interdepartmental Committee of 1942, 133

Attorney General's list of subversive organizations, 149–152

Auden, W. H., 94

Authoritarianism: core values of, 31; style of loyalty in, 31–33; and conflicts of loyalty, 42

Authoritarian loyalty: illustrated in Shakespeare's *Henry V,* 32; irrationality of, 35

Authoritarian personality, 25